Unencumbered by History

The Vietnam Experience in Young Adult Fiction

Deborah Wilson Overstreet

The Scarecrow Press, Inc.
Lanham, Md., & London
1998

SCARECROW PRESS, INC.

Published in the United States of America
by Scarecrow Press, Inc.
4720 Boston Way
Lanham, Maryland 20706

4 Pleydell Gardens
Kent CT20 2DN, England

British Library Cataloguing in Publication Information Available

Library of Congress Cataloging-in-Publication Data

Overstreet, Deborah Wilson.
Unencumbered by history : the Vietnam experience in young adult fiction /
Deborah Wilson Overstreet.   p.   cm.
Includes bibliographical references and index.
ISBN 0-8108-3535-5 (cloth : alk. paper)
1. American literature—History and criticism.   2. Vietnamese Conflict,
1961–1975—Literature and the conflict.   3. Young adult fiction, American—
History and criticism.   I. Title.
IN PROCESS   98-22140
813'.5409358—dc21   CIP

⊖™ The paper used in this publication meets the minimum requirements of
American National Standard for Information Sciences—Permanence of
Paper for Printed Library Materials, ANSI Z39.48–1984.
Manufactured in the United States of America.

Thanks, Mom

Contents

Acknowledgments

From AND ONE FOR ALL by Theresa Nelson. Copyright © 1989 by Theresa Nelson. Reprinted by permission of Orchard Books, New York.

From THE BEST OF FRIENDS by Margaret I. Rostkowski. Copyright © 1989 by Margaret I. Rostkowski. Used by permission of HarperCollins Publishers.

Excerpts from CARIBOU by Meg Wolitzer. Copyright © 1984 by Meg Wolitzer.

Excerpts from CHILDREN OF THE DRAGON by Karl Terry. Copyright © 1974 by Karl Terry.

Excerpts from COME IN FROM THE COLD. Copyright © 1994 by Marsha Qualey. Reprinted by permission of Houghton Mifflin Company. All rights reserved.

From TO STAND AGAINST THE WIND by Ann Nolan Clark. Copyright © 1978 by Ann Nolan Clark. Used by permission of Viking Penguin, a division of Penguin Books USA, Inc.

From STOP & SEARCH: A NOVEL OF SMALL BOAT WARFARE OFF VIETNAM by William Butterworth. Copyright © Copyright © 1969 by William Butterworth. By permission of Little, Brown and Company.

From TOUGH CHOICES: A STORY OF THE VIETNAM WAR by Nancy Antle. Copyright © 1993 by Nancy Antle. Used by permission of Viking Penguin, a division of Penguin Books USA, Inc.

Excerpts from TRAVELERS by Larry Bograd. Copyright © 1986 by Larry Bograd.

Excerpts from VIETNAM NURSE by Ellen Elliott. Copyright © 1968 by Ellen Elliott.

Excerpts from WAR YEAR by Joe Haldeman. Copyright © 1972, 1978 by Joe Haldeman.

Preface

This book is an inquiry into how the Vietnam War has been represented in adolescent fiction. The Vietnam War and its surrounding events were probably the most significant period in the twentieth century. Vietnam changed how Americans viewed their government and how they viewed each other. Divisions caused by attitudes toward the war still affect us today.

Young readers often know very little about the Vietnam War and America's foreign policies during that time. Novels written about the war are one source of information for adolescents to learn about this era. Because many of these novels are eminently readable, they make learning about the war more approachable. But what are young readers likely to "learn" from reading these books? Are they likely to get a historically accurate picture of the time?

This study examines twenty-eight young adult novels that represent some aspect of the war. The novels were published in the thirty years between 1967 and 1997. More than half of the novels are set in Vietnam and feature some combat. Nearly half of those novels are all combat. Six novels are set in America during the war and feature characters who join the antiwar movement, evade the draft, or enlist and go to Vietnam. The final group of novels depict returned veterans trying to make sense of their Vietnam War experiences.

The first few chapters of the book set the background for the analysis of the novels with a discussion of the relation of ideology, literature, and culture. Chapter 4 explains the three most common interpretations of Vietnam War history and examines the novels in terms of those historiographies. Chapter 5 examines five American cultural myths related to the war. The novels are analyzed for how they support or subvert these cultural myths. Chapter 6 explores representations of American soldiers, the Vietnamese, and the antiwar movement. Each of these chapters concludes with a discussion of how the date of publication may have influenced the particular aspect of the novel examined in that chapter.

Chapter One

The Culture War and Vietnam Literature

"No, let her look. It's all right. Everyone ought to see me." I'm sure those were his exact words, even though it has been more than twenty years since I heard them. My mother and I were walking through the antiseptic corridors of Maryland's Bethesda Naval Hospital as we so often did in the late 1960s. Because of my bad kidneys, I had practically grown up in hospitals. At seven, I had perfected that polite glance and half-smile that acknowledges that you've seen someone who probably doesn't care to be looked at. I had, as any well-brought-up young lady of the time, been taught not to gawk or call attention to people or ask questions that might make someone uncomfortable. I had learned not to be startled by blood or sobs or patients with tubes protruding here and there, patients in wheelchairs, patients missing limbs—the standard hospital population. But this man stopped me cold. The majority of his face was gone. An eye and an ear were missing, his mouth was little more than a gaping hole, and there was a flap of wrinkled skin that covered the place where his

1

nose should have been. He wore the not-particularly well-healed scars of a vicious burn over his chest and arms
and entire head. My mother was trying to divert my attention when he rasped out, "No, let her look. It's all right. Everyone ought to see me." This was my first living encounter with the horrors of the Vietnam War.

Growing up in 1960s Washington, D.C., in a navy family, the war in Vietnam was such a fixture in our lives from my earliest memories that its presence seemed almost natural. American "advisors" had been sent to Vietnam long before I was born. The first major battle of the war (January 2, 1963), close to a small village called Ap Bac, occurred a mere four days after my birth. The fact that two companies of North Vietnamese Army (NVA) regulars and fifty Viet Cong (VC) guerrillas had easily repelled an Army of the Republic of South Vietnam (ARVN) force that outnumbered them ten to one ominously signaled even then that it would take far more than superior numbers or technology to win this war. Unfortunately, it would be more than a decade before that signal reached the ears of those who would finally choose to say "enough."

My earliest memories of Vietnam are its ubiquitous appearances on the news that we watched every evening at dinner. Reports from correspondents in the field—soldiers on patrol, in firebases, in helicopters—were followed by Walter Cronkite reading the tallies from perverse pictograph charts of stick soldier figures exhibiting how many people had been killed or wounded that day—theirs and ours. Realizing that each of those figures represented someone's daddy not coming home—someone's daddy like mine—absolutely terrified me. Each night before I went to sleep, my mother would come into my room to say good night and for us to say our prayers. Each night after the litany of God bless Mommy, God bless Daddy, God bless Grandma . . . , we would pray for God to keep the soldiers in Vietnam safe, to let them come home soon, and most important of all to ask, Please, please God, don't make Daddy go to Vietnam. The numbing dread that I experienced each night over the possibility of my father becoming one of those figures that Walter Cronkite offered up every evening or ending up like that man in the hospital made me quietly sob myself to sleep and even now brings tears to my eyes with the remembrance.

The war in Vietnam is often called the single most crucial event in twentieth-century American history (Capps, 1990; Fromkin & Chace,

1985; Gitlin, 1987; Herr, 1977; Martin, 1987; Paterson, 1988; Wheeler, 1985). Capps (1990) hypothesizes that "virtually everything that has happened in the United States since the end of the Vietnam War can be seen as both reaction and response to the war" (p. 8). Vietnam's legacy is a torn generation once caught up in fighting the war or fighting against it—sometimes both. A major survey in 1986 showed that the attitudes American leaders had toward the Vietnam War were a consistent predictor of their foreign policy views (Holsti & Rosenau, 1986). Our tragic and disastrous involvement in Vietnam still haunts the national psyche in what is often termed the "Vietnam Syndrome."[1]

> The experience of Vietnam suffuses American life. It is in the minds of our foreign policy makers as they attempt to draw up standards for engaging in combat and to gauge the public stomach for battle deaths. It is shibboleth, memory, and curse. Americans have a hunger to remember and to try to understand the events of that era. (Wheeler, 1985, p. 748)

Literature, films, and other art forms that address American involvement in Vietnam abound in the 1990s. Two annotated bibliographies list more than five hundred novels about combat in Vietnam (Wittman, 1989; Newman & Hilfinger, 1988). These novels are accompanied by 290 personal narratives, 109 volumes of poetry, 58 dramas, 252 studies of literature and film, and countless doctoral dissertations. Obviously, there is no dearth of written material about the war, and much of this work has come fairly recently, as there was for some time a real reluctance to publish any literature that addressed Vietnam. At an Asia Society conference in 1985 on Vietnam literature, Jervis Jurjevics, a sixteen-year veteran of the publishing industry, recalled that

> we sat for years in editorial boards and marketing meetings turning down novel after novel. . . . For a period of time well into the 1970s, the Vietnam novel was really [considered] an obscenity. . . . Ironically, some of the ones turned down went on ten years later to win first novel awards. (quoted in Lomperis, 1987, p. 44)

Lomperis (1987) considers these novels to be "an effort to make sense of the Vietnam experience" (p. vii).

Sense, however, has yet to be made of the conflict that has been called everything from a "noble crusade" by Ronald Reagan (quoted in Lomperis, 1987, p. 56) to a "John Wayne wet dream" by correspondent Michael Herr (1977, p. 20)—a conflict that cost 58,000 Americans their lives and scarred an entire generation. As one participant in the Asia Society conference sadly stated, "America's soul is still split over Vietnam" (quoted in Lomperis, 1987, p. 7). How to think about, interpret, or define what happened in Vietnam and what happened to America because of Vietnam is a controversy that alternately smolders and flares in response to current events—the blanket pardon of draft evaders; the release of yet another Vietnam film; the dedication of the Vietnam memorial; American intervention in Central America, Panama, Somalia, and Bosnia; the Persian Gulf War; the election of a president who protested his country's involvement in Vietnam; POW reports; and the normalization of trade relations with Vietnam. There is, as of yet, little popular consensus regarding who did what, when, where, and most important why, for and against the Vietnam War. Former president Richard Nixon (1985) declares that "no event in American history is more misunderstood than the Vietnam War. It was misreported then, and it is misremembered now. Rarely have so many people been so wrong about so much" (p. 1). While most Americans would agree with Nixon's statement, many would be diametrically opposed about how the war was misrepresented and misremembered and by whom.

The Redefinition of America

As technology continues to make the world smaller and smaller and continues to emphasize each nation's interdependence in the global community, Americans of the last decade of the twentieth century find themselves in the position of a people whose international and intranational roles are constantly changing. Now, for example, that the perceived threat of cold war communism has dwindled and Americans find themselves instead beset with a host of smaller Third World adversaries, will America continue to act as the world's police force? How will we define our nation's role in the new world order?

On an intranational level, challenges to traditional views regarding political leadership, the role of the military, redistribution of power between genders, growing minority populations, reformulation of the nuclear family, multiculturalism, political correctness, and national values (just to name a fraction) threaten to rock America to its very core. In James Davison Hunter's (1991) intricate study of what he terms America's "culture war," he suggests that the battle over these issues is being fought on five main battlefields: the family, the schools, the popular media, law, and electoral politics. Hunter broadly defines our culture war as a "political and social hostility rooted in different systems of moral understanding" (p. 42). It is his hypothesis that on every issue, each side of the debate

> can be traced ultimately and finally to the matter of moral authority. By moral authority I mean the basis by which people determine whether something is good or bad, right or wrong, acceptable or unacceptable, and so on. Of course, people often have very different and opposing bases of moral authority and the world views that derive from them that creates the deep [divisions] between antagonists in the contemporary culture war. (pp. 42-43)

Interestingly, Hunter posits that these new divisions cut across more classic oppositions (e.g., Protestants and Catholics and Jews; Democrats and Republicans), making tentative new coalitions and alliances among former adversaries. He sees individuals as possessing tendencies toward orthodoxy or progressivism. Orthodoxy is defined as "the commitment on the part of adherents to an external, definable, and transcendent authority. It tells us what is good, what is true, how we should live, and who we are" (p. 44). These people would be cultural conservatives. Progressivism is defined as the "tendency to resymbolize historic faiths [Hunter does not mean only religion, but any belief system—feminism, Marxism, etc.] according to the prevailing assumptions of contemporary life. . . . Moral authority tends to be defined by the spirit of the modern age . . ." (p. 44). These people would be cultural progressivists. In a classic example of politics making strange bedfellows, Hunter sees a social realignment based on conservatism or progressivism with little or no regard to previous distinctions of religion or political affiliation.

The culture war that conservatives and progressivists have undertaken finally crystallizes as a "struggle over national identity—over the meaning of America, who we have been in the past, who we are now, and perhaps most important, who we, as a nation, will aspire to become in the new millennium" (p. 50). The war as Hunter interprets it is a struggle for cultural hegemony with each group desperate to define America for themselves and future generations. Significant influence on America's public culture, which Hunter believes is the very essence of our nation, is the prize that goes to the winners of the current civil war.

> Public culture . . . embodies the symbols of national identity. These symbols express the meaning of citizenship and, therefore, the meaning of patriotism and disloyalty. More important, public culture consists of the shared notion of civic virtue and the common ideals of the public good—what is best for the general happiness of the people and welfare of the republic. Beyond this, public culture is reflected in the shared standards by which the actions of individuals or communities as well as the actions of other nations . . . are evaluated and judged as either good or evil, right or wrong, just or unjust. (p. 55)

As it relates to history and education, the culture war addresses the issue of which versions of history will be passed on to the next generation. George Orwell (1949) ominously predicted this portion of the debate in his dystopian novel, *1984*, wherein "lies passed into history and became truth. 'Who controls the past,' ran the Party slogan, 'controls the future: who controls the present controls the past' " (p. 16). The battle, then, to "control the past" and through it the future is ultimately fought in the presentation of national history.

> Finally, a nation . . . embraces the collective myths surrounding its history and future promise. These myths are usually constructed through a selective interpretation of our national history, in which certain themes and events are emphasized and others played down. Such myths elaborate the moral significance of the nation's founding in the context of global history; they guide the selection of its heroes and villains; and they interpret the content of the founding documents . . . . By providing an interpretation of the past, these myths also articulate the precedents and ideals for the nation's future. They set out

the national priorities and tasks yet to be accomplished, and they envision the mission yet to be fulfilled. (Hunter, p. 55)

The curators of the National Museum of American Art at the Smithsonian Institution discovered just how tightly our collective myths and selective interpretation of our national history were embraced by powerful cultural conservatives when in 1991 they opened an exhibit entitled "The West as America: Reinterpreting Images of the Frontier, 1820-1920." The conservative opposition to the show centered on wall labels accompanying paintings that suggested the paintings were more likely to provide insight about the painters' views on the West than to reflect any authentic portrait of life on the frontier (Foner & Wiener, 1991). Challenging nearly sacred frontier myths nearly cost the Smithsonian its national funding.

What Hunter calls the "selective interpretation of our national history" (p. 55), Marxist cultural theorists call the selective tradition. Raymond Williams (1977) recognized the motivation for all culture wars, noting that "this struggle for and against selective traditions is understandably a major part of all contemporary cultural activity" (p. 117). As defined by Williams, the selective tradition is a continual and ongoing process of cultural marginalization and legitimation.

> From a whole possible area of past and present, in a particular culture, certain meanings and practices are selected for emphasis and certain other meanings and practices are neglected or excluded. Yet within a particular hegemony, and as one of its decisive processes, this selection is presented and usually passed off as "*the* tradition," "*the* significant past." (p. 115, my emphasis)

Selective traditions and hegemonies are not static entities.

> A lived hegemony is always a process. It is not a system or structure. It is a realized complex of experiences, relationships, and activities, with specific and changing pressures and limits. In practice, hegemony can never be singular. Moreover, it does not just passively exist as a form of dominance. It has continually to be renewed, re-created, defended, and modified. It is also continually resisted, limited, altered, and challenged by pressures not at all its own. (p. 112)

The meanings and practices legitimated by a selective tradition are generally those that most advantageously reflect and promote the interests, values, and worldviews of the dominant culture. Children's and adolescent[2] literature tends to present a very limited range of all possible information, thus conforming to a selective tradition (Brown, 1986).[3] The culture war, as described by Hunter, is really a war over which groups have the power to frame the selective tradition to promote their own worldviews.

One feature of a successful hegemony is its ability to appear as natural or commonsensical. Baritz (1985) attests to this fact when he states that "the less one knows of the world, the more one's own little daily rituals seem to have been decreed by God or nature" (p. 32). Thus when conservative scholars and historians claim to be objective and non-political, they are simply embracing a conservative selective tradition that has been so powerful for so long that they are only able to see their beliefs as natural and commonsensical.

Teaching popular and consensus views of American history is what cultural arch-conservatives champion. Then Chairman (this inappropriately gender-specific title was the one she used for herself) of the National Endowment for the Humanities, Lynne Cheney, urged teachers to "focus on the common historical truths" (quoted in Burd, 1992, p. 22). Though never a classroom teacher herself, Cheney (1987) also castigates teachers for what she found to be "tangible evidence of how little we are doing to make our children shareholders in their cultural heritage" (p. 16). The point she misses, even as she accuses "liberal scholars" of using "classrooms to advance their political agendas and indoctrinate their students" (quoted in Burd, 1992, p. 21), is that the conservative "common truths" and "cultural heritage" that she intends to pass to students are in themselves very political weapons in the battle for cultural hegemony. Cheney's inability to see that the cultural heritage to which she refers is her own (the one she has assumed to be natural, commonsensical, and therefore universal) and not necessarily the cultural heritage of the students is an example of how deeply ingrained the conservative hegemony can be.

Our public culture can be expressed through the very powerful conduits of our various cultural forms—e.g., art, literature, films, television programs. Authors of children's and adolescent fiction are in the position to consciously or unconsciously promote their conservative or progressive stance to their audience—America's next generation. Joel Taxel's (1992) study of children's books about Christopher Columbus reveals how ultimately polemic discussion of the content of children's literature, in particular, can become. "Because these controversies involve issues that simultaneously are aesthetic, relate to questions of historical interpretation, and often involve myths that are basic to this country's belief about itself, they are profoundly political and increasingly contentious" (p. 4). Hunter (1991) discusses the contribution of "intellectuals and other elites," including the authors of adolescent fiction, in the battle to define America.

> While ordinary people participate in the construction of their own private worlds, the development and articulation of the more elaborate systems of meaning, including the realm of public culture, falls almost always to the realm of elites. They are the ones who create the concepts, supply the language, and explicate the logic of public discussion. They are the ones who define and redefine the meaning of public symbols. (p. 59)

American cultural wars as they manifest themselves in the educational sphere assume an even more dire tone since the future of America's children is at stake. It is Hunter's opinion that schools are a

> central institution of modern life through which the larger social order is reproduced. Together, the curriculum, the textbook literature, and even the social activities of the school convey powerful symbols about the meaning of American life—the character of its past, the challenges of the present and its future agenda. In this way the institutions of mass education become decisive in socializing the young into the nation's public culture. (p. 173)

The works of fiction that students read are a part of a school's informal curriculum and as such are also a part of the socialization process.

Evidence that a culture war between conservative and progressive factions in education actually exists can be found in the issues of multicultural education and the expansion of the educational and literary canons. Cultural conservatives, viewing themselves as guardians of

America's traditions, have resisted new pedagogical ideas and newer and more inclusive interpretations of American history. Historian Joan Wallach Scott (1992) claims that conservatives have "fetishized" tradition, elevating the status of traditional definitions of America to a cultural Mount Olympus. It is her contention that cultural conservatives have

> substituted "tradition" (the embodiment of taste, culture and cumulative wisdom) for the white male privilege they so deeply desire and want to protect. To read their accounts of "tradition," one would not know that it is largely invented, always contested, and that what has counted as tradition has changed from generation to generation. Canons are, after all, heuristic devices for exemplifying the literary or the philosophical or the artistic; they are not . . . timeless and unique repositories of human truths. (p. 62)

The Culture War and Vietnam Literature

While cultural conservatives and progressives battle for the ability and position to define America's public culture or the "symbols of national identity," they also battle over the interpretation of the Vietnam War—why it was fought, what it accomplished, how it affected an entire generation, how it should inform current American foreign policy. Part of the battle is played out in literature of the war. Whose memories? Whose explanations?

In the April 1982 news conference in which then President Ronald Reagan called American intervention in Vietnam a "noble crusade," he gave a small speech explaining and justifying our nation's role in Southeast Asia (speech quoted in Lomperis, 1987, p. 56). In this speech, however, his most emphatically made points were based on facts that were wholly erroneous. Among them were statements about North and South Vietnam having always been two independent countries and statements about Ho Chi Minh preventing national elections arranged as part of the 1954 Geneva peace accords. President Reagan was certainly never famous for his meticulous memory, but these two (of many) errors serve as just a small indication that the Vietnam people remember and want to pass on reflects their own ideologies.

Asking the question "What should we tell our children about Vietnam?" Bill McCloud (1989) received vastly different answers from Vietnam era figures. Many politicians, including former Secretary of State Henry Kissinger and then President George Bush, offered the quagmire interpretation of the war as the official version to be passed on to the next generation. This position, as well as the positions of other professional historians, will be thoroughly explained in a later section of the book.

Other figures, however, had stronger words and different ideas to pass on to our children. Robert McNamara (secretary of defense, 1961-1968) most astutely realized that we "must be careful not to interpret events occurring in a different land in terms of [our] own history, politics, culture, and morals" (McCloud, p. 85). Vietnam veteran and author Larry Heinemann wished to pass on that

> we lost our naiveté—had it ripped out of our throats; had it beat out of us most dramatically—understanding finally that the government had betrayed us with a program of lies. Lyndon Johnson's (and for that matter Richard Nixon's) was a government of selfish, arrogant, old men, jolly well ready to eat its own young, both overseas and back here, to preserve its own shabby honor and species dignity. Nixon's "peace with honor" is as hollow and shallow and laughable a phrase as Chamberlain's "peace in our time." (McCloud, p. 56)

An even more impassioned sentiment was expressed by an anonymous Vietnam veteran:

> To answer your question, I would say: A warmongering, war-profiteering country sold its poor, disadvantaged, and minorities down the Mekong River while it gave free rides to everyone who came along with a sob story.
>
> I would also say that we psychotic, drug-crazed, baby-killing war criminals were left swinging in the wind by an uncaring and unappreciative country that only now is starting to pay us lip service, which does nothing more than add insult to injury.
>
> That's what you should tell your students and your children (if you dare). (McCloud, p. 9)

The current controversy to define and interpret the war in Vietnam has become almost as bitter and divisive as the war itself. Now that people finally are willing to discuss Vietnam, they also seem ready to present their information and opinions to young people. With their fascination with 1960s culture in general and Vietnam in particular, students appear to be ready and willing to listen (Kroll, 1992; Johannessen, 1992). One way that adolescents learn about the Vietnam experience is through the novels specifically written to convey that experience to them. Given their potential for enculturation and the fact that information present in novels for young readers has a tendency to conform to a conservative selective tradition, it is important to examine these novels in terms of the ideologies and attitudes that they perpetuate.

Adolescent novels that address America's involvement in Vietnam provide a model for interpreting events there. These components can be examined by a thorough investigation of both the content (narrators' and characters' statements about and reactions to the war) and form (or narrative structure[4]) of the novels. Since there is little agreement about what happened in Vietnam, what should have happened, and why, it should not be surprising that there would be little agreement about what information to include in novels about Vietnam written for adolescents. It is of great importance to analyze adolescent novels that address America's involvement in Vietnam, especially in this time of renewed contest for cultural hegemony.

The primary concern of this study is the examination of representations of the Vietnam War in adolescent fiction for the ideas that authors consciously or unconsciously offer their young readers. My own experience as a reader and teacher tells me that readers of fiction often read that fiction as if it were a statement of fact. Opinions and ideologies expressed in fiction can be taken to be expressions of truth—of the "way things really were." What do adolescent novels that address American involvement in Vietnam attempt to tell their readers?

This overarching question led to a number of more specific questions. These questions were formulated before, during, and after the initial readings of the novels in the sample:

- Are the prevailing Vietnam War historiographies reflected in these novels written for young adults?
- Do these novels support or subvert American cultural myths?

- How are the participants in the conflict described? (Specifically, the American soldiers, the antiwar movement, and the Vietnamese. Also within this question, issues of participants' race, class, and gender will be addressed.)
- Are there changes in the sample of novels relative to their date of publication?
- Are there consistencies within the narrative structures of the novels? The answers to these questions should help us to understand more fully how the war in Vietnam is interpreted for young readers.

Notes

1. The "Vietnam Syndrome" is used by the advocates of both an interventionist and noninterventionist foreign policy. It is invoked by "hawks" as something of a battle cry to urge massive intervention when necessary with no government policy to "tie the hands" of the military. It is just as frequently invoked by "doves" as an admonition to refrain from any sort of intervention whatsoever, because of the possibility of another morass like Vietnam.

2. For the purposes of this study, adolescent literature is loosely defined as literature written for approximately ten- to fifteen-year-old readers.

3. Critics and scholars often use the terms "adolescent" and "children's" literature interchangeably. For the purposes of this study, I use the descriptors "adolescent" or "young adult" because the novels in the sample are appropriate for upper elementary/middle grades readers.

4. The term "narrative structure" refers to more than simply a story's plot. I will essentially be using Christian's (1984) conception of narrative structure, which she defines as "the progression of events and the resolution of conflict. It essentially indicates what actions the characters are involved in and what they do. Characters and action work in tandem . . ." (p. 69).

Chapter Two

Literature, Ideology, and the Transmission of Values

Literature and Ideology

America's public culture is continually expressed through a myriad of forms—everything from the structure and purpose of our public institutions to our comic books. Culture is more or less a set of tools people use to make sense of their world. A person's behaviors and perceptions of the world are strongly influenced by her or his culture. However, culture is far from a static inventory of acceptable thoughts and behaviors. It is instead an ever-changing, ongoing process that constantly shifts and mutates to include some new ideas and practices while excluding others (Spradley & McCurdy, 1980). Because this book focuses on literature written for adolescents, literature as a cultural form will be the focus of this discussion of the relation of culture and ideology. It is natural to embed studies of literature within studies of culture since "real literary analysis cannot be separated from a critique of the cultural situation to

which the literary work stands as a complicated and vital response"
(Jameson, 1972, p. 181).

Marxist literary and cultural critics address, among a host of other
issues, the conditions by which literature is produced and consumed, the
relations of individuals and groups to the means of production and power,
and the permeation of ideology throughout every fiber of a culture. As
defined by Terry Eagleton (1983), ideology is not "simply the deeply
entrenched, often unconscious beliefs which people hold," but is more
accurately "those modes of feeling, valuing, perceiving, and believing
which have some kind of relation to the maintenance and reproduction of
social power" (p. 15). It is the opinion of Marxist critics Eagleton (1976)
and Raymond Williams (1977) that a nation's culture and ideology are
inextricably bound. The symbols and meanings of cultural forms over
which conservatives and progressives continue to battle are also tied to
their ideology. American studies scholar Andrew Martin (1987) further
explains that

> meaning in culture is not an innocent or value-free affair, but is a
> specific product of historically constituted social relationships. And
> because meaning is the product of social relationships and practices, and
> is not a naturally occurring phenomenon, it is also ideological. . . . I
> would contend that precisely because meaning is never inno-
> cent—because it is always a product of particular ways of construing
> reality—we need to understand ideology as being something more than
> mere "ideas." In my view, ideologies are made up of actual social
> practices, not merely ideas, and they constitute, moreover, material
> forces which produce concrete effects in both subjectivity and significa-
> tion. (p. 58)

Virtually every facet of literature from its conception to its consumption
involves an expression of ideology. Eagleton (1976) addresses literature's
beginnings when he claims that "all art springs from an ideological
conception of the world; there is no such thing . . . as a work of art . . .
devoid of ideological content" (p. 17). Linda Christian (1984) adds that
"literary production is a medium for the construction of ideology" (p. 25).
Robert Leeson (1977) asserts that "writing and publishing [have] never
been neutral activit[ies]" (p. 5). Taxel (1980) agrees that literature is
"grounded in specifiable ideological orientations," adding that an author

may or may not even be aware of this fact. "These ideological orientations are components of a central system of practices, meanings, and values—an effective and dominant culture which is 'hegemonic' in function" (p. 11). Even the form or narrative structure of literature is part of the ideology of that literature. Eagleton (1976) suggests that form "crystallizes out of certain dominant ideological structures," and that "in selecting a form . . . the writer finds his choice already ideologically circumscribed" because the "forms themselves, as well as his permutation of them, are ideologically significant" (p. 26). In discussing Macherey's thoughts on gaps in a text, Eagleton further asserts that elements *not* included in literature are also tied to ideology. "It is in the significant *silences* of a text, in its gaps and absences, that the presences of ideology can be most positively felt" (p. 34, emphasis in original). Marxist literary and cultural theorists ultimately agree that every aspect of literature and literary study carries some ideological weight.

Since the adolescent literature examined in this study could potentially be part of a school curriculum, it is appropriate to give at least a cursory glance to the ideology involved in schooling. The field of scholarship that specifically addresses this issue is sociology of school knowledge. Taxel (1980) explains that

> a fundamental assumption of the sociology of school knowledge states that the knowledge distributed by schools via textbooks, tradebooks [novels], films, etc., as well as the social relations of schooling (the hidden curriculum), represent a very limited segment of all available knowledge. Further, it is asserted that this knowledge has tended to reflect the interests and perspectives of those groups who have historically, and currently dominate society. (p. 1)

Bearing this in mind, Taxel asks us to "cease viewing curriculum materials as somehow value-neutral and instead conceive of them as 'ideologically' laden cultural artifacts representing, sometimes quite subtly, the dominant interests in society" (p. 9). Since novels written for young readers are at the very least a part of a school's informal curriculum, they must be considered part of "school knowledge."

Despite earlier notions of critics like Townsend (1969) that art and literature exist solely for their own sakes and that the mixing of politics and literature leads "only to the subversion and perversion of the art form" (quote in Taxel, 1992, p. 9), it is ultimately appropriate to discuss literature in terms of politics and ideology. Eagleton (1983) denies the possibility that any discussion of literature can avoid politics. Using an analogy of politics and past South African sports, he claims that politics and ideology have been an inseparable part of literature from the beginning.

> I am not going to argue, then, for a "political criticism" which would read literary texts in the light of certain values which are related to political beliefs and actions; all criticism does this. The idea that there are "non-political" forms of criticism is simply a myth which furthers certain political uses of literature all the more effectively. The difference between a "political" and "non-political" criticism is just the difference between the prime minister and the monarch: the latter furthers certain political ends by pretending not to, while the former makes no bones about it. (p. 209)

Theorist Peter Hunt (1991) chides authors and critics for failing to see that they "cannot be apolitical," claiming that politics and literature are inseparable (p. 142). Taxel (1995) agrees that he

> cannot imagine anyone arguing that authors of children's books, whether past or present, operate in a political and ideological vacuum and pursue their artistic vision without constraint or limitation. Like other cultural artifacts, children's literature is a product of convention that is rooted in, if not determined by, the dominant belief systems and ideologies of the times in which it is created. (p. 159)

American Cultural Myth

American cultural myths form an important and powerful means of reproducing American national identity. To recall the work of James Hunter (1991), cultural myths are "constructed through a selective interpretation of our national history"; they also "articulate the precedents and ideals for the nation's future" and "set out national priorities" (p. 55). On a smaller scale, they suggest which traits and characteristics we should value in people, what defines heroism, and how we should define ourselves in the great scheme of things.

In a study of American cultural myths that both preceded and followed America's involvement in Vietnam, Hellmann (1986) defined cultural myths as the

> stories containing a people's image of themselves in history. Extreme simplification, myths may always be debunked as falsifications of reality. But simplification is their strength, since only by ignoring the great mass of infinite data can we identify essential order. . . . A myth is our explanation of history that can also serve as a compelling idea for our future. (p. ix)

American cultural myths resonate through our perceptions of people and situations; they provide a lens through which to view the past, and suggest action for the future. They are an immensely powerful, though largely hidden, force influencing our understanding of ourselves, both as a nation and as individuals, and of the world around us. These myths comprise an informing subtext to our individual ideologies.

In his 1985 study examining American culture and its effect on the war in Vietnam, Baritz determined that war itself is a culturally specific construction. He credits American culture as a driving force behind nationalist dogma:

> In countless ways Americans know in their gut—the only place myths can live—that we have been Chosen to lead the world in public morality and to instruct it in political virtue. We believe that our own domestic goodness results in strength adequate to destroy our opponents who, by definition, are enemies of virtue, freedom, and God. (p. 27)

Our general ignorance of other countries and cultures only serves to reinforce American cultural myths even as those myths distort our vision of other cultures.

> American nationalism in its purest form thinks of the world as populated by frustrated or potential Americans. This is unique among the world's nationalisms. Thus, we believe that we can know others reasonably easily because of our assumption that they want to become us. (p. 31)

These same attitudes and cultural myths help to perpetuate a paternalistic approach to other cultures and traditions.

> We seem to think that people who have such strange ideas do not really mean them. We seem to believe that they do such things out of ignorance or poverty. They cannot help it. If they could, they would become more like us. It is apparently beyond reason to believe that anyone would follow these exotic customs for deep cultural reasons, as deep as the reasons that compel us to shake hands instead of bowing. (p. 32)

Finally, Baritz posits that war is a culturally specific event—chosen and executed consistently with our cultural myths. "War is a product of culture. It is an expression of the way a culture thinks of itself and the world. Different cultures go to war for different reasons and fight in different ways. There is an American way of war. Our Vietnam War was started and fought in ways our culture required" (p. 321). As the title of Baritz's book states, *American Culture Led Us into Vietnam and Made Us Fight the Way We Did,* but it also left us completely unprepared for losing that war.

History is, for the most part, the tale told by the victor (Schlesinger, 1992). For the first time in its martial history, America was certainly not the victor. American cultural myth in no way equipped us to make sense of defeat—especially not defeat at the hands of a small and technologically inferior adversary. German historian Walter Benjamin (1979), writing in 1930 about Germany's defeat in World War I, could easily have been writing in the 1980s or 1990s about America's defeat in Vietnam. It is his contention that when a country loses a war, it also loses the privilege of defining that war.

> . . . the winner keeps the war in hand, it leaves the hands of the loser; the winner conquers the war for himself, makes it his own property, the loser no longer possesses it and must live without it. To win or lose a war reaches so deeply . . . into the fabric of our existence that our whole lives become that much richer or poorer in symbols, images, and sources. (p. 123)

Cultural myths tell us how to think, how to act, how to fight and win wars (if not how to lose them), how to place ourselves in the world, in history. They perpetuate ideologies and they are a significant part of the spoils that will go to the victor of the culture war as envisioned by Hunter. Cultural myths are part of the same selective tradition that the dominant culture uses to effect cultural hegemony. One powerful conduit through which American cultural myths flow to the next generation is children's and adolescent literature.

Literature as the Transmission of Knowledge and Values

Literature has always been, and is only recently coming to be recognized as, a powerful tool of enculturation. It demonstrates to readers how others have behaved in specific situations, thereby allowing them the vicarious experience of those actions. Young readers are able to "try on" various decisions, settings, and time periods, experiencing along with the characters in the story. Adolescent literature can suggest to readers ways in which to behave and react. It can also teach them about other children, other adolescents, other people, other racial and ethnic groups, other cultures, other times. In fact, "literature constitutes an important source of children's knowledge about and orientation to the social world" (Taxel, 1989, p. 33).

Gordon Kelly (1974) considers literature for young readers to be a vehicle through which the adults in a group pass on their values to the younger members. He further explains that

> cultural continuity requires not simply that a group's beliefs be explained to the young . . . but that the validity and importance of the beliefs be successfully justified to, and internalized by, those who will eventually be responsible themselves for maintaining the belief system. Children's literature may be used to explain the ways in which a group defines and symbolizes the principles of order thought to structure and sustain a given way of life. (p. 154)

Rudine Sims Bishop (1990) agrees that "children's books have been one of the primary ways we have attempted to relay our values to our young people" (p. 1). The subtle, and sometimes not-so-subtle, messages sent to young readers through the literary devices of characterization, dialogue, setting, and narrative structure, often convey the values and mores that the author finds acceptable and wishes to transmit (Banfield, 1985; Kelly, 1974; Sims Bishop, 1990; Taxel, 1995). Children's and adolescent fiction from any time period can be considered a reasonable reflection of the values and attitudes of the time in which it was produced "whether history or fiction often reveal as much about the era in which the books were written as they do about the period they re-create" (Taxel, 1995, p. 160).

Martin (1987) refers to the "strict acculturation of the young" that must occur in order to maintain a system of social reality. Literature is part of the acculturation process. Christian (1984) speaks of adolescent literature as having a "confirmatory and consensualizing effect" on its readers (p. 77). The generally narrow range of values transmitted through adolescent fiction attempts to "secure the consent of readers" to the relations and interpretations presented (p. 77).

Historical fiction for young readers serves an important and unique function in its position as a link to the past. Many of those readers develop much of their sense of specific historical periods through the fiction that they read, although not all fiction stands as a shining monument to historical accuracy (Taxel, 1986). Joshua Brown (1986) claims that although children's and adolescent historical fiction "addresses a large audience that academic historians never reach," these books "are largely unrecognized and rarely discussed in professional historical circles" (p. 68). He believes that historical fiction constitutes the means through which students are most often "exposed to history outside the classroom" (p. 74).

Since cultural myth and national history so strongly influence how we perceive ourselves as Americans, our national identity, so to speak, it is no wonder that the combination of myth and history transmitted to the next generation through literature is of pressing interest. Vandell (1991) cites historical fiction as a significant method for this transmission.

> Instructing the young in the appropriate interpretation of the nation's history and national identity can thus be seen to be an important part of

the cultural transmission process. Children's fiction about the nation's past is one of the channels through which these stories, and the definitions of national identity within them, are presented to the young. (p. 30)

The Vietnam War in History Texts

It is unfortunate but hardly surprising that the selective tradition should be so clearly operating, albeit in different configurations, in generation after generation of American textbooks. Since school is the primary institution through which each successive generation is asked to accept America without fundamentally questioning its goals, values, social or economic structures or policies, it is logical that textbooks reflect this generally unquestioning attitude toward our country. Jean Anyon (1979), in her influential study of ideology in secondary school history textbooks, determined that

> the school curriculum has contributed to the formation of attitudes that make it easier for powerful groups, those whose knowledge is legiti-mized by school studies, to manage and control society. Textbooks not only express the dominant groups' ideologies, but also help to form attitudes in support of their social position. (p. 382)

Anyon found that the interests of organized labor and the working class (economic and labor history were the focus of her research) were neither thoroughly nor accurately represented in history texts. In *Guardians of Tradition,* Ruth Miller Elson (1964) examined American textbooks from the nineteenth century and also found that many groups (e.g., woman, racial, ethnic, and religious minorities, the working class) were either ignored or misrepresented. Instead, history was presented with extreme nationalistic bias in a fashion that legitimated the values and positions of the dominant culture.

Since American history textbooks generally present a very narrow and selective interpretation of American history, it is not surprising to find that their discussion of America's involvement in Vietnam is consistent with this well-established pattern. Set in the context of the fight to define the meaning and lessons of the war in Vietnam, an examination of the portrayal of the Vietnam War in history texts takes on a more serious tone. School textbooks are certainly seen as an authority on what really happened in Vietnam. In my own experience as an avid American history student in junior high and high school, Vietnam was never discussed in any class. I have no idea how or even *if* the subject was addressed in any of our texts. My history classes were always taught chronologically (always starting with early explorers), and we seldom even made it to the Civil War. In light of the studies of Vietnam in history texts, however, it might be just as well that we never made it to the mid-1800s.

Frances FitzGerald (1979) devotes a small section of her comprehensive study of American history texts to the discussion of Vietnam. She claims that the texts evade the major issues and are full of inaccuracies and misspellings and that the "majority of the best-selling texts still have no firm grip on Vietnam geography or nomenclature" (p. 124). Just as disturbing is the fact that "many [texts] contain no reference, or almost none, to the peace movement or to any of the political turmoil of the late 1960s and early 1970s" (p. 127). The war seems to be explained through what she calls the "crabgrass" theory—the war was simply there, getting out of hand, and everyone hated it. In this way, the war virtually takes on a life of its own. *It* started, Americans were troubled by *it*, *it* killed many, *it* was stopped. FitzGerald should be eminently qualified to make these evaluations since her own history of the war in Vietnam, *Fire in the Lake: The Vietnamese and the Americans in Vietnam* (1972), won a Pulitzer Prize.

In their book-length study of the presentation of the Vietnam War in history texts, Griffen and Marciano (1979) reach many of the same conclusions as FitzGerald. Speaking of the treatment of wars in general, they begin by positing that historically "interpretations . . . have always stressed the necessity of our involvement and defended the correctness and morality of America's wartime role and conduct. Almost without exception, self-righteous nationalism has been emphasized at the expense of objective, honest analysis of American policy" (p. xv). Examining twenty-eight history texts in terms of the selective tradition, Griffen and Marciano conclude that

> textbooks offer an obvious means of realizing hegemony in education. Through their pretensions of neutrality and objectivity and through their

suppression of data and alternative views, textbooks further the hegemonic process. . . . Within history texts, for example, the omission of crucial facts and viewpoints limits profoundly the ways in which students come to view historical events. . . . The treatment of the Vietnam War in American textbooks serves as one of the means by which schools perform their larger social functions. Their most basic function is to obtain an uncritical *acceptance* of the present society, thus hindering rational analyses of conflicts such as Vietnam. (pp. 163, 164, emphasis in original)

Griffen and Marciano believe that the texts are full of omissions, distortions, and misinformation regarding every facet of the war and are generally devoid of any sort of critical inquiry or analysis. None of the texts "call into question any of the major premises of American foreign policy, premises that formed the foundation of the Vietnam War" (p. 168). Referring to the increasingly popular radical historiographical interpretation of Vietnam, Griffen and Marciano discover that "the bitter reality is that the texts we examined never consider that this assessment might be accurate, or *even that it is a position which could be investigated rationally and then rejected*" (p. 169, emphasis in original).

Two later studies of Vietnam in elementary and secondary history texts reach the unfortunately familiar conclusion that the war is only given cursory coverage (Fleming & Nurse, 1982; Logan & Needham, 1985). Logan and Needham especially note that the influence of the antiwar movement was avoided in texts written specifically for elementary students. Fleming and Nurse reached some startling conclusions in their evaluation of texts written between 1977 and 1981. They found that the books were for the most part "even-handed, accurate, and judicious" and believed that those issues the authors did address were addressed well. However, immediately after this conclusion, they state that

textbooks tend to neglect or to underplay the debate between the hawks and doves over war aims and the various moral issues (the My Lai massacre, the shootings at Kent State, chemical warfare, Vietnamese civilian deaths), the amnesty dilemma, the problems of the Vietnam veteran, the physical and psychological cost of the war to America and Vietnam, and the "lessons" of Vietnam. (p. 340)

After reading this extensive list, it is difficult to imagine what of significance was actually included in the textbooks. Fleming and Nurse conclude with an incredible claim:

> Most of the textbooks in our study offer a too sketchy account of the Vietnam War. The problems tend to be the neglect of certain key topics. This omission is particularly true of war aims, moral controversies, and "lessons" of the war. However, the *deficiencies of the narrative are not those of distortion, dishonesty, inaccuracy, or bias.* (p. 343, my emphasis)

Given what we know about the selective tradition and its constant influence on history texts, it is virtually beyond comprehension that this sort of neglect and omission could be seen as anything other than "distortion, dishonesty, inaccuracy, or bias."

In conjunction with the standards movements in all academic disciplines, in the 1990s the National Council for the Social Studies set out to write a set of guidelines, or standards to list the how's, when's, and what's of social studies education. The first set of standards that addressed Vietnam (within the broader context of American history) were published in 1994. Standard 3C for fifth- through twelfth-grade students was that "students should be able to demonstrate understanding of the foreign and domestic consequences of the U.S. involvement in Vietnam" (p. 218). In direct contrast to much information skimmed or skipped entirely in the textbooks previously mentioned, the first set of national standards for social studies took an interesting approach to the teaching of Vietnam. The six subcomponents of the standard asked students to "analyze the Kennedy, Johnson, and Nixon administrations' Vietnam policy and the consequences of escalation of the war; analyze growing disillusionment with the war; assess the impact of class and race on wartime mobilization; evaluate the effect of the war on Vietnamese and Americans in Vietnam; explain the provisions of the Paris Peace Accord of 1973 and evaluate Nixon's accomplishment; and, analyze the constitutional issues involved in the war and the legacy of Vietnam" (p. 218).

These curricular objectives are quite a departure from the dismally thin information presented in the textbooks. Adolescent fiction is suggested as a means to explore different perspectives on the war. The novel *Charlie Pippin* (included in this study) is specifically mentioned.

An abrupt change in the spirit of these objectives came about in the revised edition of the standards that was published in 1996. Largely under the pressure of conservative politics, the subcomponents for this objective (and for many, if not most, of the others) were changed considerably. "Assess the impact of class and race on wartime mobilization" (1994, p. 218) became "explain the composition of the American forces recruited to fight the war" (1996, p. 124). This, at least on the surface, subtle substitution is an example of the change in tone of the revisions. "Analyze growing disillusionment with the war" (1994, p. 218), the single objective that addressed any antiwar sentiment and ostensibly the antiwar movement itself, was deleted totally.

Studies of Vietnam War Film

Despite the fact that none of the films examined were specifically directed at a young adult audience, studies of Vietnam War films are relevant here because of their similar theoretical underpinnings and because young adult students are likely to have seen one or more of the films. These types of films can create an informing subtext to the novels in this study, and to school study of the Vietnam War. From doctoral dissertations to scholarly essays, films that depict the Vietnam experience have been explored for their themes and ideologies. Unfortunately, it seems that each study draws the same sad conclusion—none of the films address, even in a cursory manner, the underlying causes of the war or any political or historical implications of the war. Quivey (1988) and Martin (1987) both believe that instead of addressing larger causes and implications of the war, films narrowly examine only its effects on individuals.

> None of these films can be said to "name names," so to speak, or to treat the historical and political roots of America's involvement in Southeast Asia. In the tradition of Hollywood's established approach to controversial topics, the consequences and liabilities of a discredited system of foreign policy, and a politically corrupting war, are displaced onto personal narratives which explore individual subjectivity. (Martin, p. 151)

The four most significant Vietnam War films are *The Deer Hunter*
(1979), *Apocalypse Now* (1979), *Platoon* (1986), and *Full Metal Jacket*
(1987) (Rasmussen & Downey, 1991). In varying studies, each has been
sharply criticized for avoiding the "political or historical bases for the war
or the Vietnamese perspective of the conflict" (Auster & Quart, 1988, p.
xiv). Auster and Quart go on to specifically indict *The Deer Hunter*
saying that "what is most disturbing . . . is that; despite its memorable
frightening images of a horrific, chaotic war, it allows Vietnam to exist in
a historical and political vacuum" (p. 65). Donald Ringnalda (1990) is
also dismayed at American films' portrayal of the Vietnamese claiming
that they are "represented as stick-figure props" with the war presented as
"an *American* tragedy, virtually ignoring America's racist actions to the
Vietnamese people" (p. 66, emphasis in original).

Examining how historical amnesia is created through a continual
process of a selective interpretation of means through which Vietnam has
been represented, Michael Klein (1990) states that

> after a war or significant social crisis that has been divisive, and
> especially during a period of conservatism following an era of radical
> social or cultural action, the history of the recent past is often reinter-
> preted. Those with access to the means of cultural production, in
> accordance with the new dominant political attitudes, are likeliest to be
> behind such major shifts in interpretation. Radical or oppositional
> moments in the history of a nation are effectively exorcised from the
> cultural memory. A process of organized forgetting takes people's
> complex past away, substituting comfortable myths that reinforce rather
> than challenge the status quo. (p. 19)

Michael Frisch (1986) concurs with "when the sky is dark with chickens
coming back to the American roost, it would seem that the last line of
defense is to slam the door of memory" (p. 11).

Frisch also discusses the notion of historical amnesia in terms of the
apolitical nature of most Vietnam War films. He interprets these films as
offerings in the cultural battle to define Vietnam, but believes that they
have little to contribute.

> Mass-mediated popular culture offers other insights into how complex
> historical experience is processed for acceptable public remembering.

Films like *The Deer Hunter* and *Apocalypse Now* said almost nothing about the history and impact of the war. But they have an enormous amount to teach, in all their pretentious posturing, about how we have been encouraged to "deal with" such a traumatic collective experience. Each film is willfully and explicitly antihistorical; in a context where the forces of history virtually scream to be noticed, solitary individuals are the heroic focus, men kept deliberately isolated from history, apparently so they can stand as metaphors for the human condition or some other abstraction the filmmakers imagined might be obscured by contact with the real world. (p. 8)

All of the many studies take to task the creators of Vietnam films for not using their powerful and influential medium to address the larger and ultimately more important issues of the war.

Finally, Linda Dittmar and Gene Michaud (1990) point out that several of the standard war movie plots are absent from the Vietnam movie canon, including significantly

the "command-level" films that were especially popular in the late 1940s . . . These films were intent on explaining "The Big Picture" to American audiences; their task was to help audiences understand and come to terms with the sacrifices of individual men and women within the larger context of defeating the global territorial and political aspirations of America's enemies. (p. 5)

The "command-level" films to which Dittmar and Michaud refer are not necessarily recommended or lauded for presenting an evenhanded treatment of World War II, but merely that they make an attempt to situate their plot lines within a larger political context.

Despite the deluge of analyses of adult representations of the Vietnam War, there have been almost no substantial studies of young adult representations of the war. Wendy Saul's (1985) article "Witness for the Innocent: Children's Literature and the Vietnam War" is the only thoughtful attempt that I have found to address "the stories we tell children about how the U.S. became involved in Vietnam, how and why we lost that war and, most important, what we as a nation have learned from the Southeast Asian experience" (p. 185). She very briefly examines eleven books, both fiction and nonfiction, that deal directly or tangentially with the war; it is beyond the scope of her eleven-page article to provide an in-depth examination of the books she includes. Saul analyzed these books for their relation to what she calls a "witness for the innocent" stance, which she characterized as a perception of war as "a terrible plague rained down upon a people who want nothing more than their families and their land. There is no notion of blame, a specific oppressor is absent, and the future is seen as simply beyond individual human control" (p. 188). She finds that many of the fiction and nonfiction books conform to this stance, thereby refusing to question issues of national motive, responsibility, and lessons learned. Comparing portrayals of American soldiers in Vietnam to those in World War II, Saul believes authors attempt to show them as "brave and personally honorable, mature and competent, as opposed to idealistic and impassioned" (p. 190).

Consistent with the reading of the novels in this study, Saul notes that "not one of the novels discussed here even suggests that the U.S. role in Vietnam was different from its role in other wars, nor that the protests of the seventies arose, at least in part, from anti-imperialist sentiment" (p. 195). This idea of America's imperialist tendencies crystallized into the radical interpretation of the Vietnam War. Saul concludes by noting that

> all the Vietnam novels, even those swaddled in the rhetoric of hope, propagate a hope completely divorced from issues of power. Real war is not generally waged nor ended on issues of personal safety, yet it is only such issues that the accounts described here address. While Taxel found a body of literature about the American Revolution which described that particular war as central to the foundation of our national character, beliefs and laws (books which emphasize ideological issues through both form and content), the literature on Vietnam appears to treat the Southeast Asian conflict as an isolated incident, without a past, and having only a tenuous and dream-like relationship to our national future. (pp. 194-195)

Chapter Three

Young Adult Literature about the War

Researcher Stance

None of the studies mentioned in chapter 2 address the fact that the "texts" examined are at least partly interpretations of the researcher's own creation of the literary work of art. Rosenblatt (1978) states that researchers

> evidently think that they are being "objective" when they discuss identifiable elements of the text. They do not include in their theoretical assumptions recognition of the fact that even the most objective analysis of [a text] is an *analysis of the work as they themselves have called it forth*. (p. 15, my emphasis)

Thinking that you are dealing with a text objectively is an easy trap in which to fall because the illusion of a text as a physical object containing the literary work and its potential meanings is a powerful one.

If your interpretation of a text re-creates your identity, as Norman Holland (1975) believes, or if you fill in Iser's (1974) textual gaps with material consistent with your own worldview, then offering some information about your stance and position as a researcher seems crucial. Peshkin (1988) addresses researcher bias in much the same spirit, contending that *all* research, even ostensibly "objective" research, is permeated by subjectivity and researcher bias.

> I hold the view that subjectivity operates during the entire research process. The point I argue is that researchers, notwithstanding their use of quantitative or qualitative methods, their research problems, or their reputation for personal integrity, should systematically identify their subjectivity throughout the course of their research. [Their biases] have the capacity to filter, skew, shape, block, transform, construe, and misconstrue what transpires from the outset of a research project to its culmination in a written statement. (p. 17)

Peshkin urges researchers to explore, examine, and finally state their own biases and perspectives, since they inevitably influence all stages of research.

Reader response theorists agree that a reader's concerns and preoccupations strongly influence his or her interpretation of a text (Holland, 1975; Rosenblatt, 1978). Political and social ideas are bound to come to bear even more forcefully on the reading of any fiction that deals specifically (if not explicitly) with a controversial event. Marxist cultural critic Terry Eagleton (1983) discusses the impossibility of a non-ideologically influenced interpretation of literature saying that "the reader does not come to the text as a kind of cultural virgin, immaculately free of previous social and literary entanglements, a supremely disinterested spirit or blank sheet on to which the text will transfer its own inscriptions" (p. 89).

As a qualitative researcher examining the presentation and explanation of America's involvement in Vietnam as represented in adolescent literature, I have analyzed the literary work that I have created through my transactions with the texts. Reader response theorists, such as Rosenblatt (1978), envision readers "transacting" with a physical text with the combination of text, reader, and context forming a literary work of art.

Rosenblatt suggests a circuit metaphor to illustrate this transaction when she states, "a specific reader and a specific text at a specific time and place: change any of these, and there occurs a different circuit, a different event," or a different literary work of art (p. 14). Each reader during each reading brings a particular filter through which different responses are created. Rosenblatt sees that "interests, expectations, anxieties, and other facts based on past experience affect what an individual perceives" (p. 19). She adds that "the transaction will involve not only the past experience but also the present state and present interests and preoccupations of the reader" (p. 20).

The background from which I have read and interpreted the texts is consistent with the radical interpretation of the events surrounding the Vietnam War (this historiography and others will be explained at length in chapter 4). Although I come from a conservative military family, my political worldviews differ sharply from my family's. I have analyzed and interpreted the novels in this study as one who wholeheartedly agrees with the radical historians' interpretation of America's Vietnam policies. I generally perceive America's foreign policy as consistently interventionist, replete with covert colonialism and economic imperialism, with covert involvement in Central America and overt invasions of Grenada and Panama standing as recent examples. America's involvement in Vietnam, while part of a rabid communist containment policy, is also an example of an at best morally questionable interventionism. Even though I have no direct experience with combat in Vietnam myself or even through relatives or friends, I have always been overwhelmingly disturbed by what happened there and by what happened here because of our involvement in Vietnam. Incidents in my childhood such as those described in the first pages of this book (i.e., my meeting the wounded vet in the hospital, worrying about the possibility of my military father being sent to war) comprise my indirect experience with the war. Having grown up in late 1960s and early 1970s Washington, D.C., surrounded by antiwar, civil rights, and women's rights marches, protests, and the occasional riot, I have always been interested in America's international and intranational policy decisions and how they are perceived.

The Novels

After assembling potential novels to be included in the sample, two criteria were established. First, each novel's Library of Congress call number had to begin with PZ 7—designating a nonadult novel. Second, each novel had to have "Vietnamese Conflict" as either its first or second subject listing. ("Vietnamese Conflict" is the standard subject heading used by Library of Congress catalogers.) For novels not classified by the Library of Congress (both older and more popular—less "literary" novels are not always classified), a JUV FIC (juvenile fiction, or its equivalent) listing must be given. Also, the main plot line of the novel had to involve some aspect of America's involvement in Vietnam. Actual combat, the antiwar movement at home, the effects of war on boys of draft age, the effects of the war on veterans and their families, the effects of the war on families who lost loved ones in Vietnam, and returning veterans coming to terms with their experiences in Vietnam—all are examples of acceptable plot lines.

These two simple criteria unfortunately eliminated many recommended novels because they either addressed Vietnam in only a tangential manner or were obviously written for an adult audience and were not appropriate for younger readers. No novels that fit the criteria were eliminated from the sample. One real limitation of the criteria is the somewhat arbitrary nature of the Library of Congress system for cataloging the subject listings of works of fiction. Several seemingly appropriate novel choices either were not given a "Vietnamese Conflict" subject listing by the Library of Congress or that subject listing was the third or higher subject. The following twenty-eight novels met all criteria and formed the sample for this study:

(1967). *Special Forces Trooper.* Joe Archibald.
(1968). *Orders to Vietnam: A Novel of Helicopter Warfare.* William E. Butterworth.
(1968). *The Man in the Box.* Mary Lois Dunn.
(1968). *Vietnam Nurse.* Ellen Elliott.
(1969). *Stop & Search: A Novel of Small Boat Warfare Off Vietnam.* William E. Butterworth.

(1969). *Nurse in Vietnam.* Nell M. Dean.

(1971). *One Day for Peace.* Alexander Crosby.

(1972). *Cross-fire.* Gail Graham.

(1972, 1978). *War Year.* Joe Haldeman.

(1974). *Children of the Dragon.* Karl Terry.

(1978). *To Stand against the Wind.* Ann Nolan Clark.

(1980). *Where the Elf King Sings.* Judie Wolkoff.

(1984). *Caribou.* Meg Wolitzer.

(1986). *Travelers.* Larry Bograd.

(1987). *Charlie Pippin.* Candy Dawson Boyd.

(1988). *Fallen Angels.* Walter Dean Myers.

(1989). *Pocket Change.* Kathryn Jensen.

(1989). *And One for All.* Theresa Nelson.

(1989). *The Best of Friends.* Margaret Rostkowski.

(1990). *Long Time Passing.* Adrienne Jones.

(1991). *Echo Company #1—Welcome to Vietnam.* Zack Emerson.

(1991). *Echo Company #2—Hill 568.* Zack Emerson.

(1991). *Echo Company #3—'Tis the Season.* Zack Emerson.

(1992). *Echo Company #4—Stand Down.* Zack Emerson.

(1993). *Tough Choices: A Story of the Vietnam War.* Nancy Antle.

(1994). *Come in from the Cold.* Marsha Qualey.

(1995). *The Road Home.* Ellen Emerson White.

(1997). *Sing for Your Father, Su Phan.* Stella Pevsner and Fay Tang.

Research Categories

Each book in the sample was read many times. Phrases, sentences, paragraphs, and passages of any necessary length were isolated and placed in one of the following categories:

- Literary elements (including setting, plot, point of view, characterization)
- References to the causes of the war
- How and why individual Americans came to be in Vietnam
- Representations of all Vietnamese (North and South, civilian and military)
- Attitudes toward and characterizations of war

- Attitudes toward and characterizations of the military establishment
- Attitudes toward and characterizations of the antiwar movement
- Narrative structures

These categories were established after a preliminary reading of the novels in the sample. The categories and the research questions emerged from the theoretical frame and background of the study as well as the historiographical accounts reviewed.

Research Questions

The research questions that drove this analysis were:

- Are the prevailing Vietnam War historiographies reflected in these novels written for young adults?
- Do the novels support or subvert American cultural myth?
- How are the participants in the conflict described? (Specifically, the American soldiers, the antiwar movement, and the Vietnamese. Also within this question, issues of participants" race, class and gender will be addressed.)
- Are there changes in the sample of novels relative to their date of publication?
- Are there consistencies in the narrative structures of the novels?

By systematically identifying passages from these novels to discuss and evaluate, inferences can be drawn about how the Vietnam War has been represented for young adult readers.

Narrative Structures

As mentioned in an earlier chapter, the novels have been analyzed in terms of both their content (narrators' and characters' statements about and reactions to the war) and form (or narrative structure). It should be noted that this division is really artificial and used only for the sake of clarity. In her 1984 study, Linda Christian considers narrative structure to be more than simply a story's plot. More explicitly it is defined as "the progression of events and the resolution of conflict. It essentially indicates what actions the characters are involved in and what they do. Characters and action work in tandem. . ." (p. 69).

The twenty-eight novels in the sample were easily separated into three categories based on narrative structure consistencies and similarities. Only one novel could potentially fit into more than one category. For the twenty-seven other novels, the distinctions were clear and prominent. *The Road Home* (1995) is divided into two sections— Part One: The War is included in one category; Part Two: The World is included in the other. (For a detailed summary of each novel in the sample, please refer to Appendix C.) Broadly described, the three categories are Combat novels, Response to the War novels, and finally Returned Vet novels. These groupings were created in the qualitative tradition of allowing categories to emerge naturally from the data—that is, the categories emerged as it became apparent to me that certain groups of novels shared a general narrative structure pattern.

Combat Novels

The seventeen novels in this category are all set in Vietnam during the war and include some combat. There are three distinct subcategories within this largest group of novels. The first subcategory (hereafter referred to as the Duty novels) is comprised of five novels that begin in America (one in Australia) detailing the protagonists' training before coming to the war. All characters, despite their personal feelings toward this war in particular, have a great sense of duty about serving their country. All protagonists are American or Australian, and although important to the story, only a few scenes of combat are included. This group contains the widest array of combat assignments of any of the categories. Included are two novels about nurses, *Vietnam Nurse* (1968) and *Nurse in Vietnam* (1969); the only novels concerning helicopter pilots, *Orders to Vietnam: A Novel of Helicopter Warfare* (1968) and the navy's riverine patrol, *Stop & Search: A Novel of Small Boat Warfare Off Vietnam* (1969); and finally a novel describing Green Beret counterinsurgency training, *Special Forces Trooper* (1967).

The second subcategory of combat novels focuses on Vietnamese or Montagnard (tribal inhabitants of Vietnam's Central Highlands—not ethnically Vietnamese) protagonists and will hereafter be referred to as the Vietnamese Perspective novels. In each of the five books in this subcategory, Vietnamese or Montagnard characters try to come to terms with combat, American characters, and America's involvement in their country. In three of the novels, *The Man in the Box* (1968), *Cross-fire* (1972), and *To Stand against the Wind* (1978), Vietnamese or Montagnard protagonists befriend an American character in attempting some understanding of the war. The two final novels, *Children of the Dragon* (1974) and *Sing for Your Father, Su Phan* (1997), detail characters in North Vietnam trying to make sense of American actions and the war in general.

I have named the third and final subcategory of combat novels the Platoon novels because of their surface similarity to the Oliver Stone film *Platoon*. In these novels, we meet the protagonists either in the airplane on the way to Vietnam or as they deplane in Vietnam. These novels are predominantly comprised of combat action. Included here are *War Year* (1972, 1978),[1] *Fallen Angels* (1988), *Echo Company #1—Welcome to Vietnam* (1991), *Echo Company #2—Hill 568* (1991), *Echo Company #3—'Tis the Season* (1991), *Echo Company #4—Stand Down* (1992), and Part One "The War" of *The Road Home* (1995). This subcategory contains the only series books written about Vietnam—the *Echo Company* books. *The Road Home*, while not an official *Echo Company* book, is nonetheless by the same author and is a continuation of the *Echo Company* story and characters. For the purposes of a discussion of narrative structure, the four series books are treated as four episodes of the same story. There appears to be no real conclusion at the end of each book, and each subsequent book would make little sense if the previous book had not been read. In fact, the second book in the series, *Hill 568*, begins just minutes after the end of the first book, *Welcome to Vietnam*, in the same place, with the characters still having virtually the conversation they were having when *Welcome to Vietnam* ended.

Response to the War Novels

The six novels that make up this category are all set in America during the war. In each novel, the protagonists struggle to make sense of the war and the effect that it has on their lives. Characters choosing to join the antiwar movement, evade the draft, or enlist and go to war in Vietnam are all profiled here as well as the events that lead up to these important life-altering decisions. Included in this category are *One Day for Peace* (1971), *Caribou* (1984), *And One for All* (1989), *The Best of Friends* (1989), *Long Time Passing* (1990), and *Come in from the Cold* (1994).

Returned Vet Novels

The novels in the final category of the sample are all set in America and all feature characters who experienced combat in Vietnam. In each case, the Vietnam vets and/or their families try to understand the meaning of the war in both personal and national terms. Four of these novels are set after the war (taking place from 1978 to 1987) and the others while the war continues (1968 and 1969). This struggle by the vets and/or their families to comprehend the meaning of the war and the effect it continues to have on the vets and everyone who loves them comprise the overall narrative structure of the novels in this category—*Where the Elf King Sings* (1980), *Travelers* (1986), *Charlie Pippin* (1987), *Pocket Change* (1989), *Tough Choices: A Story of the Vietnam War* (1993), and Part Two "The World" of *The Road Home* (1995).

These categories delineated by the novels' narrative structures will serve as an organizing device when discussing the novels in terms of each research question. For example, in chapter 4, the first research question (regarding the novels and the historiography of the war) will be addressed. As a method of organization and for clarity's sake, the novels will be discussed grouped in these narrative structure categories.

Note

1. Interestingly, Joe Haldeman's novel, *War Year,* was published in 1972 and 1978 in different editions. The stories are identical up to their last several pages. in the 1972 edition, the first person narrator watches his best friend being killed in a helicopter crash and then returns home a few weeks later. In the 1978 edition, the first person narrator sends his friend off in the same helicopter (which doesn't crash) and then is himself killed in an ambush a few hours later.

Chapter Four

Vietnam Historiography and Literature

The Nature of Historiography

Many Americans hold the conviction that "history" is an account of the past—objectively written from known and provable facts. These "facts" exist in an academic limbo, waiting for a historian to arrange them in some sort of chronological order to accurately depict the events of the past. According to historian Edward Hallett Carr (1961) "the belief in a hard core of historical facts existing objectively and independently of the interpretation of the historian is a preposterous fallacy, but one which it is very hard to eradicate" (p. 10).

The facts that survive any event are surely a minute fraction of all the possible knowledge that could have been retained. By what process does something become a historical fact? The facts must obviously be relevant to the concern of a particular historian at a particular time. Unfortunately, these surviving facts often are chosen for retention in a manner consistent

41

with the selective tradition as envisioned by Eagleton (1976) and Williams (1977) .

> From a whole possible area of past as present, in a particular culture, certain meanings and practices [and historical facts] are selected for emphasis and certain other meanings and practices [or historical facts] are neglected or excluded. Yet within a particular hegemony, and as one of its decisive processes, this selection is presented and usually successfully passed off as "*the* tradition", "*the* significant past" [*the* history]. (p. 115, my emphasis)

According to Williams, interpretations of history (or historiographies) legitimated by a selective tradition would be those that most advantageously reflect and promote the interests, values, and worldviews of those in power.

Few events in America's history provoke as much disagreement among historians as the Vietnam War. The great number of historians who have sought to explain the war are unable to even agree on what the facts are much less on what these facts might mean. The volume of disagreement is consistent with production theorist Gramsci's notions of resistance. Production theorists maintain that individuals and groups can resist hegemonic processes by asserting their own experiences and beliefs as legitimate. Each historian will choose different sets of facts on which to base her or his writing of history. Carr (1961) explains that historians' perspectives will influence their collection of facts from which to work:

> [Historical] facts are really not at all like fish on the fishmonger's slab. They are like fish swimming about in a vast and sometimes inaccessible ocean; and what the historian catches will depend partly on chance, but mainly on what part of the ocean he chooses to fish in and what tackle he chooses to use—these two factors being, of course, determined by the kind of fish he wants to catch. By and large, the historian will get the kind of facts he wants. *History means interpretation.* (p. 26, my emphasis)

Thus, according to Carr, there is no *objective* history or one *true* history that stands as a touchstone around which historians may conform or deviate.

Despite the fact that Carr understands that all historians will create their histories differently, he does maintain the belief that available historical fact constrains interpretation. Using the analogy of viewing a mountain from different angles, he points out that the actual shape of a mountain doesn't change. But is there an "actual shape" of history? Of course not, but historical interpretation, or historiography, must reside within factual boundaries.

There are as many interpretations of the causes, merits, outcomes, and implications of the Vietnam War as there are historians who examine it. In a case such as this, where even the facts cannot be agreed upon, it would be foolhardy to expect otherwise. The interpretations of Vietnam historians can generally be gathered into three major categories.[1] No two historians agree on each point of the history of America's involvement in Vietnam, but for classification purposes, I have grouped historians sharing similar views into three predominant interpretations of the war.

The Quagmire School

The quagmire interpretation of America's involvement in Vietnam consists of many distinct perspectives, but can be summed in several statements. America's foreign policy in Southeast Asia was well meaning, if not well informed.[2] In an attempt to contain expanding Asian communism

> American leaders from Truman to Johnson had undertaken a series of incremental steps in Indochina which ended in a disastrous U.S. involvement. This came about by chance, not design, and if any of the presidents had known where his policies were leading the nation, he never would have approved them. (Divine, 1988, p. 81)

Two eminent historians popularized terms that essentially provided the quagmire school with a vocabulary to discuss Vietnam. David Halberstam in *The Making of a Quagmire* (1965) coined the term "quagmire" to metaphorically conceptualize the entire U.S. involvement in Southeast Asia. Arthur Schlesinger, Jr.[3] in his often quoted (1967) work *Bitter Heritage: Vietnam and American Democracy 1941-1966* popularized the phrase "the politics of inadvertence," which he used to describe the uninformed and incremental steps just cited (Divine, 1988)—each step logically, if tragically, followed from those that had come previously.

The overriding theme in all quagmire historiographies is that America's involvement and eventual defeat in Vietnam came about gradually through a "series of relatively rational foreign policy decisions made by well-meaning administrators whose intentions were basically sound, which nevertheless lead inadvertently into the irrational quagmire of a land war in Vietnam" (Martin, 1987, pp. 92-93).

Critics of the quagmire interpretation cite the lack of any assignment of responsibility (or blame) as just one of many weaknesses of this theory. While obviously no single person could be held completely responsible for the gross destruction and enormous loss of life in Vietnam, Schlesinger, for example, faults no one or no group for their decisions. Various historians have in turn laid blame at the feet of the presidents, the advisors, and the military leaders. Quagmire historians and advisors writing about America's involvement in Vietnam generally excuse everyone, including themselves, for their roles in the tragedy. Other critics, such as Barbara Tuchman (1985) and Frances FitzGerald (1972), claim that our government officials—presidents and their advisors—were far from ignorant about events in Vietnam and thus their decisions could not be considered uninformed, and that America was not sucked into a quagmire against its collective will. FitzGerald (1972) states that in fact, ". . . the United States created the war" (quoted in Fromkin & Chace, 1985, p. 727).

Former president of the Students for a Democratic Society (SDS) and antiwar organizer Todd Gitlin (1987) remembers the vehemence directed at the antiwar groups, even from those quagmire subscribers who were dovish: ". . . the national pragmatism which though the war ought to be liquidated as a bad investment, a 'mistake,' a 'mess,' was incensed at students who insisted it was a crime" (p. 414). So, while much of the nation saw the war in Vietnam as a bad idea and eventually a tragedy, few were ready to accept any questioning of the morality of America's actions.

Another major criticism of the quagmire position centers on its lack of examination of one principle question—was the Cold War goal of containing communism at any cost a realistic or even morally acceptable one? This question is simply not addressed by these historians. The domino theory of the systematic fall to communism of one after another neighboring country is taken as an unquestioned and acceptable given.

The Revisionists

Often revisionist historians seek to reinterpret history as a broader and more inclusive representation—helping to legitimate the voices and views of historically marginalized groups in the overall picture of America's past. In terms of the revisionist work in Vietnam historiography, this is far from the case. Conservative historians have undertaken a considerable task in their rewriting of America's involvement in Vietnam. This "Ramboloney" (as Stephen Pelz called it in 1990) basically consists of an attempt to portray the war in a positive light. The essence of this interpretation of events in Vietnam is that the war was a "noble crusade against communism" that should have, and indeed could have, been won.[4] While many of the proponents of this revisionist position have always been staunch conservatives, the steadily increasing conservatism and aggression of America's domestic and foreign policies during the successive Reagan and Bush administrations did much to foster an environment that would breed and perpetuate this sort of historiography. Revisionists fault the liberal press, antiwar demonstrators, and spineless politicians as the principal villains in the Vietnam debacle.

> Indeed, many supporters of the American involvement in Indochina blame the media for stopping the war just at the point, they claim, when America had got it won. General William Westmoreland, the commander of the troops there, is only one of those who claim that the war was won militarily, but was lost because the United States no longer was willing to stay the course. (Fromkin & Chace, 1985, p. 728)

Richard Nixon, in his 1985 book, *No More Vietnams*, reiterates Westmoreland's view—America actually did win the war in Vietnam, but because of the indefensible and borderline seditious actions of the press, the demonstrators, and the Congress at home, the peace was lost. Even though many military analysts do not agree with Nixon that America actually had won the war in Vietnam, some do agree that American forces could have won and that defeat "wasn't inevitable" (Divine, 1988, p. 85). In his 1980 *A Soldier Reports*, Westmoreland claims that the military's hands were tied by politicians in a no-win, containment-only policy.

Revisionist historians also address the issue of the morality of America's actions in Vietnam. "While [these historians] admit that the use of chemical defoliants, the free-fire zones, and the heavy air bombardments killed many civilians, they claim that this war was no worse in that respect than other twentieth century conflicts" (Divine, 1988, p. 86). Guenter Lewy, in *America in Vietnam* (1978), claims that in a strictly legal sense, no war crimes were committed in Vietnam and that Americans shouldn't feel guilty about their country's involvement there. Norman Podhoretz in *Why We Were in Vietnam* (1982) goes one step further by completely standing the question of ethics on its head and placing any immorality connected with the war at the feet of the antiwar movement. "[Podhoretz] claims that those who opposed the Vietnam War acted immorally by giving aid and encouragement to the enemy, ignoring the totalitarian nature of the North Vietnamese government, and exaggerating the damage done by American raids on North Vietnam" (Divine, 1988, p. 87). Westmoreland more than concurs with Podhoretz. Despite the extraordinarily dubious logic of this position, one need only remember Americans' election year questioning of Bill Clinton's participation in antiwar demonstrations during his college years to understand the pervasiveness of Podhoretz's position even today.

The cry of "no more Vietnams" has an ominous meaning for these revisionist historians. The lessons they take away from Vietnam revolve around how America should behave the next time that it chooses to involve itself in the internal politics of another sovereign state. Historians who subscribe to this position seem to feel that America should always be ready to completely obliterate any enemy and that first complete support must be rallied (or wrenched) from the American public. Here, "no more Vietnams" is far from a demand for a new isolationism, but instead a call for America to always be ready to win (apparently at any price) any conflict it enters.

Critics of the revisionists easily find many holes in these historiographies. The first, and essentially most important, criticism is of the assertion that America could have won or, according to some historians, actually *did* win the war in Vietnam. The primary task here would be to define what is actually meant by "winning" a war. Few would dispute the fact that America possessed vastly superior military technology, a larger military, and many more resources than its smaller and less equipped adversary. If left to operate in total independence, it is quite possible that the American military could have destroyed both the North Vietnamese Army and the Viet Cong (VC) guerrillas, also wiping out much, if not most, of the Vietnamese civilian population along with them. But would that have constituted winning? If our objective in Vietnam was to stop the establishment of a communist government, killing the entire populace seems more than a bit extreme. Even though they were outnumbered and outgunned, the guerrillas never showed any inclination to stop fighting, nor is there any reason to assume that they would have if America had continued its efforts.

> To have won the war, moreover, the U.S. would have had to reform significantly the Saigon government, which claimed little popular following and existed at Washington's sufferance. The clique of southern leaders routinely jailed critics, fixed elections, refused land reform, and, as nationalists, ignored or rejected American advice. A series of conspiracies, coups, attempted coups, and American covert actions destabilized Vietnamese politics, while America's client, Ngo Dinh Diem [the nonelected and American supported president of South Vietnam], polarized politics by smashing the Buddhists, leaving the extreme choices of the NLF [National Liberation Front—North Vietnam] or the Saigon regime. (Paterson, 1988, p. 7)

There is little reason to believe that even if at any time American forces had even been in control of the populace and government of Vietnam that prewar problems would not have reappeared as the Americans departed. Paterson (1988) concludes that the war in Vietnam was virtually unwinnable:

> But even if the U.S. had overcome [its] litany of problems, victory would have remained elusive, because American leaders proved woefully ignorant about Indochina. They knew little and seemed not to want to know about the Vietnamese people and their ancient culture, particularly their traditional and largely successful resistance to foreign influence. (p. 12)

The notion that the American press was somehow so rabidly liberal that it provoked strong antiwar feelings in the general American population is definitely not consistent with fact. Prior to the Tet Offensive early in 1968, the majority of the American press—both print and broadcast—was solidly and unquestioningly behind the war effort. In fact, radical historians fault the press in the early war years for not being far *more* critical. After Tet the press was more prone to question America's motives and actions in Southeast Asia, although many still did not.

Revisionists, like their quagmire counterparts, leave the notion of the causes of the war unquestioned. There is little discussion of the validity of a war policy designed around the containment of communism. Critic Andrew Martin (1987) neatly summarizes the myriad faults of this revisionist stance, claiming that it conveys an extremely distorted picture of the war.

> . . . there is little or no reference to the political system of South Vietnam—to a system that was created and maintained by American power and which was, in practice, oppressive and unpopular with the vast majority of those who lived under it. At the same time, no attention is given to the war's violent contradictions, where whole provinces were destroyed so that they might be saved, where more bombs were dropped than in World War II and Korea combined, where over 10 million South Vietnamese refugees were created, along with almost 2 million South Vietnamese casualties and where more than 58,000 Americans were killed in action. (p. 100)

The revisionist and quagmire historiographies have in common their unquestioned interpretation of the cause of the war—communist containment.

The Radicals

The final group of historiographers of the Vietnam War make their observations from a significantly different standpoint than the other two groups. These radical historians are critical of America's involvement in Vietnam on *every* level. Where quagmire historians see American involvement as blind, gradual steps into an unmanageable quagmire, and conservative revisionist historians see American military might thwarted by the leftist press and communist-infiltrated student organizations, radical historians see America's involvement in Vietnam as yet another episode in a long series of interventionist and imperialist foreign policy decisions.[5] It is their general contention that despite the fact that the United States has never overtly established colonies in the classical European tradition, it has nevertheless exerted enough political, economic, and military influence to create covert colonies through American dominated surrogate regimes that had come to power through American covert operations and that were maintained with American money and military might (Pelz, 1990).

Radical historian William Appleman Williams (1980) believes that Americans have always seen themselves as vehemently anticolonial, but also considers this to have been largely self-deluding.

> [Throughout American history, policy makers] became less candid about their imperial attitudes and practices. They talked ever more about "extending the area of freedom," supporting such noble principles as "territorial and administrative integrity" and "saving the world for democracy"—even as they destroyed the cultures of the First Americans, conquered half of Mexico, and relentlessly expanded their government's power around the globe. (p. ix)

Correspondent Michael Herr (1977) agrees in recognizing America's expansionist policies when he asserts that "you might as well say that Vietnam was where the Trail of Tears was headed all along" (p. 49).

The extreme communist containment policies that emerged from the Cold War drove the United States to becomes the world's police force. Establishing covert colonies through surrogate regimes to prevent Third World countries from choosing communism accounts for a large part of the American empire. Neil Sheehan (1988), writing about the career of John Paul Vann, an early American advisor to the South Vietnamese government, summarized Vann's (and largely, the American public's) beliefs about American policies that are essentially interventionist:

> Vann's political credo was the set of beliefs characteristic of the United States that had emerged from World War II as the greatest power on earth, the view of self and the world that had carried America to war in

Vietnam in the fullness of this power. To Vann, other peoples were lesser peoples: it was the natural order of things that they accept American leadership. He was convinced that having gained the preeminence it had been destined to achieve, the United States would never relinquish the position. He did not see America as using its power for self-satisfaction. He saw the United States as a stern yet benevolent authority that enforced peace and brought prosperity to the people of the non-Communist nations, sharing the bounty of its enterprise and technology with those who had been denied a fruitful life by poverty and social injustice and bad government. He assumed that America's cause was always just, that while the United States might err, its intentions were always good. He was simplistic in his anti-communism, because to him all Communists were enemies of America and thus enemies of order and progress. (p. 7)

Disturbances or revolutions in the Third World were often attributed to communist influence and were thus considered threatening to the United States. Williams (1980) explains America's intervention in foreign revolutions in terms of our own revolution.

> . . . the American Revolution (including the conception and implementation of the Constitution) represented the perfect revolution. Americans came very quickly to view themselves as having discovered the ultimate solution to mankind's long search for the proper way to organize society. Jefferson encapsulated the outlook in his famous remark that America was the "world's best hope."
>
> That belief had two imperial consequences. *First,* the behaviour of other peoples (including their revolutions) was judged by its correspondence with the American Way. The weaker the correlation, the greater the urge to intervene to help the wayward find the proper path to freedom and prosperity. *Second,* the faith in America's uniqueness coupled with the failure of others to copy the perfect revolution generated a deep sense of being *alone.* Americans considered themselves perpetually beleaguered, an attitude that led on to the conviction that military security was initally to be found in controlling the entire contenient—and ultimately prompted them to deny any distinction between domestic and foreign policy. (p. 53, emphasis in original)

Evidently, the revolution in Vietnam neither met this criteria properly nor corresponded to the "American Way."

Gabriel Kolko (1969), writing eloquently during the war, perhaps said it most forcefully when he concluded that

> . . . ultimately, the United States has fought in Vietnam with increasing intensity to extend its hegemony over the world community and to stop every form of revolutionary movement which refuses to accept the predominant role of the United States in the direction of the affairs of its nation or region. (p. 132)

With regard to the notion of "no more Vietnams," Thomas Paterson (1988) bleakly describes the radical perspective of the inevitability of many more "Vietnams."

> According to this reasoning, the United States is destined to repeat Vietnam-type experiences for several reasons. Americans will likely insist on remaining "Number One," whatever that means, and this psychological factor compels an activist, interventionist foreign policy. Americans will continue, as well, to exaggerate the Communist threat and thus interpret local crises derived from internal sources as Cold War contests demanding impositions of the containment doctrine. So long as a national security bureaucracy perpetuates a war-making machine and the imperial presidency [Reagan/Bush when Paterson was writing] overwhelms the checks-and-balances system and misleads the American people through deliberate "disinformation," Vietnams will darken America's future. (p. 4)

Radical historians, unlike their quagmire and revisionist counterparts, dispute not only the primary cause of the Vietnam War, accepting the given communist containment as only a surface explanation, they also question the overall morality of American involvement in Vietnam.

Unlike competing historiographical interpretations of other events or periods in American history, the quagmire, revisionist, and radical positions on the war in Vietnam have existed simultaneously rather than in turn.[6]

Historiographies and Adolescent Fiction

Examining adolescent novels that address the Vietnam War and its aftermath for their historiographical stances will help to address and uncover the ideology that Eagleton (1976) and Taxel (1980) claim is inherent in all literature. Eagleton (1976) states that "there is no such thing . . . as a work of art . . . devoid of ideological content" (p. 17), and Taxel agrees that literature is "grounded in specifiable ideological orientations" (p. 11). The "ideological orientations" in the sample of novels are apparent in the historiographical stance expressed in each novel.

The historiographical and ideological stance taken in each novel is not always stated in an unmistakable and straightforward manner. Each novel's narrative structure and content work together to demonstrate its historiographical stance. Situations, characters' reactions to those situations, internal narration, and dialogue are all conduits through which interpretations of the causes, merits, outcomes, and implications of the war can flow.

In turning to the twenty-eight novels in the sample, historiographical interpretations of the war were not always immediately apparent, but emerged eventually. As was explained in the narrative structure section of chapter 3, what follows is a discussion of the three historiographies—quagmire, revisionist, and radical—and their manifestations in the novels will be organized around the three narrative structure groups (Combat novels, Response to the War novels, and Returned Vet novels).

Combat Novels—Duty Subcategory

Given that these novels all take place *during* the war, it is reasonable that none of the Combat novels of any subcategory will be able to address the overall implications of the war on American life and history. The Duty novels contain a wealth of information and attitudes toward the causes, purposes, and merits of the war in Vietnam. The rather simplistic attitudes displayed in the Duty novels is reminiscent of the attitudes expressed by John Paul Vann quoted earlier in this chapter. *Special Forces Trooper* (1967) follows Stan Rusat through his special forces training in the States to his tour of duty in Vietnam as an ARVN (Army of the Republic of South Vietnam) and CIDG (Civilian Irregular Defense

Group—Montagnard) advisor. Stan knows exactly why the American military is involved in Vietnam—to fight the "shackles of Communism" (p. 153). He refers to the war as a "civil war" but rationalizes American intervention with lofty platitudes: "The reason for the presence of all Green Berets in [Vietnam], with no exception was the preservation of human freedom" (p. 143).

Back in the Special Forces training portion of this novel, we are told that the

> Special Forces teams were conducting psychological warfare to win the people before the Vietcong did. The term Unconventional Warfare had given way to the designation, Counterinsurgency, a program aimed at healing rifts, social and political, in a population stemming from class, ethnic, religious, or linguistic differences. (p. 6)

When the Green Beret trainees go on a "war games" exercise in the woods of North Carolina, they are told that they will be helping the peasant people of the "mythical country of Pineland, an emerging nation seeking a democratic government" (p. 59). Obviously, Pineland is a thinly veiled substitute for Vietnam.

Orders to Vietnam: A Novel of Helicopter Warfare (1968) is the story of Bill Byrnes, a warrant officer and helicopter pilot. When his father, a general, insists that Bill attend West Point, Bill decides eventually to become a pilot. His training takes him to Vietnam where, after extensive combat experience, he becomes a commissioned officer. Bill briefly questions the ultimate purpose of the war when weighed against the loss of American life. A confrontation with Captain Hawker reveals the only reasons given in the entire novel for American involvement in Vietnam:

> "He was a soldier. He got paid for driving helicopters. He knew what the score was, just like you and me. Soldiers get killed. That's the name of the game."
> "That makes it right?"
> "I didn't say that," Hawker said. "I didn't . . ."
> "For that lousy little hilltop? Who wants it?"
> "What is your solution for the problem of communist expansion, Mr. Byrnes?" Hawker asked. "To give in to fatherly Uncle Ho?" (p. 117).

It is taken as a given that readers would understand how and why "communist expansion" would present a problem for Americans.

Stop & Search: A Novel of Small Boat Warfare Off Vietnam (1969) follows protagonist Eddie Czernik from high school through Navy ROTC to his duty as a river patrol boat pilot. Nowhere in *Stop & Search* is communist expansion mentioned. In the only exchange in the novel that even vaguely alludes to a cause of the war in Vietnam, patrol boat pilot Eddie Czernik's grandfather urges him to kill communists when he arrives in Vietnam:

> "They are no good, the Communists. Of all the madmen who have tried to rule the world, they are the worst. They deny God and dignity. If it bothers you to kill them, Little Eddie, consider that it would not bother them at all to kill you, and that they will be trying very hard to do that. Hunt them as you would a rabid dog." (p. 56)

We are given no reason for the grandfather's vehemence against communism, nor is communism in any way explained in any of the Duty novels. We can gather only that it is evil incarnate and must be stopped at any cost.

Putting an end to communist expansion appears to be the characters' interpretation of American intervention in Vietnam in both of the nurse novels. The first novel, *Vietnam Nurse* (1968), tells the story of Australian nurse Joanna Shelton's search for her missionary/physician father who is missing in the jungles of Vietnam. He was actually on a mission for the Americans to establish talks between the governments in Washington and Hanoi. Joanna is escorted on her search by a Green Beret unit. *Vietnam Nurse*'s Joanna Shelton pities the Montagnard characters whom she meets in the Highlands of Vietnam and the coarse and turbulent life that they lead. "Peace won't cure all of this overnight, but a country at peace had the time and energy to do a little housecleaning, and Vietnam could certainly do with that. And the first stop is to clear it of Communists" (p. 1). Joanna doesn't explain how ridding Vietnam of communism would help the Montagnards, nor does she speculate on the prospect of how ridding Vietnam of Americans might help. Green Beret Captain Wayne Moore agrees with Joanna's interpretation that the purpose of the war is to stop communist expansion. He also accurately predicts escalating American involvement. "[Wayne] felt that, in time, the U.S. would be totally committed, would be pouring troops and money into the South in an attempt to stem the continuous infiltration of Communists from the North" (p. 148).

Nurse in Vietnam (1969) tells the story of U.S. Air Force nurse Lieutenant Lisa Blake's tour of duty at Clark Air Force Base in the Philippines and her eventual romance with Green Beret Captain Mace Thomas. The novel only hints at the idea of communist expansion by tying it to Vietnamese "freedom." Lisa believes that Americans are fighting in Vietnam because they are "the forces that were defending freedom around the world" (p. 9). The whole of the purpose of the war from the perspectives of the characters in *Nurse in Vietnam* is a "struggle to keep men free" (p. 12). In a particularly stilted scene, a wounded and dying soldier dictates his last letter home to Lisa, his nurse. He explains to his children his (and presumably America's) reasons for fighting in Vietnam:

> I am not the only daddy who won't be coming home, because others like me will also die in the line of duty. You see, the people in this little country of Vietnam do not live in a free country like America. So American soldiers are helping them to win their freedom. I came over to fight knowing that I might be killed, but I also knew that by doing my part I might save you children from having your freedom taken from you. (p. 120)

This nameless soldier doesn't explain from whom the Vietnamese are trying to win this freedom or how the potential "freedom" of the Vietnamese people could in any way be linked to the freedom of children in America. This bizarre and nebulous connection between the freedom of Vietnam and America is also mentioned by Lisa when she thinks of American soldiers fighting in Vietnam as "men who defended *their* country" (p. 10, my emphasis).

Combat Novels—Vietnamese Perspective Subcategory

Only one of the five novels in this group was actually authored by a writer who lived in Vietnam during the war. The other novels can provide only an American interpretation of a Vietnamese outlook on the causes and implications of the war in their country. In *The Man in the Box* (1968) we see the first mention of Americans being in Vietnam at the invitation of the (South) Vietnamese. This is the story of a Montagnard boy, Chau Li, and the Green Beret, David, whom he saves. David has been captured by the VC and after having been tortured is being held in a tiny bamboo box in Chau Li's unnamed village as a means of intimidating its residents. Even though Chau Li's friend Ky and the village teacher continually refer to the Americans as "invaders," Chau Li maintains another perspective. Immediately before the final battle scene in which the entire village is destroyed, some of the older villagers try to discourage Chau Li from fighting along with the Americans:

> "Be careful. You do not know these weapons [that the Americans] have put in your hands. I do not see why you want to go out and mix in this."
> "I do not. We have asked these men to come here to help us, not fight for us. Now we must go and do our part." (p. 146)

Of course, the Montagnards had never asked for American help and ultimately whether the South Vietnamese asked for it is even debatable. There is nothing else in the novel that addresses why Americans were asked to come help or what they may have been helping to do.

Cross-fire (1972) is a virtual echo of *The Man in the Box* (1968) in its neglect of any sort of discussion of causes or purposes of the war or American involvement in the war. In *Cross-fire* (1972) an American soldier, Harry, is separated from his unit after a firefight. Awaking alone in the jungle, he comes across four Vietnamese children whose entire village has just been destroyed by American bombers. The novel follows Harry and the children as they attempt to figure out each other's actions and motivations. Also like *The Man in the Box*, *Cross-fire* reiterates the notion that American troops were in Vietnam at the request of the Vietnamese; but this time, there is some American frustration that Americans might be doing too much of the fighting—very probably a result of a later publication date. When Harry is alone in the jungle with the four Vietnamese children he has found, he thinks: "Damned Vietnamese. They ask us to come over here and fight their lousy, stinking war for them" (p. 108). Harry apparently has no opinion about the causes or purposes of the war—just that the Vietnamese have asked the Americans to come.

The Vietnamese characters in *To Stand against the Wind* (1978) have some very curious attitudes toward American intervention in their country. This story is told in one, long flashback after Em (the ten-year-old protagonist) and his remaining family have emigrated to America. Em recalls the events leading to his family's departure from Vietnam, from the war's encroaching influence on their lives to the eventual death of most of his family when an American air strike destroys his unnamed village. Even though Em and his family members state how much they have resented the rule of previous invaders, they welcome the Americans who are "coming to help run our government"—presumably at the request of the South Vietnamese (p. 30). There is some discussion, although only in the third person internal narration, of the causes of the war.

> As Em had grown older, he had become aware of the unrest among the people. The Vietnamese had always resented foreign domination—Chinese and later French—but they had always fought bitterly among themselves as well. They were patriotic, but their loyalty was to the land rather than to the people. Local elected officials and many secret societies and committees and factions had always existed side by side. Finally the country *became divided* into Northern communists and Southern noncommunists. In the South, there were some sympathizers of the communists, and in the North of the noncommunists. Then in the South there were the Vietcong, who were sympathetic to the Northern communists. (p. 11, my emphasis)

The rather vague "became divided" makes the division at the seventeeth parallel appear to have happened spontaneously as opposed to something foisted on the American people by Western governments. The American involvement in the war takes on a quagmire tone in the internal narration when the Americanization of the war is described.

> True, almost all the French were gone, but the North and South were arguing bitterly. The Vietcong were siding with the North. Powerful nations were giving aid to the North while the military of the United States came to the South. At first they came to advise and train the Vietnamese. Here and there military bases were built. More and more Americans came. (p. 33)

The one American character in *To Stand against the Wind*, Sam, a news reporter, reiterates the idea of an incremental American involvement gone awry in a conversation with a village elder: "[the war] is as confusing to me as it is to you. Most of us don't know why we got into this mess and why we don't get out of it" (p. 41). Other than these vague statements about the North and South arguing and becoming divided, nothing about the causes of the war or appropriateness of American involvement is mentioned.

The final two Vietnamese Perspective novels are both set in North Vietnam, which obviously provides a significantly different viewpoint from which to comment on the war. The didactic *Children of the Dragon* (1974) takes every opportunity to express thoughts on the causes, purposes, and potential outcomes of the war. This is the first novel in the Combat category that addresses any larger political issues behind the war and the fact that the "Vietnam" war actually extended into both Cambodia and Laos. The preface to the story gives a short chronology of Vietnamese history focusing mainly on varying foreign invasions of Vietnam. The Mongols, the Chinese, the French, and the Americans are all listed as invaders, although no recriminations are made. *Children of the Dragon* (1974) tells the story of Tri, a young Vietnamese boy sent from Hanoi to live with his Grandmother in the country to be safe from the constant American bombing of civilians. Tri and his cousin Hoa attend school and enjoy the pastoral life of rural North Vietnam. Grandmother Te tells her grandson Tri a story about ancient Vietnam with clear implications about the American war. "This province you are visiting, little Tri, is called Thai Binh. The name means Lasting Peace. We Vietnamese are always looking for peace, but we have been attacked by war makers throughout our history. We always fight back" (p. 2).

There is much talk of freedom for the Vietnamese in *Children of the Dragon*, but this time it is the freedom for the Vietnamese people to live without foreign intervention in their country. Grandmother remembers the misery of the old days before "we won our independence in the North" (p. 19). She neither states nor implies from whom this freedom was won—although perhaps she means from the French who were the most recent colonizers of the Indo-Chinese peninsula—Vietnam, Cambodia, and Laos. Both Grandmother Te and Teacher Vo from the village school perceive the war in Vietnam as a fight for the freedom of South Vietnam and North Vietnam to be a single country again. Grandmother Te explains:

> Now the United States is in the southern part of Viet Nam and our country is divided. Today there is a South Viet Nam and a North Viet Nam where there has always been one country. . . . Soon the South will be free and Viet Nam will be one country again. Then our people will know peace. (p. 5)

In a geography lesson at school, Teacher Vo echoes Grandmother Te's sentiment:

> Here it is on the map. Do you see the 17th parallel? It divides Viet Nam in two parts—the North and the South. We Vietnamese did not make that boundary. Other countries divided Viet Nam. But the people in the North and South are fighting to be one country again. Then we can take the dividing line off the map. (p. 31)

This is the first and only mention in the Combat novels of the historical fact that Vietnam was indeed divided by the Geneva Accords in 1954 by representatives of countries other than Vietnam. It is quite a different take on the war to envision it as one people—both North and South, falsely divided by outsiders, fighting to regain control over their own destiny. *Children of the Dragon* does not, however, address any issues of the causes or purposes of America's perspective of intervention in Vietnam.

While *Children of the Dragon* is explicitly political, *Sing for Your Father, Su Phan* (1997) is quite the opposite. This short autobiographical novel was co-authored by Su Phan (who has subsequently changed her name to Fay Tang), the daughter of a Chinese merchant family who lived in a small village in North Vietnam during the war. This novel details her family's experiences. Chung Bo, the merchant father, is arrested by "the Communists" and put in prison for seven years because he did not embrace communism. His wife and children spend these years trying to scratch out a living and survive the distant war that is only visited upon them through occasional American bombing raids. The young characters in this novel are largely ignorant of and uninterested in the war. The only comment about the war is made by a school friend of Su Phan's, Chung Bo's young daughter:

> "I wish they'd fly somewhere else!" Lien exclaimed. "I hate the noise those planes makes."
> Some boys standing nearby hooted with laughter. "Planes? Those are bombers, you stupid girl!" one of them said. "Don't you know there's a war going on?"
> "Well, yes. But what has that to do with us?" Lien replied.
> "Do with us?" The boy shook his head. To his friends, he said, "Do you believe this?" He looked back at Lien. "Wake up. We've been fighting for years and it'll probably go on forever." (p. 15)

There is some resentment toward the Americans, even though the resentment ultimately seems more like an irritation than the feelings one might hold for an enemy who bombs the village you live in. Later in the same conversation, another character adds matter-of-factly, "We'd have won long ago if it weren't for the Americans butting in, taking the South's side and bombing us." Many characters' comments make it sound as if "the Communists" are the true enemy—which ultimately makes little sense. If the communists are the enemy, then wouldn't the South be an ally? Never do characters discuss the causes or purposes of the war. There is never an explanation of communism even though the word is used frequently—and frequently as an accusation.

Sing for Your Father, Su Phan makes several mentions of the previous French colonial government that ruled Vietnam for many years prior to the war and the maintenance of which contributed to the start of the Vietnam War. Several characters speculate that Chung Bo's arrest was at least partially because of his previously friendly relationship with the ruling French government. Even though neither do so in any depth, *Children of the Dragon* and *Sing for Your Father, Su Phan* are the only novels that mention French involvement in Vietnam.

Combat Novels—Platoon Subcategory

It might be expected that the Platoon novels would contain the most information about the nature of American involvement in Vietnam, given that they are the stories of the actual Americans involved in Vietnam, told during their involvement. With the exception of *Fallen Angels* (1988), however, very little straightforward information is actually given. *War Year* (1972, 1978) is the only novel in the sample written by a Vietnam vet. This first person narrative follows nineteen-year-old draftee John Farmer from his arrival in Vietnam through his tour of duty as a combat engineer in the Central Highlands, close to Pleiku—including his eventual wounding in a firefight and his subsequent hospital stay. There is virtually no mention of the cause or purpose of the war that nearly consumes John. He is there. The war is there. Everyone tries to get home in one piece. No characters express thoughts or speculations regarding why they have been sent thousands of miles from home against their collective wills to risk their lives.

Fallen Angels (1988) is a first person narrative that follows seventeen-year-old African American Richie Perry from his arrival in Saigon through his tour of duty near Chu Lai. Through Perry, we become acquainted with the other men in his squad, as they endure the traumas of a jungle war with no front lines. *Fallen Angels* is perhaps the novel in which the most information about the perceived causes and purposes of the war is given—although many contradictory perceptions are given. In a contrived scene, Perry's squad is in an unnamed firebase when a television crew happens by. The news reporter asks each person, in turn, their reasons for fighting in Vietnam. Lieutenant Carroll, the platoon leader, replies that the soldiers "had to demonstrate that America stood for something, and that's what [they] were doing" (p. 77), although neither Carroll nor the narration states what he thinks America stands for. Radical historians might agree that American interventionism is *exactly* what America stands for, but I don't think that is what Carroll intended. Sergeant Simpson, the squad leader, "said that we were trying to free the South Vietnamese people to do what they wanted to do" (p. 77). This statement implies that the South Vietnamese people were being oppressed in some manner and that the Americans were fighting the oppressors. In that case, perhaps American soldiers should have fought the corrupt government of South Vietnam in equal proportion to the VC. "Brunner said he was fighting because he hated communism" (p. 77). It is doubtful, however, in light of Corporal Brunner's other comments, that he would even know what communism was. When the television crew reaches Private Lobel, he gives the domino theory as the purpose of the war: ". . . if Vietnam fell to the Communists then the rest of Asia might fall" (p.

77). There is never any questioning of this dubious Cold War logic. Finally, the camera crew comes to Perry and his answer is the most curious and enigmatic of all. "I said that we either defended our country abroad, or we would be forced to fight in the streets of America" (p. 77). Vaguely reminiscent of the dying soldier's letter in *Nurse in Vietnam* (1969), Perry equates American soldiers fighting in Vietnam with defending *our* country. There is never any sort of explanation for this logic or connections that underpin this non sequitur.

Later, Perry and another grunt, Johnson, reflect on the abstract nature of fighting "communism":

> "I guess somebody back home knows what they're doing," I said. "What it means and everything. You talk about Communists—stuff like that—and it doesn't mean much when you're in school. Then when you get over here the only thing they're talking about is keeping your ass in one piece."
>
> "Vietnam don't mean nothing, man," Johnson said. "We could do the same thing someplace else. We just over here killing people to let everybody know we gonna do it if it got to be done."
>
> "That might be a good reason to be over here." I said.
>
> "That's for people like you to mess with," Johnson said.
>
> "I don't know about that."
>
> "Then why you messin' with it?" (p. 148)

In this exchange it appears to be Johnson's contention that the entire point of American intervention in Vietnam is the demonstration of American military might—muscle flexing, so to speak. Johnson also implies that there is little purpose in questioning the reasons that America was in Vietnam.

The revisionist notion that the war was or could have been won militarily, but not politically—or more popularly put: win the war, but lose the peace—is expressed by Major Leff when he addresses the platoon, saying that they "have to remember that there's as much of a psychological war going on over here as there is a physical war" (p. 173). Leff creates an artificial division in war—the psychological war *is* the real war as much as the bullets and bombs are. He also doesn't go on to explain how this could happen or what could be done to prevent it.

The final interpretation of the purpose of the American involvement in Vietnam comes from the chaplain in a Purple Heart ceremony conducted in the hospital after Perry has been wounded. After the presentation of medals,

> the chaplain said that everything we did we did for the highest reasons that men knew.
> "You are defending freedom," he said. "You are defending the freedom of Americans and of the South Vietnamese. Your acts of heroism and courage are celebrations of life, and all America thanks you." (p. 215)

Perry doesn't question or reflect in the internal narration on anything that the chaplain says. There is no explanation of how killing Vietnamese in Vietnam could be construed as defending the freedom of Americans. Earlier in the novel, there is more than one instance in which entire hamlets of Vietnamese civilians have been destroyed and their inhabitants killed. How was their freedom defended? How could any of these actions be construed as having a "high" reason or being a "celebration of life"?

The *Echo Company* series focuses on eighteen-year-old draftee protagonist Michael Jennings as he travels from Saigon to join his unit near Chu Lai. The series follows Michael as he takes over the point position in the squad and eventually takes the whole company to a stand down on the base in Chu Lai. The only real mention of the purpose or cause of the war in *Echo Company #1—Welcome to Vietnam* (1991) comes early on as draftee Michael Jennings travels to Chu Lai shortly after his arrival in country. Michael interprets American involvement in Vietnam in terms of the domino theory, but laces his explanation with some healthy cynicism.

> Michael wasn't exactly an expert on the war—other than knowing he didn't want to be in it—but, the basic situation was that it was a civil war. South Vietnam wanted to be independent, and democratic—so they said—and North Vietnam wanted to take over the whole country, and make it communist. The DMZ [demilitarized zone, something of a misnomer] was sort of a no-man's-land separating the two halves of the country. The Geneva Convention had something to do with all of this, but Michael wasn't sure what.

> He was even more vague on why the United States was here at all
> but apparently—so they said—communism was a fate worse than death,
> and if South Vietnam fell, the rest of the world might follow. Like, one
> country at a time. America was going to save the world. So they said. (p.
> 29)

All in all, not a very satisfactory explanation. Again, there is no questioning of the logic behind the domino theory. The first idea that Michael expresses about South Vietnam wanting to be independent and democratic is also not wholly accurate. The Diem government in Saigon (and all of its coup-produced successors) had few, if any, democratic leanings. Leadership in the North wanted the country split through Western intervention to be reunited under one government, but was mainly prevented from doing so by the American presence.

In *Echo Company #2—Hill 568* (1991), Michael continues to question the purpose of stopping communism and even the meaning of communism itself. During a particularly brutal battle to take "Hill 568" on Thanksgiving Day, Michael thinks, between attempts up the hill, about the justification of killing people over differing preferences for economic systems.

> People. He was trying to kill *people*. . . And—they were the
> enemy. And—Communism was bad.
> He laughed weakly, keeping his head down behind a splintered log.
> That's why he was here. When he should be home, eating turkey, and
> fighting with Dennis and Carrie about who was going to do the dishes.
> Because some big shots somewhere thought that Communism—a
> concept he would probably have trouble defining on a social studies
> test—was bad. He, personally, didn't care if they were godless Communists—as long as they left *him* alone. (p. 199, emphasis in original)

Although Michael doesn't understand why he should have to risk his life to rid the world of communism, he doesn't pursue the matter any further. The final *Echo* books (1991, 1992) reiterate the idea that the war is being fought to stop communism. Michael eventually thinks that he is "risking his life for freedom and democracy," but he doesn't say whose (*Echo #4*, p. 109).

The Road Home (1995) is unofficially the fifth book in the *Echo* series. Written by the same author (who penned the *Echo* books under the pseudonym Zack Emerson), Part One (The War) of the novel begins shortly after *Echo Company #4—Stand Down* concludes. (Part Two—The World is included in the Returned Vet section.)

After Michael Jennings steps on a mine and has a traumatic above-the-knee amputation, he is brought to the evac hospital where he had recently visited Rebecca Phillips, a nurse whom his squad had rescued in the bush. In a scene surprisingly similar to the one in *Fallen Angels* (1988), a general awards Michael his Purple Heart instead of Perry's chaplain. The general comments, "On behalf of the U.S. Army, I hereby present you this Purple Heart, for wounds received in action, in the defense of the Republic of South Vietnam" (p. 159). This oblique comment about "defending" South Vietnam is the only mention of why American soldiers were in Vietnam.

All in all the domino theory is mentioned most frequently in the Platoon novels as the leading cause for American intervention in Vietnam. Often included is the idea that Americans are fighting for freedom and democracy. Inexplicably, American freedom and democracy are sometimes quite mysteriously tied to action in Vietnam.

Response to the War Novels

Novels in this category could easily lend themselves to detailed historiographical accounts of the war, given their narrative structure. Since characters are responding and reacting to the war and sometimes to their potential participation in it, this structure seems particularly created to examine historiographical issues. In *One Day for Peace* (1971), Jane Simon tries to understand the purpose of the war that has taken the life of her friend. After becoming convinced that the war is wrong, Jane and some of her friends organize a peace march that culminates in the ceremonial planting of a tree in a downtown park. Jane writes to the president for an explanation and receives a pamphlet entitled *Why We Fight in Vietnam,* which will ostensibly answer her questions. An excerpt from the document reads:

> We are fighting to assist the people and Government of the Republic of Vietnam to defend themselves against aggression. We are

there, at their request, to help them maintain their right to direct their
own affairs free from external influence.

By early 1965, it became clear that unless the U.S. and other
nations introduced major combat forces to assist the Republic of
Vietnam in military action against growing external aggression, South
Vietnam would be taken over by force. If that had happened, there can
be no doubt whatever that, by the dynamics of aggression, Communist
Chinese and North Vietnamese subversive efforts against the rest of
Southeast Asia would have been increased and encouraged. We would
also have seen a drastic reduction of the will and capacity of the
remaining nations of Southeast Asia to resist their pressures. (p. 20)

It is hard to even know where to begin in commenting on this passage.
Since South Vietnam wasn't a nation until Westerners at the 1954 Geneva
Convention deemed it so, it is difficult to imagine how anything from
North Vietnam could be considered "external" aggression. Radical
historians would argue that the lion's share of external aggression came
in the form of American troops. There is again no discussion of the
viability of or justification for containing communism. Since there was
previously neither democracy nor communism in Vietnam, radicals might
also argue that American forces were attempting to impose democracy in
much the same way that they accused the North Vietnamese of trying to
impose communism.

Jane's father agrees when she claims that none of the government
information really answers her question. He also points out what he
considers to be inaccuracies in the government information.

The fact is, Vietnam is one country, temporarily separated into north
and south after the Vietnamese threw the French out. The French had
set up a corrupt government that the people hated, and we've done the
same thing. The South Vietnamese government we support is not only
corrupt—it's antidemocratic, too. We're afraid to let the people of the
country throw the tyrants out and set up their own government. Now we
talk about aggression—but we're the only aggressors. (p. 22)

Jane's father has taken a radical historiographical stand on interpreting
American involvement in Vietnam.

The 1989 novels *The Best of Friends* and *And One for All* have the
virtually parallel narrative structure of two potentially draftable high

school seniors who disagree about the war. In both novels, one boy enlists in the army and one grows to vehemently oppose the war. *And One for All* (1989) is the story of Wing Brennan, a high-tempered, weak student who enlists in the marines in a snit after failing a high school English test. Wing's friend, Sam Daily, becomes an antiwar activist in Washington. The majority of the characters in *And One for All* espouse communist containment as the purpose of the war. Sam Daily, the one antiwar character in the novel, points to the influence of the military-industrial complex and the profit incentive in the escalation of the war effort.

> "We don't have any business over there," Sam insisted. "It's a civil war—it doesn't have anything to do with us."
> "Bull, Daily—those North Vietnamese are Communists—what're you going to do, sit back and let 'em take over the world?"
> "Bull yourself, Brennan—that's just a line the rich guys made up—the ones who manufacture weapons. They're the only ones getting anything out of this war." (p. 35)

Although Sam insists that the war in Vietnam is a "civil war," he doesn't explain what he means by this.

The Best of Friends (1989) is the story of Will Spencer and his best friend Dan Ulvang. Dan is a history student who studies the historical and political context of the Vietnam War and who eventually comes to challenge his draft board father by returning his draft card. As a noncollege-bound high school senior, Will eventually joins the army, with little discussion as to what his decision might entail. Characters in *The Best of Friends* provide a variety of information about the perceived purposes and causes of the war. Dan and his father (who is a Korean War veteran) argue over the purpose of the war. Again we see the same unexplained connection of fighting in Vietnam and defending the freedom of America that was present in both *Nurse in Vietnam* (1969) and *Fallen Angels* (1988).

> "You know as well as I do that we're fighting in Vietnam to protect our way of life against the Communists. Our freedom. Your freedom to go to school. Your freedom to protest. We must support democracy in Vietnam."

> "There's no democracy over there. We didn't allow South Vietnam
> to hold free elections in 1956. That's when they lost democracy. We
> interfered then. And we're interfering now. (p. 93)

Dan is correct in his assertion that the elections called for in the 1954
Geneva Convention were prevented by the Americans and the South
Vietnamese government (because it was widely known that a communist
government would be freely elected by the Vietnamese population), but
he oversteps when he claims that at this point the South Vietnamese "lost"
democracy. The governmental structure in South Vietnam was at no time
democratic. Perhaps it would have been more accurate to say that they lost
the potential for democracy. As before, there is no explanation of the
supposed tie between American freedom and the American intervention
in Vietnam, even as another character claims that "we're fighting for *our*
way of life over there" (p. 93). Later in the same argument, Dan's father
claims that communist containment or the domino theory is another
reason for the war:

> "Let me tell you the truth." Dad leaned forward, pointing his pipe
> at Dan. "Wherever you have Communists, democracy is in danger. Look
> at Hungary and Poland in 1955, at Czechoslovakia just last year. Now
> Vietnam."
> "The Viet Cong aren't Communists. That's a myth."
> "Myth! Where did you get that? Ho Chi Minh is an ally of the Red
> Chinese and you know it."
> "That's what Nixon wants us to believe, so we'll all shut up and
> support the war."
> "You're saying the President is lying?"
> "Yes. If you call propaganda lying. That's all it is—propaganda so
> we'll all back the war." (p. 94)

Embedded in this discussion of containment is some inaccurate information about the nature of Vietnamese communism. The VC were indeed
communist, as was Ho Chi Minh and the government of North Vietnam.
They were not, however, allies of the "Red" Chinese. China and Vietnam
had been adversaries for centuries.

In an attempt to historically situate American involvement in
Vietnam, Dan does some reading about the background of the war. He
comes to a conclusion that sounds much like the radical historiography of

the war and explains his opinions to two classmates—one who has enlisted and one who is contemplating it.

> "To start with, Americans are not exactly loved in Southeast Asia, whatever your recruiter told you. We've been messing up their country since WWII, fixing elections, buying off officials, even"—Dan paused and looked at both of them—"murdering people who got in our way. Every president since Truman has been messed up in it. We've done everything we could to destroy democracy in Vietnam. Is that what you mean by the American way of life?" (p. 100)

This speech represents the only real attempt in the entire sample of novels to situate American involvement in Vietnam within a larger political/historical layout.

Come in from the Cold (1994) is the story of Maud and Jeff, who both have lost family members to the war. Maud's older sister, Lucy, a longtime antiwar activist, was killed when she set a bomb to blow up a college physics building. Jeff's older brother, Tom, was killed in combat in Vietnam. They become closer as they begin to participate in antiwar protests together. Maud and Jeff see the irony in American war policy. While Jeff looks at the Mississippi River in Minnesota he speculates on American attitudes of control. "Power and money, again. Men used them to strangle the world's greatest river. And the kind of thinking that says we can do that . . . was the kind of thinking that says it's okay to bomb a little country in order to free it" (p. 108).

Like *Children of the Dragon* (1974), *Come in from the Cold* acknowledges that the "Vietnam" war didn't remain in Vietnam. Even with his jaded view of the American government, Jeff is incredulous when information about American troops being deployed in Cambodia is revealed. "Today the president of my country expanded an illegal war by invading Cambodia . . . for the purpose of destroying Communist strongholds" (pp. 127, 124). This is the only characterization of the war as "illegal."

Neither *Long Time Passing* (1990), a story that tangentially explores some antiwar activity at Berkeley in 1969, nor *Caribou* (1984), a story in which Becca Silverman's brother Stevie goes to Canada to avoid the draft, ever attempts an explanation of the war. *Caribou*'s potential draftee Stevie Silverman doesn't want to go to Vietnam because he might get hurt. His father assumes that if America is fighting a war, it must be for a "good cause," although if Mr. Silverman knows what that is, he isn't saying.

Returned Vet Novels

This final category of Returned Vet novels seems the most ideally suited, in terms of narrative structure, to thoughtfully examine and explore historiographical issues of the purposes, causes, outcomes, and implications of America's war in Vietnam. But, like *Caribou* (1984) and *Long Time Passing* (1990), *Where the Elf King Sings* (1980), *Pocket Change* (1989), and *The Road Home* (1995) venture virtually no interpretive observation on the causes or purposes of the war. *Where the Elf King Sings* tells the story of young Marcie Breckenridge's family's attempt to come to terms with Marcie's Vietnam vet father's post-traumatic stress disorder (PTSD)-induced alcoholism. *Pocket Change* is the sample's only other PTSD novel. But in this case, Josie Monroe's Vietnam vet father's PTSD manifests itself in long flashbacks, culminating with her father "protecting" his three-year-old son by breaking out the windows in the house and shooting at the "VC" that he sees on the lawn. In her (1985) article "Witness for the Innocent," Wendy Saul blasts both *Caribou* and *Where the Elf King Sings* for lacking this interpretation.

> Both Wolitzer's [*Caribou*] and Wolkoff's [*Where the Elf King Sings*] books beg for a political explanation of events. Why were the lives of Marcie's dad and Stevie Silverman so horribly disrupted? Sensible children and their fictional counterparts seek to understand how and why their nation finds itself in such difficulties, but not the characters in these novels. Although both books end on a high note, the hope they proffer is based on personal gratification and resolution rather than political understanding and commitment. (p. 193)

The Road Home (Part Two: The World) (1995) doesn't discuss any causes or purposes of the war, but it is significant in that it's the only novel to explore or even acknowledge the experiences of female Vietnam vets.

Teenage Jack in *Travelers* (1986) tries to understand the attitudes of A.J. Karlstad, his dead father, toward Vietnam. As Jack reads his father's letters and speaks to his father's friends, he comes to the conclusion that

A.J. began his service as a fighter pilot thinking that the war was a good idea—although we are never told why. Jack discovers that eventually his father turned against the war. But through Jack's conversations with his father's friends, we see that A.J. seemed finally to hold the classic quagmire position that the war was only a bad idea *after* it became excessively destructive and obviously unwinnable. There is no reason to believe that if the war bad been imminently winnable that A.J. Karlstad would have changed his previously gung-ho opinion.

Young protagonist *Charlie Pippin* (1987) chooses to do a school social studies project on the Vietnam War in order to try to understand the experiences of her vet father and uncle—both of whom refuse to talk to her about what the war was like. As Charlie learns about the war that so shaped the father and uncle who influence her life, she comes across information that both characterizes the war as a "civil war" and explains its purpose as the containment of communism. Mr. Pippin (Charlie's father) and Uncle Ben, both Vietnam vets, continue to argue about the war twenty years after their return. Mr. Pippin thought that fighting a war to contain communism was a fine idea. Uncle Ben disagrees about the war being a good idea only in that America wasn't willing to do everything possible to win. He doesn't think that American intervention in Vietnam was a questionable idea, only that the government handled the war badly in its unwillingness to go the distance. In this aspect Uncle Ben holds a revisionist viewpoint.

A nice feature of *Charlie Pippin* (1987) is a discussion and definition of communism. Since the word is so often bandied about in discussions of the war, Charlie feels that she needs to know more about communism before she can have any true understanding of the war. She does some reading and research and shares her concept of communism with readers. Though rather simplistic and one-sided, this represents the only discussion of the nature of communism itself in any of the novels in the sample.

The last novel in the sample is *Tough Choices: A Story of the Vietnam War* (1993). The returned vet in this case is Mitch Morgan, who is picked up at the airport on the way home from Vietnam at the start of the story. Mitch has difficulty in readjusting to civilian life and is angered to see his younger (nearly draft-age) brother involved in protesting the war. Eventually Mitch cannot believe that he will ever have success in readjustment and decides to return to Vietnam—telling his family that the war brought out the best in him. The purpose of the war in Vietnam as discussed in *Tough Choices* (1993) is purely communist containment. There is, however, one character who questions the inherent morality of this position. Emmett, a young antiwar activist, and his brother Mitch, a Vietnam vet who has been home from Vietnam for only a few days, argue about the validity of containment:

> "Everything about this war is bad."
>
> "I hope you mean the Viet Cong, too," Mitch said.
>
> "I don't know," Emmett said. "Are they really the enemy? They are just Vietnamese people who want Communism in their country and are willing to fight for it."
>
> "And what about people who don't want Communism?" Mitch asked. "What about the people who want to own land, and not share everything with the government? People who want to be able to say what they please?" (p. 40)

Mitch's perception of life in a noncommunist Vietnam is not exactly an accurate one. It is certainly debatable whether peasants ever owned land, and the idea of free speech was never accepted even by the American-supported Diem government. Ironically, if the Vietnamese had been allowed to hold the free and democratic elections in 1956 that had been arranged by the Geneva agreement in 1954, the populace would have democratically elected a communist government. These elections were largely prohibited by American intervention in the South Vietnamese government. This, however, represents one of the few exchanges in which the notion of the containment of communism is questioned.

Generalizations

Overall, the twenty-eight novels in the sample show a lack of historiographical information in both content and narrative structure. Not one novel depicts a specific historiographical stance incorporating all consistent information from that viewpoint into the story. Historiographical interpretation generally remains limited to an occasional comment or conversation rather than as the main component around which the content or narrative structure revolves. The Duty novels generally interpret the war as an American effort to stop communist expansion with an occasional and unexplained link of freedom in Vietnam to freedom in

America. The Vietnamese Perspective novels contain the only mention of the American presence in Vietnam being at the invitation of the Vietnamese. *Children of the Dragon* (1974) is the only Combat novel to mention that North and South Vietnam had been created by a division imposed by the Geneva Convention. Sam in *To Stand against the Wind* (1978) is the only character to interpret American intervention in terms of a quagmire. He mentions that the Americans slowly became involved in Vietnam and now don't know how to extricate themselves from the situation. The Platoon subcategory follows the lead of the Duty novels in that it focuses mainly on containing communist expansion as the purpose of the war. Vietnamese freedom and the inexplicable tie to American freedom are also addressed. Only in the *Echo* books is there any small questioning of the sensibility of a communist containment policy. Protagonist Michael Jennings cynically observes that policy makers must think that communism was a "fate worse than death," and although he has his doubts, he doesn't pursue the matter.

Only three of the six Response to the War novels give any hint of a historiographical stance. Characters in two novels, *One Day for Peace* (1971) and *The Best of Friends* (1989), suggest the radical interpretation of the war. Mr. Simon and Dan Ulvang both see the war as an American attempt to interfere in the internal politics of another country. They both mention that Vietnam was split into two countries by the West.

Again, in the Returned Vet category, only three of the six novels display some sort of interpretative stance. This is particularly surprising given the narrative structure of these novels. Since they all address Vietnam vets and their families attempting to come to terms with the vets' experiences in Vietnam, it would seem the ideal structure through which to examine and explore what the war in Vietnam was supposed to have been about. This, however, is not the case. The war is characterized as a civil war in which America became involved to prevent communist expansion. A nearly revisionist stance is depicted by Uncle Ben in *Charlie Pippin* (1987), when he expresses his belief that the war was lost only because of America's lack of will to do what must be done to win. Finally, a character in *Tough Choices* (1993) vaguely questions the inherent morality of a communist containment policy when he wonders if the United States has the right to prevent a country from being communist.

The most frequent cause of the war expressed in this sample of novels, regardless of their narrative structure category, is communist containment. Neither the legitimacy nor the viability of this policy is ever seriously or thoughtfully explored. Unfortunately, the adolescent novels examined here are not alone in their lack of historiographical comment. Countless critics of Vietnam War narratives, both literary and cinematic, have condemned these often emotionally powerful representations as being apolitical and ahistorical—"existing in a political and historical vacuum" (Auster & Quart, 1988, p. 65). In discussing Vietnam War films, Frisch (1986) claims that each film is "willfully and explicitly antihistorical; in a context where the forces of history virtually scream to be noticed, solitary individuals are the . . . focus, men kept deliberately isolated from history" (p. 8). Dittmar and Michaud (1990) agree with Frisch's assessment noting that "most Vietnam War films place themselves squarely at ground level, focusing on men in combat. . . . They avoid historical specificity, [and] repress politically sensitive issues . . ." (p. 5). Martin (1987) also observes the focus on the individual instead of the larger issues within American film:

> None of these films can be said to "name names," so to speak, or to treat the historical and political roots of America's involvement in Southeast Asia. In the tradition of Hollywood's established approach to controversial topics, the consequences and liabilities of a discredited system of foreign policy, and a politically corrupting war, are displaced onto personal narratives which explore individual subjectivity. (p. 151)

Although these critics are referring to adult films, their conclusions can easily be extended to these adolescent novels. None of the novels attempts to provide any sort of larger picture of the "historical and political roots" of the war.

There can be only speculation regarding this apparent lack of historical and political situating on the part of authors and filmmakers. Given the economically driven nature of both the film and publishing industries, perhaps only safe, apolitical narratives that make no recriminations are marketable. It is also a possibility that authors and filmmakers are unwilling to do the research required to situate a novel of film both historically and politically. If authors or filmmakers are unclear about their own historiographical ideologies, then it would be extraordinarily difficult for them to frame a narrative within a cohesive historiography.

It would seem, finally, that when narratives do not ask larger political questions about the purposes and underlying morality of American intervention in Vietnam, the process of a conservative and status quo selective tradition has functioned inviolate. By marginalizing through consistent neglect these issues of moral culpability and political responsibility, the war in Vietnam is represented as something that need not be examined on a large scale. The interests of those in power are served through having a young generation of potential soldiers and war supporters who are not shown characters challenging the political military decisions of the past. In discussing the implications of elements *not* included in a text, Eagleton (1976) claims that "it is in the significant *silences* of a text, in its gaps and absences, that the presence of ideology can be most positively felt" (p. 34, emphasis in original).

Historiography Related to Date of Publication

Obviously two factors must be considered when examining the historiographical stance of the novels in this sample: first, the date of publication and, second, the time in which the novel is set. It would hardly be appropriate to expect a novel *written* during the war to express opinions about lessons learned from the war. Also a novel that is *set* during the war—i.e., all of the entries in the Combat and Response to the War categories—could scarcely address whether the war was won or lost or give reasons for this victory or defeat.

There appears to be little consistent pattern in the relation of date of publication to historiographical interpretation in the novels. The nine novels written and published while American troops were in Vietnam (*Special Forces Trooper*, 1967; *Orders to Vietnam*, 1968; *Stop & Search*, 1969; *The Man in the Box*, 1968; *Vietnam Nurse*, 1968; *Nurse in Vietnam*, 1969; *One Day for Peace*, 1971; *War Year*, 1972; and *Cross-fire*, 1972) all utilize either Combat or Response to the War narrative structures and capitalize on the policy of communist containment as the purpose for the war and let it go at that—that is, when they address the purpose of the war at all. Americans fought for freedom in Vietnam (theirs and somehow ours) at the request of the South Vietnamese government. The notable exception is *One Day for Peace*, wherein a character expresses the radical historiographical interpretation that perhaps American involvement in Vietnam is imperialist.

With the exception of *Children of the Dragon* (1974), which interprets the war as a struggle of the Vietnamese people, both North and South, to rid their country of invaders and be free to reunite, the novels from the mid-1970s through the 1980s, regardless of their narrative structure (*To Stand against the Wind*, 1978; *Where the Elf King Sings*, 1980; *Caribou*, 1984; *Travelers*, 1986; *Charlie Pippin*, 1987; *Fallen Angels*, 1988; *And One for All*, 1989; and *Pocket Change*, 1989), cling to communist containment as the purpose of the war—when the purpose is even examined. Not until 1989 in *The Best of Friends* does a character again venture a radical interpretation of the war—eighteen years after the first time in *One Day for Peace* (1971).

The nine novels published in the 1990s (*Long Time Passing*, 1990; *Echo Company #1—Welcome to Vietnam*, 1991; *Echo Company #2—Hill 568*, 1991; *Echo Company #3—'Tis the Season*, 1991; *Echo Company #4—Stand Down*, 1992; *Tough Choices*, 1993; *Come in from the Cold*, 1994; *The Road Home*, 1995; and *Sing for Your Father, Su Phan*, 1997) again look to communist containment as the sole discussed motivation for American involvement in Vietnam.

All in all there is an amazing consistency within these twenty-eight novels. With only a few notable exceptions, the bulk of all three historio-graphical interpretations of the Vietnam War are ignored in the novels. There is little sense of a quagmire-like situation, or of a war that would have been won if not for the acts of the antiwar movement and the liberal press, or of an implication that American intervention was essentially imperialist. Just as quagmire and revisionist historiographies are criticized for their refusal to question the feasibility and morality of a Cold War-inspired communist containment policy, these novels must also be criticized.

Notes

1. The historiographical interpretations of Vietnam grew out of positions regarding American policy in Southeast Asia that many people held in the 1960s and 1970s. Many who were moderately critical of American intervention and often involved in the antiwar movement (called peace liberals by Charles deBenedetti) came to be associated with the quagmire interpretation. Another group associated with the antiwar movement and vehemently opposed to American action in Vietnam (called the anti-imperialist left by deBenedetti) came to be associated with the radical interpretation. The successive Kennedy, Johnson, and Nixon administrations' position on the war came to be associated with the revisionist position. The main point is that these varying interpretations of the war are not academic creations, but are in fact logical evolutions of positions that people held *during* the war in Vietnam. For a more detailed discussion, see deBenedetti, Charles. (1990). *An American Ordeal: The Antiwar Movement of the Vietnam Era.* Syracuse, NY: University Press.

2. These are especially good explanations of the quagmire interpretation of the war:

Gelb, L.H. & Betts, R.K. (1979). *The Irony of Vietnam: The System Worked.* Washington, DC: Brookings Institution.

Halberstam, D. (1965). *The Making of a Quagmire.* New York: Random House.

Halberstam, D. (1972). *The Best and the Brightest.* New York: Random House.

Nolting, F. (1988). *From Trust to Tragedy: The Political Memoirs of Frederick Nolting, Kennedy's Ambassador to Diem's Vietnam.* New York: Praeger.

Schlesinger, A.M., Jr. (1967). *Bitter Heritage: Vietnam and American Democracy, 1941-1966.* Boston: Houghton Mifflin.

3. Arthur Schlesinger, Jr. was originally a Kennedy aide who supported American involvement in Vietnam. It was only in the years after Kennedy's assassination that Schlesinger became something of a critic of the war. In *Bitter Heritage* (published in 1967, four years after Kennedy's death), when Schlesinger discusses the "politics of inadvertence," he has become at least a moderate critic of American policy in Vietnam.

4. These books explain the revisionist interpretation of the war:

Lewy, G. (1978). *America in Vietnam.* New York: Oxford University Press.

Lomperis, T.J. (1993). *The War Everyone Lost—and Won: America's Involvement in Vietnam's Twin Struggles.* (2nd ed.). Washington, DC: CQ Press.

Nixon, R.M. (1985). *No More Vietnams.* New York: Arbor House.

Palmer, B., Jr. (1984). *The 25-Year War: America's Military Role in Vietnam.* Lexington: University Press of Kentucky.

Podhoretz, N. (1982). *Why We Were in Vietnam.* New York: Simon & Schuster.

Summers, H.G., Jr. (1984). *On Strategy: A Critical Analysis of the Vietnam War.*

Novato, CA: Presidio Press.

Westmoreland, W.C. (1980). *A Soldier Reports*. (2nd ed.). New York: Dell.

5. These texts present especially good explanations of the radical interpretation of the war:

Donovan, J.C. (1974). *The Cold Warriors: A Policy Making Elite*. Lexington, MA: Heath.

Herr, M. (1977). *Dispatches*. New York: Knopf.

Kolko, G. (1969). *The Roots of American Foreign Policy: An Analysis of Power and Purpose*. Boston: Beacon Press.

Kolko, G. (1985). *Anatomy of a War: Vietnam, the United States, and the Modern Historical Experience*. New York: Pantheon.

Pelz, S. (Winter 1990). Vietnam: Another Stroll Down Alibi Alley. *Diplomatic History*, pp. 123-130.

Sheehan, N. (1988). *A Bright, Shining Lie: John Paul Vann and America in Vietnam*. New York: Random House.

6. These texts offer a great deal of information about American attitudes toward the war:

Divine, R.A. (Winter 1988). Vietnam Reconsidered. *Diplomatic History*, pp. 79-93.

Fromkin, D. & Chace, J. (1985). What *Are* the Lessons of Vietnam? *Foreign Affairs, 63*, 722-746.

Gitlin, T. (1987). *The Sixties: Years of Hope, Days of Rage*. New York: Bantam.

Paterson, T. (Winter 1988). Historical Memory and Illusive Victories:

Vietnam and Central America. *Diplomatic History*, pp. 1-18.

Salisbury, H.E. (Ed.). (1984). *Vietnam Reconsidered: Lessons from a War*. Philadelphia: Harper & Row.

Wheeler, J. (Spring 1985). Coming to Grips with Vietnam. *Foreign Affairs, 63*, 747-758.

Chapter Five

American Cultural Myth and Literature

Cultural myths play a vital and integral, although largely below surface, part in the reproduction of a nation's identity. They "articulate the precedents and ideals for the nation's future" and "set out the national priorities" (Hunter, 1991, p. 55). McKeever (1989) agrees, adding that "national myths do not perform their prime function of uniting a people merely by offering a preferred version of the past: they also incorporate a utopian vision of the future" (p. 44). This "preferred" interpretation of national history is created through the same process of selective tradition that Hunter (1991), Eagleton (1976), and Williams (1977) all describe.

There is a significant body of literature examining American cultural myth in total, but it is, of course, beyond the scope of this study. American myths that have been explored in terms of the Vietnam War are the most relevant here. Realizing that "a people cannot coherently function" without their national mythology intact, Hellmann (1986)

claims that "Vietnam is an experience that has severely called into
question American myth" (pp. ix-x).

The Frontier Hero and Myths of
Regeneration and Proficiency

Hellmann (1986) identified the frontier myth as our central national
myth. In its prototype, the frontier myth "features stalwart frontiersmen,
entering the vast wilderness alone or in small bands, who draw on the
virtues of nature while battling its savage denizens in order to make way
for settlements of yeoman farmers" (p. 8). The traits and characteristics
of the frontier or western hero set forth to be admired and emulated as
essentially American are "self-reliance, democratic idealism, homespun
practicality, adaptability, ingenuity, humor, and generosity" (p. 27).

Hellmann hails the early 1960s as the return of the frontier hero in the
form of the Green Beret and the Peace Corps. He cites the American
press's romance with Kennedy's newly reemerged elite arm of Special
Forces, recalling that "by 1962 this image of a resurgent American
character had crystallized into a portrayal of the Green Beret as a
contemporary reincarnation of the western hero" (p. 45). Because he
wanted the Green Berets to epitomize rugged individualism, Kennedy had
gone to battle against the bureaucratic Pentagon to wrest control of these
special units away from the regular army. The national press was so
enthralled with this elite corps that their "resonant imagery presented the
Green Beret as a rebirth of America's central mythic hero" (p. 45).

> What indeed distinguished the Green Beret from earlier versions of the
> western hero was the sheer ease with which he encompassed savagery
> and civilization. . . . The Green Beret took the paradox of the genteel
> killer, the death-dealing innocent, far beyond the previous incarnations
> of the western hero, for he spent much of his time engaged in the
> missionary work of the Peace Corpsman. . . . As a single hero repre-
> senting the ideal answer to the New Frontier to the calls for renewal, the
> Green Beret of the periodical press occupied in a single timeless
> moment the whole of American myth. (p. 47)

The majority of the first thousands of troops to be sent to Vietnam by President Kennedy as "advisors" were Green Berets.

The image of the frontier hero encompasses more a cluster of personality traits than an actual scenario. To reiterate: "self-reliance, democratic idealism, homespun practicality, adaptability, ingenuity, humor, and generosity" (Hellmann, p. 27). His adaptability plays an extremely important role in his ability to survive in that often the frontier hero must learn and practice the ways of his enemy in order to ultimately conquer that enemy. Figures who are clearly examples of frontier heroes abound in American literature, legends, folktales, and popular culture—from Davy Crockett, Daniel Boone, Wyatt Earp, and Hawkeye (Nathaniel Bumppo), to Bruce Willis's character John McClane in the *Die Hard* movies—good ole boys one and all.

The mythical image of the frontier hero is subverted when he exhibits characteristics in opposition to those listed. For example, when a character either becomes or begins as dependent, cynical, impractical, unable to adapt to or figure out a situation, and loses his overall good nature, he embodies the antithesis to the frontier hero. When characters like a frontier antihero populate novels and/or eventually prevail, there is definite subversion of the frontier hero. A frontier antihero would not be an evil villain, but rather a weak and ineffectual man.

Margaret Stewart's (1986) study of American cultural myths within the tradition and framework of general frontier mythology reveals two distinct and related myths—the myths of regeneration and proficiency. The regeneration myth is essentially a scenario in which the frontier hero stars. The myth fundamentally involves the defense of civilization from potential enemies—tracing its most ancient roots to stories of heroes fighting dragons to save princesses and other fair maidens. The American version renamed "regeneration through violence" is an integral part of the frontier myth.

> Its structure is formed by the relationship between three stock characters: a *victim*, often a white woman captive or a white farm or settlement; an *assailant*, usually a person of color or a "renegade" white; and a *hero*, a white man who is an intriguing amalgam of the other two. The hero is a fighter like the antagonist, but essentially decent like the victim. (p. 3)

American involvement in Vietnam was initially interpreted in terms of the regeneration myth. The South Vietnamese played the part of the defenseless *victim*; the evil communist North Vietnamese and the Viet Cong (VC) played a vicious and ruthless *assailant*; and the American military (originally mostly Green Beret advisors) were clearly the *heroes* sent to defend the helpless South Vietnamese against the inhuman North Vietnamese. War viewed through the lens of the regeneration myth is perceived as a "sacred, purifying, culturally regenerative quest for victory against a sinister foe" (Rasmussen & Downey, 1991, p. 178).

The myth of regeneration through violence is subverted when the *hero* becomes too much like the *assailant* in that he becomes too savage or when a battle to defend a helpless *victim* becomes too destructive. The accompanying notion that war (in this scenario) is sacred is subverted when the war becomes purposeless or becomes only a struggle for survival.

The myth of technical proficiency essentially addresses job performance. Americans tend to have the deepest respect for anyone who preforms with exceptional skill. Traditional heroes are admired "not only for [their] chivalry, but also for [their] skill" (Stewart, p. 14). Hellmann also points out that frontier sharpshooting was practically seen as a sign of natural virtue. In explaining the myth of proficiency, Stewart maintains that it

> dispenses with the question of ultimate goals and concentrates instead on the skillful manipulation of techniques, on the competent, efficient performance of the task at hand. The "regeneration through violence" myth separates means and ends into two distinct morally significant entities: the ends (regeneration) justify the means (violence). The technicist paradigm, in contrast, collapses the two elements into one. The means *are* the ends. Proficiency is equated with goodness; professionalism becomes its own justification. This new ethic [is] embodied in the phrase "just doing my job. . . . Skill in work, whether it be shooting a weapon, keeping a situation map up to date, or advising a battalion, is an index to character." (p. 14, also Stromberg, 1974, quoted in Stewart, emphasis in original)

The proficiency myth has two main facets: the innate respect Americans hold for anyone who performs with excellence and the equation of skill and goodness. In a neatly reciprocal relationship, the frontier hero is good at things *because* he is good, and conversely, he is good *because* he is good at things.

The proficiency myth can be subverted in several ways. First, because bureaucracy and its accompanying policies and regulations impede proficiency, if bureaucrats or characters who adhere too tightly to the idea of "going by the book" prevail, then the proficient hero has been subverted. Second, if the *assailant* from the regeneration myth performs with an excellence equal to or greater than the *hero,* then the equation of skill with goodness is unbalanced.

In his famous personal narrative, *Dispatches* (1977), journalist Michael Herr related a true story that shows the respect Americans hold for anyone doing a good job—even when that person is the enemy.

> Two hundred meters away, facing the Marine trenches, there was an NVA [North Vietnamese Army] sniper with a .50-caliber machine gun who shot at the Marines from a tiny spider hole. During the day he fired at anything that rose above the sandbags, and at night he fired at any lights he could see. You could see him clearly from the trench, and if you were looking through the scope of a Marine sniper's rifle you could even see his face. The Marines fired on his position with mortars and recoilless rifles, and he would drop into his hole and wait. Gunships fired rockets at him, and when they were through he would come up again and fire. Finally, napalm was called in, and for ten minutes the air about the spider hole was black and orange from the strike, while the ground around it was galvanized clean of every living thing. When all of it cleared, the sniper popped up and fired off a single round, and the Marines in the trenches cheered. They called him Luke the Gook, and after that no one wanted anything to happen to him. (pp. 125-126)

When the *assailant* from the regeneration scenario is invested with great proficiency, the skill equals goodness equation is undermined. In this instance and many others, Americans are in the uncomfortable position of giving grudging respect to their enemies. In turning to the twenty-eight novels in the sample, frontier hero figures and examples of regeneration and proficiency myths were easily identifiable.

Combat Novels—Duty Subcategory

Frontier heroes and myths of regeneration and proficiency abound in the Combat novels. Of the five novels that comprise this first group of Combat novels (those that include the prewar training of the diversely assigned characters), Joe Archibald's (1967) *Special Forces Trooper* is the richest source of myth. The first half of this novel explains in great detail the exacting training given to Green Berets at Fort Bragg, North Carolina. The second half of the novel follows protagonist Stan Rusat into the Central Highlands of Vietnam, to Luc Co on the Cambodian border, where he and fellow advisors train and lead both Army of the Republic of (South) Vietnam (ARVN) and Civilian Irregular Defense Group—mainly Montagnard (CIDG) units. The fact that Stan and his fellow Americans are all Green Berets immediately capitalizes on the image of the frontier hero, with one soldier even referred to as "a latter-day Davy Crockett" (p. 57). Consistent with Hellmann's ideas of Green Berets perceived as engaging in "the missionary work of the Peace Corpsman" (p. 47), these Special Forces soldiers are presented training the Vietnamese and Montagnard peasants to be barbers, tailors, blacksmiths, and teaching them better agricultural techniques. Remembering how he came to join the Green Berets, Stan thinks:

> The motto of the Green Berets: *To Liberate from Oppression.* Back at Camp Dix he had been inspired and motivated by a piece of literature left behind by the recruiting sergeant. It said that recent events in the world political picture have underlined the need for a new breed of American soldier, one skilled in the techniques of unconventional warfare. The United States had the answer. Intensively trained to a higher degree than any other soldier on earth, he stands today on the frontiers of democracy across the world. (p. 39)

Stan, Vince, Harry, and all of the other advisors immediately adapt to the jungle lifestyle of their charges and are natural leaders of men. They easily smooth the feuds between the Vietnamese and Montagnard soldiers.

The regeneration scenario is immediately apparent upon the Green Berets' arrival in the Central Highlands. The Americans and CIDG are to protect several nearby villages from the ravages of the VC. It appears that the Americans are also there to protect the ARVN and CIDG from the VC. As the Americans (the internal narration of this novel never privileges readers with the thoughts of anyone besides American characters) at Luc Co await an expected VC attack, Stan compares the situation to American history. "Modern warfare, he thought, had been set back over 200 years. He had been whisked back through a time tunnel to a primitive stockade on the Kentucky frontier. All around him the savages were getting ready to attack" (p. 162).

The only small subversion of this myth occurs after a particularly bloody, although successful battle. The defense of Luc Co has become so destructive that Stan wonders "if he would ever be exactly all right again. Can a man take a walk through the lower regions and still stay the same as he used to be?" (p. 178). Although at that moment Stan begins to question the brutality of the war, he quickly dismisses the thought by appearing indeed to "be exactly all right again."

The Green Berets are inherently good soldiers. Their proficiency is exhibited time and again throughout the novel. In one instance a force of forty-five ARVN and three Americans come under VC attack. The ARVN commanding officer (who outranks all Americans) gives a sound and direct order, but the highest-ranking American countermands the order, insisting that the troops do the exact opposite of what the ARVN commander ordered. Even though Sergeant Cantenbine has no more information about the situation than the ARVN commander, Cantenbine's order saves the day and all the soldiers—showing his skill.

Stan and his fellow Green Berets rail at the rules that keep them from fighting the war in the way that their common sense tells them would be the most proficient. The bureaucratic rules that control the war frequently impede the Green Berets' actions. In one scene, a Green Beret sergeant says he is frustrated because he knows the VC are hiding in Cambodia, but the American government won't allow him to pursue them across the border. Showing proficiency's tenuous relation to rules, in a later incident, a wounded Montagnard boy isn't evacuated to an American hospital because of a Vietnamese rule against transporting civilians. The American commander tells his lieutenant that "there was never a lousier, more complicated war" and that the Americans "should have taken that boy out regardless of the rules" (p. 131).

In the second half of the proficiency myth, the VC are presented as guerrillas whose amazing skill and disciplines are to be admired, even if their politics and policies are to be abhorred. They operate stealthily in the night, even to the point of harvesting their crops in darkness. They are presented as intelligent and ubiquitous, infiltrating any American camp—right under the noses of the Green Berets.

The next two books in this group are both from the same author, William Butterworth: *Orders to Vietnam: A Novel of Helicopter Warfare* (1968) and *Stop & Search: A Novel of Small Boat Warfare Off Vietnam* (1969). Butterworth is the only author to create protagonists who are not members of the Special Forces. *Orders to Vietnam* details Bill Byrnes's training as a warrant officer and a helicopter pilot, then follows him to Pleiku, where he joins an aviation battalion. Given the pervasive presence of the helicopter in Vietnam, it is surprising that more novels don't explore this facet of the war. *Stop & Search* begins on the Alabama coast as Eddie Czernik begins his training as a small boat captain. The novel follows him through college Navy ROTC to the Mekong Delta as part of the navy's riverine forces—a segment of the American forces in Vietnam who are seldom profiled in novel or film. Their most widely seen portrayal is in the film *Apocalypse Now*, as a riverine patrol boat ferries Captain Willard up the Nung River.

Butterworth's book capitalizes much less frequently on the mythical ideas of regeneration and proficiency than did *Special Forces Trooper* (1967). Both Bill and Eddie have natural and innate skills at helicopter and boat piloting, respectively. This is, of course, a part of the image of the frontier hero. Not only does Bill have great skill as a pilot, he also is extremely gifted with all types of guns. In one scene, Bill has brought his own sidearm with him to Pleiku—something he knows is strictly against regulations. After he demonstrates his deadly proficiency with it, he is allowed to keep the gun.

The narrative structures and setting of Butterworth's two novels reduce their ability to tap into the regeneration scenario. Being billeted on a large base in Pleiku or spending the entire Vietnam section of the novel in a patrol boat isn't as conducive to the protection of the defenseless as perhaps an infantry story would be. In *Stop & Search,* Eddie does, however, maintain attitudes that tend to subvert the idea that war is a sacred quest. Eddie and his fellow shipmates never express an opinion about the purpose of the war and to them it appears rather purposeless. After a crew member is killed when the patrol boat has a firefight with a VC junk, Eddie thinks that the war "didn't quite seem worth [Gunner's Mate Chernoff's] life" (p. 133).

The final Duty books are two novels that address the experiences of nurses in Vietnam: Ellen Elliott's *Vietnam Nurse* (1968) and Nell Dean's *Nurse in Vietnam* (1969). The "Vietnam nurse" of the first title is Joanna Shelton, an Australian nurse whose missionary/doctor father is missing in the jungle close to Dalat. Dr. Shelton had been unofficially trying to set up peace talks between authorities in Hanoi and Washington. Joanna has been called by the American government to pick up her father's work. Accompanied by a Green Beret unit, Joanna, who grew up in Vietnam, is to try to locate her father and establish contact with the government in Hanoi. In this novel, Joanna is not a mythic figure, but the leader of the Green Beret unit, Captain Wayne Moore, certainly is. In the internal narration, Joanna thinks of Wayne as

> a fascinating man, the type of man who was a challenge, because by his very strength and aloofness, his obvious male ego and confident masculine superiority, he became a mystery, so that one wondered constantly what lay beneath the tough-soldier exterior, what kind of man Wayne Moore really was. (p. 88)

A frontier hero through and through. Other members of the Green Beret unit are presented as frontier heroes as well. For example, Wayne describes Corporal Koerner's abilities to Joanna:

> Corporal Koerner, Miss Shelton, was born to do this sort of thing [track, elude, and kill the enemy], in the same way that other men are born to be lawyers, policemen, and doctors. He's a natural, like an animal, with an animal's reflexes and a sixth sense when it comes to danger. (p. 79)

Juxtaposed against the frontier virility of Wayne Moore and his Green Berets is Dr. Steve Donovan, an Australian doctor in love with Joanna who has come along on the expedition. Steve's emotionality and macho posturing first cause him to appear weak, and finally cost him his life. After the whole unit is captured by the VC and is on a forced march through the jungle, Steve proposes to Joanna. She agrees only to keep him quiet. Later in camp, when the VC leader, Phat, speaks politely to Joanna,

> Steve suddenly surged to his feet, pushing between Joanna and Phat. His jaw jutted stubbornly and his blue eyes were bright with anger. "Leave her alone, you swine! Can't you see she's exhausted? Is this the way the brave Viet Cong operate, getting tough with helpless women?" (p. 137)

After this exchange Phat punches Steve and Steve strikes Phat in return. The other VC shoot and kill Steve. In contrast to the knowledge of Wayne, the frontier hero, Steve failed to properly understand the situation and appropriate reactions, and this failure cost him his life.

When it comes to the regeneration scenario, *Vietnam Nurse* has all elements in place: a *hero* in the form of Wayne Moore, a perfect *victim*—a white woman, and a vicious *assailant*—the Viet Cong. True to the prototype of this myth is the Green Beret's ability to become something like their enemies in order to conquer them. The Green Berets being "highly trained experts in guerrilla warfare and counter-insurgency" are able, if not to win the war, at least to keep Joanna safe throughout the mission (p. 49).

Not only are the American soldiers proficient warriors and survivalists, but the VC are as well. Once again portrayed as having the utmost discipline and skill, the VC are adversaries to be respected.

> There was no sight or sound of the VC. And that, Joanna knew from what she had overheard the Americans say, was when you least expected them to strike, when one least expected them, when one's sense and reflexes were dulled by constant false alarms. That, Roswell, Koerner, Allison, and Mijor claimed, was the crux of the VC war. The Popular Army, together with its American "advisors," made ninety-nine ambushes and nothing happened, and so they relaxed. And all the time the VC had been watching and waiting. On the hundredth night they attacked in strength. (p. 92)

This novel set up Steve Donovan for scorn and death because of his lack of proficiency and frontier skills, and rewards the VC with the respect of the Green Berets because of VC skill.

In *Nurse in Vietnam* (1969), the last Duty novel, the nurse is USAF 1st Lieutenant Lisa Blake. The title is somewhat misleading because Lisa is actually stationed at the hospital at Clark Air Force Base which is close to Manilla in the Philippines. The novel follows Lisa through her acclimation to military nursing and on her occasional trips into Vietnam as a flight nurse. Like Joanna Shelton, Lisa has her own Green Beret captain to function as a frontier hero and protector. Captain Mace Thomas meets Lisa while recuperating from a broken leg at Clark's hospital. She is in awe of his fierce loyalty to his men and thinks of the "supreme compliment" her dead fiance, Clint, had paid the "Special Forces, the men in the Green Berets: 'A fearless bunch of good guys with guts'" (p. 15). Merely by being a Green Beret, Mace takes on the image of the frontier hero.

Not until the latter part of the novel are these particular Green Berets actually cast into a regeneration scenario. Mace and several of his men are separated from the rest of the unit when one is badly injured. When Lisa goes along with a doctor to treat the men (not knowing, of course, that Mace is with them), their helicopter is shot down. Only when Mace and Lisa are reunited in the leper colony where he had been hiding does the regeneration scene become truly apparent. He risks his life in order to secure the rescue of the Americans from the leper village for the sake of protecting them from the VC.

American soldiers are thought to be the very model of proficiency in *Nurse in Vietnam*. Captain Mace Thomas, Green Beret, explains to Lisa how good he and other Green Berets are at their jobs:

> Well, I think I'm pretty important to my unit, every Special Forces soldier is. We're the men who are trained in jungle fighting, underwater techniques, hand-to-hand combat. That's what's important in the kind of war we're fighting in Vietnam. Without a doubt [the Green Berets] are considered the most multiskilled, enlisted men in the forces today. You see, if one of the medics gets waxed—that means killed—a demolition engineer can take over his job, and the unit can carry on. (p. 50)

Lisa hardly needed to be convinced of the Green Berets' amazing talents, but when Mace brings a few wires and pieces of wood back to the village intending MacGyver-like to assemble a radio, she exclaims, "Sometimes I think you Green Beanies are charmed. Green Beanies can do anything. *Anything*" (p. 186, emphasis in original).

Viet Cong guerrillas are the subject of a grudging respect, as is consistent with the other novels. They are perceived as deadly, vicious, and extraordinarily disciplined. When Lisa talks to Bart, a wounded reporter in the hospital, he quickly corrects her naive notions of "VC Charlie":

> "I'm outlining a feature story I'm going to do on Viet Cong Charlie."
> Lisa told him, "I've heard so much about VC Charlie that I feel like I already know a good deal about him. Usually he's just a village boy with wrong ideas."
> "I wouldn't define him that way," Bart returned tersely. "Charlie's no dumb cluck. He's a pretty sophisticated person. And he's brave. Out of 40 or 50 village men, the 2 or 3 recruited by the VC are the very best of the lot—the strongest individuals and those with the most highly developed sense of competition. When they go into the forest, they take little along except their courage and will to compete." (p. 64)

The VC are certainly portrayed as worthy opponents.

The only example of the subversion of a myth in either of the nurse novels occurs when Lisa learns more information from the wounded reporter, Bart. Here the Americans' proficiency is undermined again by Washington bureaucrats. In discussing Air America, the CIA-run airline that Bart calls a "chartered airline in Vietnam and Laos," he mentions that the planes and pilots are unarmed. Unarmed because that's the rule. Despite the fact that this is wholly erroneous information (Robbins, 1988), the indictment to proficiency was again a preponderance of rules.

Combat Novels—Vietnamese Perspective Subcategory

The Vietnamese in whose country this devastating war was fought are seldom given any representation in adolescent novels about the war. The Vietnamese, when included, are often just faceless masses or unseen enemies—novels rarely have even a single, named Vietnamese character. The five novels in this subcategory are a small attempt to give something of an Asian perspective on America's involvement in their country. While none of the novels were authored by Vietnamese writers, *Sing for Your Father, Su Phan* (1997) was cowritten by a Chinese immigrant who lived in North Vietnam during the war. Each novel presents a story in which a Vietnamese, Montagnard, or Chinese character is the protagonist or co-protagonist. Mary Lois Dunn's (1968) *The Man in the Box* represents the only attempt to show the perspective of a Montagnard character. Montagnard ("mountain people"—a name given by the French) is a general name given to the many tribal groups who inhabited the mountains of the Central Highlands of Vietnam. They are not ethnically Vietnamese, nor are their languages and customs familiar to or accepted by the Vietnamese. Men from these groups were trained by the early American Green Berets and called CIDG or "strike forces" with their main purpose being something of a border patrol between Vietnam and Cambodia. They were also to gather intelligence about NVA and VC activity and to foil VC cadres, whenever possible.

Set in an unnamed village, *The Man in the Box* is the story of Chau Li, a young boy whose tribal leader father was tortured and killed by the VC. When the VC bring a captured and brutalized American, David Lee, into the village in a tight bamboo cage (the same one used to kill his own father), Chau Li decides, at great personal risk, to save him. Chau Li hides David in a cave and nurses the wounds inflicted by David's torturers, finally reuniting him with his Green Beret unit. Even though Chau Li is the clear protagonist of the story, David manages to exhibit frontier qualities despite his serious injuries. Being a Green Beret automatically confers some frontier hero status, and the description of Green Beret activity is consistent with Hellmann's Peace Corps notions. Talking about his mission before his capture, David says "I had a team. Ten Americans, sixteen Vietnamese officers. We trained the men of the [Montagnard] village to defend themselves, their families, and the crops" (p. 96). He is a good and decent man, who by sheer strength of will manages to walk down a jungle-covered mountain filled with VC guerrillas despite the fact that all the bones in both feet have been crushed. David fluently speaks Chau Li's language, incorrectly referred to as Montagnard. Montagnard is a general term, used much like "Indian" in this country. Just as there is no tribal group called "Indian," there is also no language or dialect called "Indian"—and by extension, no language called "Montagnard."

While the Green Berets in general are not presented as the protectors of the Montagnards or the Vietnamese, David is shown tenuously as the protector of Chau Li. *In* a smaller version of the regeneration scenario, when David asks Chau Li to return with him to America and be his adopted son, he and Chau Li easily fill the *hero* and *victim* roles.

The final scene is a classic and horrible subversion of the regeneration myth. The Green Berets and ARVN have set up a command post in a small Montagnard village. Captain Louis subverts the regeneration myth when he thinks that the Vietnamese "bring us here to help them and what they get is killed" (p. 138). When the village is nearly overrun in the ensuing firefight, the Green Berets call in an air strike. The entire village and surrounding jungle are bombed, napalmed, and of course, destroyed. The village and people that the Green Berets had tried to help were destroyed because of their presence—the few not killed by the VC were killed by the American air strike.

Gail Graham's (1972) *Cross-fire* tells the story of Harry, an infantry soldier, who awakens after a firefight alone in the jungle. He comes across four young Vietnamese children whose village has just been leveled by an American air strike. The novel follows these characters as they try to decide what to think about each other and what to do. Interestingly the third person narration shifts with each chapter between Harry's and Mi's (the twelve-year-old girl and oldest Vietnamese child) point of view. This novel doesn't capitalize on many myths. Harry is certainly not a frontier hero (also not a Green Beret), nor is he an impressive soldier or survivalist.

The regeneration scenario is used in both the structure and content of the novel. Harry envisions the entire war as one huge battle wherein the Americans' purpose is to defend the South Vietnamese against the communists. On a small level, Harry being the only adult with four orphaned Vietnamese children in the jungle is another manifestation of this same scenario. The myth is quickly subverted by the fact that Harry doesn't want these children with him, nor does he especially like them. Even though he sees the larger war in terms of fighting for the South Vietnamese, his small part of the war is struggling to stay alive—another subversion. Finally and brutally, Harry and all of the children are killed by frightened and overzealous Americans, which shows that no one is being protected.

Ann Nolan Clark's (1978) *To Stand against the Wind* tells, in flashback, the story of how a small family of Vietnamese immigrants came from South Vietnam to America, focusing on their experiences from the beginning of the war until they left Vietnam. Ten-year-old Em and his family are rice farmers in the Mekong Delta. They befriend Sam, an American reporter, and the novel details life in their unnamed hamlet and the war's increasing infringement on their way of life. No frontier images are presented. Only the idea of war being sacred and regenerative is addressed and, in this novel, denied. The "savage" (p. 75) and "evil" (p. 87) war is perceived as little but wanton destruction. Sam muses on the effects of war, explaining that "war leaves scars. Scars are deep and ugly. They take a long time to heal" (p. 46). Em's mother agrees, flatly stating that "war is evil. It makes all it touches evil" (p. 87). Sam stays in Vietnam and continues to report because he "want[s his] countrymen to know what they're doing to the land and the people half a world away from our peaceful shores" (p. 68). Hardly the model of regeneration, it is difficult to imagine who might have been protected as "the war continued. The body count, the uncounted burned and crippled, and the thousands of orphaned and abandoned children, the burned hamlets, the destroyed roads and waterways grew steadily in number. . ." (p. 93). The American presence and the war in general in this novel serve only to undermine these myths.

Karl Terry's (1974) *Children of the Dragon* follows Tri, a young boy from Hanoi who is sent to live in Dai Lai, the country village of his Grandmother Te, because of the constant American bombing of civilians in Hanoi. Tri and Hoa, his female cousin, go to school, do chores, quote Ho Chi Minh's poetry, and enjoy a pastoral country life until the war's end. No American characters are included in this short novel. In subtle ways, however, several myths are subverted. Instead of Americans playing the part of the *hero* in a sacred and regenerative war against vicious *assailants,* the Americans are referred to as invaders who are keeping the South Vietnamese from obtaining their freedom and independence. Throughout the entire novel, war is seen only as a destructive and brutal interruption to the pastoral and idyllic life of North Vietnam.

Finally, Stella Pevsner and Fay Tang's (1997) *Sing for Your Father, Su Phan* is also set in North Vietnam. The protagonist, Su Phan, and her family are Chinese immigrants. The war is discussed in such vague and amorphous terms that no mythology can be isolated.

Combat Novels—Platoon Subcategory

The Platoon novels all focus on the extensive combat experiences of "grunts"—low-ranking infantry troops with nary a Green Beret in sight. Joe Haldeman's (1972, 1978) *War Year* is unique on several fronts. This is the only adolescent Vietnam novel to be written by a Vietnam vet; it's the first novel to have a draftee as its protagonist (Haldeman was also drafted); and it's the only one in the sample to have been published in two editions with two different endings—first edition in 1972 (the protagonist lives and his best friend is killed) and second edition in 1978 (the best friend lives and the protagonist is killed). The novel follows draftee John Farmer from his arrival in Vietnam to joining his unit near Pleiku as a combat engineer (a solider who deals with explosives). His miserable experiences with both the military and the war provide the content of the novel. Since the story focuses on drafted grunts and not Green Berets, as might well be imagined, the frontier hero is nowhere to be found. As opposed to frontier bravery, John admits that the war "scared me shitless. I was so scared I wanted to puke" (pp. 2, 24). Military bureaucracy abounds, and John is sent back to his combat unit after an injury far before he is physically able, because of a snafu in the rules. Impeding any hope of proficiency, the ponderous army rules and hierarchies sometimes seem as much an enemy to the soldiers as the VC.

Contrary to the notion of war being a sacred and regenerative endeavor, the war as presented in *War Year* serves only to subvert the myth. As early as page 14, John is told at Camp Enari in Pleiku by his commanding officer to listen carefully to his instructors because "they're all combat veterans, and they'll be trying to teach you how to stay alive for a year" (p. 14). Not how to win the war, or help the Vietnamese, but only to stay alive. The war is constantly described as something to endure, never a glorious undertaking to vanquish the VC and protect the South Vietnamese. In an exchange with an older soldier, John realizes that many Americans are killed by American bombs and napalm—that not only can the Americans not protect the South Vietnamese, they cannot even protect themselves from other Americans. John describes his part of the war as some sort of terrifying and pointless camping trip:

> . . . we moved around for a couple of weeks without so much as a peep from Charlie. Just walked around the boonies all day, dug in at night, got up in the morning, and humped all day again. . . . It's funny. I never could get up much hate for the enemy. Like I say, this is [President] Johnson's fuckin' war, let him fight it. (pp. 83-84)

John Farmer sees the war as pointless and something at best to be endured.

Walter Dean Myers's (1988) *Fallen Angels* is perhaps the best known adolescent novel about the Vietnam War. Dedicated to his brother who was killed in Vietnam, Myers's novel follows seventeen-year-old Richie Perry from his arrival at Tan Son Nhut airport in Saigon to his joining his unit near Chu Lai. *Fallen Angels* is the only Combat novel to use a black protagonist. No one character in Perry's unit emerges in the full-blown image of a true frontier hero, but most of the men, from time to time, exhibit some frontier characteristics. Like western frontier heroes learning the ways of Native Americans in order to fight them better, Monaco suggests that "you got to be like the Cong to get him" (p. 275). When Johnson, a low-ranking but highly competent soldier, challenges Brunner, a higher-ranking but less competent soldier, the squad is immediately ready to follow Johnson. The scene is later repeated with Johnson and the extraordinarily incompetent Captain Stewart, and again the squad is ready to follow Johnson, recognizing his innate and powerful leadership abilities showing the egalitarian and democratic ideals of the frontiersman.

It is the general consensus of the squad that the Americans are in Vietnam to defend the South Vietnamese from the invading communists, which plays nicely into the regeneration scenario. Perry and his friends do eventually question the accuracy of their assumptions and their role in the *hero*, *victim*, *assailant* choice. Perry questions the need for pacification missions:

> We were supposed to smile a lot and treat the people with dignity. They were supposed to think we were the good guys. That bothered me a little. I didn't like having to convince anybody that I was the good guy.

That was where we were supposed to start from. We, the Americans, were the good guys. Otherwise it didn't make the kind of sense I wanted it to make. (p. 122)

Pacification missions demonstrated to Perry that perhaps the Vietnamese had not accepted the Americans in their role of *hero*. Perry realizes that the Americans cannot act in a capacity to protect and save the Vietnamese from the VC, because they cannot tell them apart. After General Westmoreland issues a directive to "maximize destruction" of the enemy, Peewee replies "What the fuck does that mean? We get a Cong, we supposed to kill his ass twice?" (p. 228). But Perry has quite a different take on the idea:

I wondered what it did mean about "maximizing" destruction. Would it mean that we would simply kill more? But who would we kill? Maybe we would be quicker to shoot in the hamlets. Maybe we would stop pretending that we knew who the enemy was and let ourselves believe that all the Vietnamese were the enemy. That would be the easy way. The women, the babies, the old men with their rounded backs and thin brown legs. They would be the enemy, all of them, and we would be those who killed the enemy. (p. 229)

In two devastating scenes, Myers subverts and destroys the mythic notion of war as a regeneration—*heroes* protecting *victims* from evil *assailants*. Perry's squad reaches a hamlet that they are supposed to secure against the VC only to find that it has already been destroyed by Americans.

There was a sense of panic in the air. We had our weapons ready. Sergeant Simpson was telling us not to kill the civilians. I didn't consciously want to kill anybody, anything. But I felt strange. The sight of all the bodies lying around, the smell of blood and puke and urine, made my head spin, pushed me to a different place. I wanted to fire my weapon, to destroy the nightmare around me. I didn't want it to be real, this much death, this much dying, this waste of human life. I didn't want it. . . . We could have killed as easily as we mourned. We could have burned as easily as we put out the fires. We were scared, on the very edge of control, at once trying to think of what was right to do and hating the scene about us. (pp. 176, 178)

Days earlier after another firefight in another hamlet, helicopters are called in to pick up the squad.

> It took the chopper another five minutes to get to us. What we hadn't done to the village, it did. It leveled the huts. There were Vietnamese, mostly women and old men, running for their lives. Few of them made it more than a few feet as the chopper guns swept everything in their path. These were the people we had come to save, to pacify. Now it was ourselves that we were saving. God have mercy. God give us peace. (p. 127)

This last passage deals a death blow to any idea in this novel that the war is to protect the South Vietnamese.

Perry realized that the terror men experienced in the jungle made for dangerous soldiers. "You never saw anything. There was never anything there until it was on top of your ass, and you were screaming and shooting and too scared to figure out anything" (p. 295). This terror was perhaps what led to Americans dying from "friendly fire." Immediately after a firefight,

> Scotty nudged me and pointed toward [Lieutenant] Doyle. Doyle [who has just ordered an artillery strike on the position] had his helmet off and was screaming into the radio. He was gesturing wildly and then he stood up and looked toward the target area. The radio man stood and looked, too. The machine gun on the right opened up again, and Doyle started screaming.
>
> "Cease fire! Cease fire!" Doyle was jumping around and waving both of his arms over his head.
>
> "Oh shit!" Scotty turned around and leaned against the sandbags.
>
> "What's up?" I asked.
>
> "I hope not what I think it is," Scotty said.
>
> We waited as Doyle walked a little ahead of his position, hands on hips, and looked out to the field ahead of us. Behind us I heard choppers. I turned and saw them headed for us. They went by us out to the target zone.
>
> "Hey, Scotty, did we. . .?"
>
> "Yep, we just shot the shit out of the first platoon." . . . The guys that our artillery blew away didn't have a reason to die. They hadn't

died facing the enemy. They just died because somebody else was scared, maybe careless. They died because they were in Nam, where being scared made you do things you would regret later. We were killing our brothers, ourselves. (pp. 102, 106)

Obviously the war as presented in *Fallen Angels* is no sacred quest to protect innocents from evil. It has become a destructive and surrealistic nightmare where the only goal is survival. When accompanying a pacification team on a mission to a nearby hamlet, Perry's closest friend, Peewee, questions showing Disney movies to the Vietnamese children. "What the fuck am I doing running around over here protecting Donald Duck?" (p. 140). Hardly a sacred cause.

The proficiency myth fares little better in *Fallen Angels*. Perry has faith in American proficiency—the idea that doing a good job is enough. In trying to compose a letter to his younger brother Kenny, Perry writes that when

> the killing started, there was no right or wrong except in the way you did your job, except in the way that you were part of the killing.
> [The war] was exciting, too. It was that, the knowing that we would win, and the excitement that overcame the being scared. If we just did our job, we would be all right. (p. 269)

But, just doing that job turns out to be quite difficult because the ideals of proficiency are constantly undermined by incompetence and bureaucracy. Perry isn't supposed to be in combat because of a knee injury, but a paperwork snafu assigns him to a combat unit. The unwieldy military bureaucracy forces an injured man into combat and rotates soldiers in and out of the war in one-year periods, impeding the proficiency of the American army. Individual incompetence in American soldiers is despised, making such soldiers the easy target of the VC and Americans alike. When Lieutenant Gearhart accidentally sets off a trip flare, giving away the squad's position on ambush and nearly getting the entire squad killed, he is met with threats of extreme retaliation for endangering the squad and damaging their proficiency.

> "Who set the first flare off?" Monaco asked. "We got somebody here working for Charlie?"

"It just . . . I made a mistake," Gearhart said.

"Don't be making no more mistakes, man, because I'll frag your ass in a hot damn minute!" Monaco spat on the ground. (p. 164)

The only real proficiency (along with the respect it merits) is attributed to the VC. In the eyes of Perry's squad, the VC, unlike the Americans and the ARVN, are the most fierce and proficient warriors in the war. In conversations among squad members, the VC attain an almost superhuman status. "The Congs know everything," Johnson simply states (p. 271). Perry "had heard stories about artillery fire taking off the entire top of a mountain and then having the Congs come out of the ground. Their bunkers were deeper than ours, a lot deeper" (p. 236). Referring to the VC's ability to remain completely unseen, Peewee says "the only time I seen a live, straight-money Cong was that guy they was questioning. As far as I'm concerned, the Congs could sneak they asses clear out the damn country, and we'd be here fighting for two more years" (p. 133). In a conversation one evening, some of the squad discuss the frightening notion of coming face-to-face with a VC guerrilla:

"Hey, y'all hear about the dudes collecting ears from dead Congs and wearing them around their necks?" Monaco asked.

"That's rough stuff," Lobel said.

"It ain't nothing to mess with a Cong once he dead," Johnson said. "You cut the mother's ears off while he still alive and kicking—then you doing something."

"And what you gonna say to Mr. Cong when he catch your ass with them damn ears?" Peewee said. "'Scuse me, Mr. Cong, I just taking these here ears to the lost and found?" (p. 275)

In general, the VC are thought to be worthy, if not overwhelming, opponents with amazing and admirable military abilities.

Four of the remaining Platoon novels are the *Echo Company* (1991, 1991, 1991, 1992) books written by Ellen Emerson White under the pseudonym Zack Emerson. These series books follow draftee Michael Jennings from his arrival at Tan Son Nhut to joining his unit close to Chu Lai—virtually the exact date and location of *Fallen Angels* (1988). These novels, *Echo Company #1—Welcome to Vietnam* (1991), *Echo Company #2—Hill 568* (1991), *Echo Company #3—'Tis the Season* (1991), and

Echo Company #4—Stand Down (1992), will be addressed as one
continual story, which in fact they are. Although many characters
occasionally exhibit a range of frontier characteristics, only one emerges
in the constant image of the frontier hero. Sergeant Hanson, the black
squad leader, is a quiet, handsome, good-natured, intelligent, nearly
superhuman soldier who never misses anything, always looks out for his
men, and displays the natural leadership abilities that make the squad trust
and follow him.

Only in the third book, *'Tis the Season*, does Hanson meet his frontier
equal in the form of Lieutenant Rebecca Phillips, an army nurse. While
stranded alone and injured in the jungle after a helicopter crash, she
demonstrates virtually every characteristic of a frontier hero. She is
extraordinarily brave, tough, knowledgeable, practical, and maintains her
sense of humor and honor even in life-threatening situations. Having
sustained a broken nose and compound fracture of the ankle after her
helicopter is shot down, she takes a gun from a dead soldier and starts off
through the jungle, avoiding trails knowing that they might be booby-
trapped. She eventually kills a Vietnamese man, but not before he shoots
her in the arm. When she is found by Hanson's (and Michael's) squad,
she orders the medic to give her his forceps so that she can pull the bullet
from her arm before she is returned to the evac hospital where she is
stationed. The entire squad is in awe of her toughness.

The regeneration scenario is not found in the *Echo* books. Michael
vaguely mentions that he thinks Americans are supposed to be in Vietnam
to protect the South Vietnamese from the North Vietnamese, but he has
his doubts. There are virtually no Vietnamese characters in the books that
the Americans might be protecting. The idea of war as a sacred undertaking is given a little more consideration, although much of that is in its
subversion.

At different times, Rebecca refers to the war as "pointless," "stupid,"
and "corrupt" (*Echo #3,* pp. 15, 61). Michael thinks about the randomness
of his combat experience and realizes that the war he thinks of as
"pointless" is hardly the exalted and morally correct experience that
American culture implies it to be (*Echo #1,* p. 28).

> It rained all morning, and they walked all morning. Nothing much
> happened, except that they all got even more tired, and even more wet.

> The VC were probably sitting in their damned tunnels, nice and dry, eating lunch, and having a good laugh about the dumb, muddy Americans, walking around the jungle like there was some point to it all. (*Echo #2,* p. 38)

Michael wonders about any war's ability to be meaningful when he thinks: "No one knew better than someone who had been in combat how horrible war was, but Michael was sure that *this* war was more stupid and wasteful than usual. More pointless" (*Echo #4,* p. 3, emphasis in original).

Michael and the other grunts resent not so much the fact that war wasn't in reality as they had been made to believe it would be through American mythology, but that it was ever implied to be glorious or sacred at all.

> Fuck John Wayne, for making it seem so—glamorous. So filled with dignity, and scope, and—logic. Like everything had a point, and if you *did* die—and everyone else would see it coming a long way off, and be prepared—it was always heroically, neatly, and in a blaze of color a trumpeting soundtrack music.
> Like hell. (*Echo #2,* p. 25, emphasis in original)

Not only do the grunts resent that war has ever been made to seem sacred, but they move past resentment into sadness when they realize that no one in America is even interested.

> "You think they know, in the World [America], there's kids lying in the jungle, using mud for a pillow" [Michael] asked.
> "Don't think they care," Viper said.
> Even more depressing. But, probably true. They were all cruising around in cars, going to football games, eating buckets of hot buttered popcorn at movies. Doing whatever they wanted, whenever they wanted. Figuring any guy dumb enough to get himself sent to Vietnam wasn't worth worrying about. What did they care, as long as *they* got out of it? (*Echo #2,* p. 137, emphasis in original)

The men's bitterness carries through all four books of the *Echo* series with the idea of the Vietnam War being anything other than "a constant and chaotic nightmare"—senseless and horrifically destructive, standing as a constant subversion of the regeneration myth (*Echo #4,* p. 4).

As is consistent with the other Platoon novels, the *Echo* books ascribe most images of proficiency to the VC. Michael invests them with superhuman powers as he stands watch one night: "He could hear branches rustling. Just the wind, or Charlie, smart, and swift, and tricky as hell? Supposedly, they could sneak right up to you without making a sound, and you wouldn't see them until the second before you died" (*Echo #1,* p. 63). Several months later Michael's entire company is involved in a huge firefight to take Hill 568. When the NVA/VC bunker complex situated within the hill appears impervious to American firepower, Michael demonstrates the archetypal American respect for anyone who demonstrates outstanding skill:

> . . . nothing seemed to be working on the bunkers—not grenades, or LAWs [light antitank weapons], or even the recoilless rifles—and despite the shrapnel and bullets flying everywhere, knocking wood and rocks all over him, Michael felt a flash of admiration for whoever had built the damned things. Hours of artillery and air strikes, and they were still standing. And there were men still *in* there, fighting. Jesus Christ, maybe they *weren't* human. (*Echo #2,* p. 200, emphasis in original)

While American characters are not presented as bumbling idiots, they are constantly thwarted by both military bureaucracy and carelessness. When truly proficient frontier hero Sergeant Hanson is replaced by Sergeant Quigley for political reasons, Michael thinks to himself that it was "typical of the Army to waste one of the few born leaders he'd met [in Vietnam]" (*Echo #4,* p. 143). Rebecca is also prevented from any real hope of proficiency in nursing by massive army red tape since "she had come to Vietnam with a Post-Op MOS [military occupational specialty]; had *wanted* to be an OR nurse; and had, naturally been assigned to Emergency/Receiving" (*Echo #3,* p. 3, emphasis in original). Rebecca, however, sees far more than military regulations standing between Americans and elusive proficiency:

> Friendly fire. Accidents. Mistakes. She wondered, often, if people back in the World know how many of the casualties here were just plain accidents. Dumb, preventable accidents. Two guys would start fooling around on top of an APC—armored personnel carrier—and one of them would slip off and get crushed underneath the tank's treads. A weapon

would fall onto a hootch floor, discharge, and hit someone. A grenade pin would get caught in a hanging vine, pull out, and a couple of kids would get blown to pieces. Someone would sit on an unexploded mortar round, and it would go off. Someone else would walk into a helicopter's rotor blades. While they were spinning.

Guys would get drunk, and angry—and there were too many lethal weapons around, within easy reach. Or they would be playing football, someone would throw a long pass and someone else would run right into a roll of concertina wire. They got bitten by spiders and snakes and scorpions. Stung repeatedly by bees. Caught in the undertow. Slammed against the rocks. Covered with second-degree burns.

One night a drunk kid tried to climb a palm tree, fell, and broke his neck. Jeeps crashed. Trucks crashed. *Helicopters* crashed. Wires shorted out and electrocuted people. Smoke grenades went off in people's faces. Gasoline and sparks came into contact. Explosives and detonators. Claymores turned in the wrong direction. Loads of crates fell. Bunkers collapsed. Boats sank. Cables snapped.

And—there were drug overdoses. Nobody worried much about marijuana—hey, Summer of Love, man—but there was opium, and heroin, and morphine, and—every drug imaginable. And they were all *cheap*. Easy to find. Making it too easy to take too much of the wrong thing. (*Echo #3*, p. 79, emphasis in original)

The *Echo* books are only ready to attribute any real proficiency to the VC.

The *Echo* series is unofficially continued in Ellen Emerson White's *The Road Home* (1995). The first half of this lengthy novel picks up shortly after *Echo #4*. Rebecca has always seen the war as pointless, but as her tour continues, she becomes more bitter. The regeneration myth is subverted when Rebecca reflects on how apathetic everyone involved has become. "It was the *casual* aspect of the callousness that bothered her the most. The war made it too easy to stop giving a damn. The war bade it easy even when you *did* give a damn" (p. 46, emphasis in original).

Interestingly, there is a bizarre subversion of the frontier hero in *The Road Home*. Michael Jennings (the protagonist of the *Echo* series) and Rebecca have remained close. He writes this letter to her at the evac hospital in Chu Lai from the bush where his unit is fighting.

Everyone was in bad shape—we hadn't lost anyone for a pretty long time, and suddenly, we lose a bunch of guys at once—but we have to pull out and hump another couple of hours for no damn reason that I *could see. Finnegan's totally out of it, all pale and shaky and not talking to anyone, and so when we're digging in, I just thought, hell with it, went over, and did it. I thought I might not hurt him as much if I used my .9 mm, so I did. He* is *okay, right? He's lying there all surprised and bleeding, and I'm yelling like my gun went off by accident, but everyone knows it didn't. After the medevac left, about ten guys shook my hand.* (p. 108, emphasis in original)

Michael summons all the frontier hero qualities he has and uses them to shoot a fellow soldier to get him out of the bush. In some respects the frontier myth is upheld, because Michael has seen what needs to be done and is willing to do it—regardless of how unpleasant it may be. However, shooting a friend is not generally a frontier hero approach to a situation.

Rebecca also cannot see the war as a regenerative act. Never fond of the war herself, she views the situation as continually deteriorating. Becoming more senselessly destructive.

> The fighting and dying were as bad as ever, and there was a constant little buzz of rumors about the way the situation was deteriorating out in the field, mostly stories about village incidents, some of which were so bad that she assumed they couldn't possibly be true. Although they *were* getting more and more civilian casualties. On the other hand, they were the victims of VC and NVA fire at *least* half of the time.
>
> They were also starting to get more alcohol poisonings and drug overdoses. White guys hurting black guys, and vice versa. A sudden, frightening rash of officers being attacked by their own men. *Killed* more often than not. Jesus. It was as though everyone in the country was going simultaneously crazy. (p. 79, emphasis in original)

Response to the War Novels

The six novels in this category are all set in America during the Vietnam War and explore characters' reactions to events in Vietnam and the effect of those even on lives in America. In general, the cultural myths of frontier heroes, regeneration scenarios, and amazing proficiency do not play a significant role in these novels. Not one of the novels in this category gives us a character in the image of a frontier hero or, for that matter, a subversion of this image.

Since none of the main characters in the novels in this category have endured war firsthand, their perceptions of war in general, and the war in Vietnam in particular, have come from sources other than personal experience. Among these sources are movies, television, the experiences of parents and other family members, and the great body of American cultural myth that surrounds our collective cultural thoughts on war. In an interesting although predictable split, characters who think of the war as a sacred undertaking, a necessary evil, are frequently the protagonists' fathers. In all of the cases where war is cast in the regeneration scenario, it is an older father—himself a veteran of Korea or World War II—who tends to see fighting a war as a duty to one's country. This is, of course, a view not necessarily shared by the younger generation—those who would actually fight the war.

Set in 1970, Meg Wolitzer's (1984) *Caribou* is the story of Stevie and Becca Silverman. Stevie's birthday has been chosen first in the draft lottery—virtually guaranteeing that he will indeed be drafted. Although he holds no political beliefs whatsoever, Stevie chooses to go to Canada instead of allowing himself to be inducted. Both Mr. and Mrs. Silverman are veterans of World War II. Recalling his own military service with pride—"helping defeat Hitler's men," Mr. Silverman perceives serving one's country as part of the military as a patriotic duty (p. 90). Thinking of the possibility of Stevie being drafted, Mr. Silverman tells the family that "Stevie will be going to help put an *end* to it. He'll be fighting for a good cause. It's something to be proud of. I remember when I went off to fight [in WWII]. I remember the way I felt when I put on my uniform for the first time" (p. 16, emphasis in original). Mr. Silverman cannot understand why his son and daughter do not share his opinion.

Margaret Rostkowski's (1989) *The Best of Friends* chronicles the story of a brother and sister, Dan and Sarah Ulvang, and their best friend, Will Spencer. Dan, a budding historian, researches the history and causes of the war. Sarah is an emerging antiwar activist. Both Dan and Sarah have as their nemesis their father, Roald Ulvang, Korean War veteran and head of the local draft board. Much like Mr. Silverman, Roald Ulvang is a staunch and unquestioning supporter of the American effort in Southeast Asia. He considers a man's service in Vietnam as a "sacrifice for his country" (p. 90). In discussing the nature of the war in Vietnam, Mr.

Ulvang clearly perceives the situation cast in terms of the regeneration scenario.

> "Dad, don't you ever worry about the guys you draft?" Sarah asked. "Even the ones who don't want to go?"
>
> "Sure we do. We're human. But we know it's a necessary evil. And we know what the alternatives are."
>
> "What are the alternatives?"
>
> Sarah looked over her shoulder at Dan. He never used that tone of voice with Dad.
>
> "Communism. You know as well as I do that we're fighting in Vietnam to protect our way of life against the Communists. Our freedom. Your freedom to go to school. Your freedom to protest, Sarah. We must support democracy in Vietnam." (p. 93)

None of those who support the notion that war is somehow a sacred duty to protect the helpless against the evil portray war in a glorified fashion. They do all cast it in terms of a necessary evil.

The myth of war as a sacred or regenerative act is often undermined in the novels of this category by young protagonists who have no desire or inspiration to fight. Alexander Crosby's (1971) *One Day for Peace* tells the story of how young Jane Simon and her friends organize a huge peace parade when Jane's friend, Jeff the milkman, is killed in Vietnam. Throughout this novel, we are told that the war is in no way regenerative and is only destructive. Jane writes to the president to find out what the war is about. Receiving a pamphlet entitled *Why We Are Fighting in Vietnam,* Jane thinks: "There was something odd about this. The bulletin said we're supposed to be helping the people of Vietnam. But the newspapers say we're killing them, every day" (p. 21). It is Jane's father's opinion that this war is too destructive:

> "I don't blame you for crying," [Dad] said. "Everybody should cry about this war."
>
> "But why don't we stop it?" I asked. . . .
>
> "Jane, I think it's our fault—I mean the fault of people like us and all our neighbors, rich and poor, white and black. We haven't accepted any responsibility. We have let the President and the generals do as they like. And what they have done is wrong." (p. 5)

At the closing ceremony of the peace parade, Mr. Tarantino gives a speech before planting a tree as a symbol of peace.

> When I see our great country destroying a small country across the Pacific Ocean, I am sick. Why should we kill the men and women and the children of that little country? What have they ever done to us?
>
> I cannot find the answer in the newspapers. I cannot find the answer on television. My friends, I think our government is deceiving us. And perhaps many of us find it comfortable to be deceived.
>
> But not the children. It is very hard to fool the young. We are here today because the children know this war is wicked. (p. 103)

Mr. Tarantino's ideas definitely subvert the myth that the war in Vietnam is regenerative.

In Theresa Nelson's (1989) *And One for All*, Sam Daily has become very involved in the antiwar movement, much to the horror of his best friend, Wing Brennan, and the whole Brennan family. Mr. Brennan is a World War II veteran who perceives participating in war as a sacred duty to one's country, and war itself to be an honorable undertaking. He requires the entire family to watch President Johnson's 1966 State of the Union Address, which mainly called for the country's support of American action in Vietnam. Sam purposely attempts to subvert the idea that war is sacred or regenerative by distributing flyers that he wrote. The flyer begins:

HELP BRING ABOUT PEACE IN SOUTHEAST ASIA—WHAT YOU CAN DO TO HELP:
1. READ!! The United States is currently involved in an immoral war, in which thousands of innocent men, women, and children are being needlessly slaughtered, day after day. We are not getting the full story. The American news coverage has been largely limited to press releases handed out by our government which has a vested interest in keeping the conflict alive. War is good for business, the theory goes. But it is a deadly business that has at its heart the taking of human life.

Attached you will find copies of articles by leading newspapermen not only from America, but from countries all over the world. Included are interviews with veterans who have witnessed these atrocities firsthand. READ THEM!! LEARN THE TRUTH!! (p. 111, emphasis in original)

The characters of the novels in the Response to the War category who feel that American involvement in Vietnam serves only to kill Vietnamese obviously subvert, consciously or unconsciously, the regeneration scenario in which American *heroes* protect South Vietnamese *victims* from VC and North Vietnamese *assailants*.

The myth of technical proficiency does not appear with any significance in any of the novels in this category. It is neither supported nor subverted in terms of American characters. No amazing proficiency is attributed to the VC or NVA in these novels—in fact, the Vietnamese are hardly mentioned.

Returned Vet Novels

The final category of novels share as their unifying structure returned Vietnam veterans who are, along with their families, trying to come to terms with their experiences in Vietnam. The novels are set from 1968 to 1987. Somewhat surprisingly, even though the novels all contain Vietnam vets, they do not rely on American myths where characters with frontier qualities populate regeneration scenarios or have extraordinary proficiency. None of the Returned Vet novels produces a single frontier hero. The only novel to subvert the mythical image of a frontier hero is Larry Bograd's (1986) *Travelers*. Seventeen-year-old Jack Karlstad searches out his KIA (killed in action) fighter pilot father's friends in order to learn more about the father he never knew. A.J. Karlstad, Jack's father, joined the army feeling that it was his patriotic duty. Only after arriving in Vietnam did he begin to think that the war was a terrible thing. When A.J.'s best friend in Vietnam, Flip McKenzie, tells Jack that both he and A.J. wanted desperately to leave a war they thought was wrong, he begins to subvert the image of a frontier hero. "If A.J. and I hadn't given a fuck about the dishonorables, if all that mattered was to stop our part in the killing and get out. . . . If . . . if . . . if" (p. 133). Flip believes that a moral character (or frontier hero) wouldn't have let worries about a dishonorable discharge stand in the way of doing what he knew to be morally right.

Only one novel in the Returned Vet category casts the war in Vietnam in terms of the regeneration scenario. Nancy Antle's (1993)

Tough Choices: A Story of the Vietnam War follows Mitch Morgan from his return from a tour of duty in Vietnam to his eventual reenlistment and return to Vietnam. Mitch believes strongly in the American war effort and perceives the war in terms of the Americans protecting the victimized South Vietnamese peasants by "fighting the Communists" who want to rule their lives (p. 12). No characters in the Returned Vet novels, especially not the vets themselves, perceive war as a glorious endeavor. There are many examples of the regeneration scenario and its attendant belief that war is sacred being subverted by characters in the novels of this category. The war becomes too destructive—killing the very people it is meant to save, or becomes purposeless—soldiers merely struggling to survive. A scene from *Tough Choices* most clearly shows a subversion of the regeneration scenario. Mitch's younger brother Emmett is a vehement antiwar protestor. Fifth-grade sister, Sam (the story's first person narrator) and Emmett discuss whether the war effort is actually protecting the Vietnamese civilians. Emmett is preparing signs to take with him to a dramatization of Vietnamese civilians being killed.

> "It's [the dramatization] supposed to show how terrible this war is for the people of Vietnam. The people we're supposedly trying to save."
> "Soldiers are fighting the war," I said, "not regular people."
> "Who do you think all the bombs get dropped on? Do you think the soldiers check first to see if there are any innocent people among the Viet Cong?"
> "Oh, shut up," I muttered. But he'd gotten me thinking. I'd watched the 6:00 news every night during dinner with Mom and Emmett. Most of the time there was film of soldiers firing their guns into trees. Or running for cover. Sometimes there were pictures of injured Vietnamese people, but I'd never thought that our soldiers might be responsible. (p. 19)

It had never occurred to Sam, or to many Americans, that this war may not, in fact, be consistent with regeneration mythology.

Returned vet Bill Breckenridge, of Judie Wolkoff's (1980) *Where the Elf King Sings*, battles with alcoholism and post-traumatic stress disorder (PTSD) as a result of his war experiences. After his wife has thrown him out of the house because of his drinking, he writes a letter to his twelve-year-old daughter, Marcie, explaining his perception of the war. He tells her that he and most of his men didn't want to be in Vietnam and had no idea why they'd been sent. Then after surviving the horror of combat, that he returned to accusations of an ungrateful American public. Bill perceives the war as a traumatic exercise where the primary goal was staying alive—not conquering an evil foe.

His feelings are echoed in the other novel in the Returned Vet category that addresses PTSD, Kathryn Jensen's (1989) *Pocket Change*. When a sudden onset of flashbacks more than fifteen years after his return from Vietnam triggers bizarre and frightening behavior in her father, Josie Monroe contacts a vet counselor for help. Dr. Whitehead, himself a Vietnam vet, tells Josie much the same thing that Bill Breckenridge (*Elf King*) tells his daughter Marcie. In trying to explain part of the reason for PTSD, Dr. Whitehead tells Josie that most probably her father witnessed enormous devastation and was probably constantly surrounded by death. In both of these passages, survival is a more realistic goal than the sacred battle against a sinister enemy.

Jack Karlstad (*Travelers*) is told by one of his father's pilot friends that A.J. had come to question if the war was a sacred and just endeavor. A.J. had entered the war with it cast (in his mind) in full mythical regalia.

> Jack, I don't know if you know this, but your dad, as I remember, was a real hawk. Now I met him soon after he arrived—maybe he changed his mind after I left. But he couldn't accept the idea that America was misusing its power. That for the *first* time in our history a war wasn't going to solve anything, that perhaps we were fighting for an unjust cause. (p. 90, my emphasis)

While it is certainly not a given fact that the Vietnam War was the "*first* time in our history . . . we were fighting for an unjust cause," A.J. did in fact come full circle in his beliefs about war as a sacred undertaking. He confides in a much later letter to his wife that he has completely changed his opinions about the war.

> He's [A.J.'s new copilot] all gung-ho, like I must've been when I got here. How can I tell him what I know? I've reached the conclusions that we are the war. I am the war. And the war is evil. The damage we've

done is evil! Victory is impossible. We're no longer here to win, merely
to "contain and pacify." (p. 157)

Although this passage raises questions about whether A.J. would have
considered the war "evil" if victory *had* been imminent, it certainly shows
this character's disbelief in the mythological sacredness of war. The myth
of American proficiency is neither supported nor subverted. Neither the
VC nor NVA, when mentioned, are invested with the superhuman
abilities that are seen especially in the Combat novels.

Generalizations

There are some within and across category generalizations to be made
about the myths of frontier heroes, regeneration scenarios, and technical
proficiency and how the novels support them. The Duty novels consistently support the idea of American soldiers as frontier heroes. They all
have natural ability, practicality, and adaptability. Three of the five novels
use Green Berets as protagonists or coprotagonists, which automatically
capitalizes on the mythic image of the Green Beret soldier.

The only Green Beret and frontier hero in the Vietnamese Perspective
novels is David Lee from *The Man in the Box* (1968). Other characters are
either not American or not especially frontier-like. Throughout the
Platoon novels, various characters exhibit frontier qualities, but only
Sergeant Hanson and Lieutenant Rebecca Phillips (both from the *Echo*
books) emerge as true frontier heroes. These novels are not necessarily
populated by frontier antiheroes who subvert the frontier hero mythology,
but instead by characters who only occasionally exhibit frontier qualities.

As for the Response to the War and the Returned Vet categories, no
characters are introduced that could be considered frontier heroes. While
this is less surprising in the Response to the War category because most
protagonists are not adults and are not cast in situations where their
frontier qualities would be demonstrated, it is somewhat more surprising
in the Returned Vet category. None of the vets in the novels are invested
with frontier hero qualities.

The regeneration myth, which gives war a nearly sacred status and
interprets armed conflicts in terms of *hero*, *victim*, and *assailant* roles, is
addressed with much more frequency than the frontier myth. Within the
Duty novels, the war in Vietnam is constantly considered to be configured

in the classic regeneration scenario. Protagonists in William Butterworth's two novels, *Orders to Vietnam* (1968) and *Stop & Search* (1969), briefly question whether the war is worth the loss of friends' lives, but in the end the myth is upheld.

That is certainly not the case in the Vietnamese Perspective novels. In four of the novels, the regeneration myth is subverted when the war becomes too destructive and eventually destroys those that it purported to defend. The Platoon novels follow the lead of the Vietnamese Perspective group. In each of the novels, the regeneration myth is subverted. Characters in *Fallen Angels* (1988) and the *Echo Company* (1991, 1992) books begin the war believing that the overall conflict fits the regeneration model, but they soon conclude that the war is devastating to the very people it was meant to protect. Also, in all seven novels, the soldiers' main goal is survival—staying alive for their year in-country—not protecting the Vietnamese or ridding the land of an evil enemy.

The Response to the War novels each have a character who envisions America's involvement in Vietnam in terms of a sacred regenerative quest and at least one who argues that the intent may be for the war to be regenerative, but in fact it has become so destructive that it is not. In four of the novels in this category, the character who perceives the war as sacred or regenerative is an older male who is himself a war veteran (of the Korean War or World War II). In *One Day for Peace* (1971), it is an American government pamphlet that states the regenerative nature of the Vietnam War. The idea that the war is somehow beneficial or necessary is denied and therefore subverted by younger characters—four who are becoming active in the antiwar movement. A character in *Caribou* (1984) chooses to go to Canada instead of being drafted, but his motivations are wholly connected to his fear for his own safety—not a protest against a war that is too destructive.

Characters in the Returned Vet novels also subvert the myth of war as sacred and regenerative with their beliefs that the war destroyed the very people it was supposed to save. Several of the returned vets remember their war experience mainly in terms of something that they struggled to endure, with survival being the main motivation—again, like the Platoon novels, not protecting the Vietnamese or vanquishing the VC.

The myth of technical proficiency is only consistently addressed in the Duty and Platoon novels, with virtually no mention in the Vietnamese

Perspective, Response to the War, or Returned Vet categories. The four Combat novels that have Green Beret protagonists or coprotagonists, *Special Forces Trooper* (1967), *Vietnam Nurse* (1968), *Nurse in Vietnam* (1969), and *The Man in the Box* (1968), all attribute dazzling technical proficiency to the Green Beret characters. The men are frontier heroes and they are good at what they do. In virtually every novel in both the Duty and Platoon groups, the proficiency myth is subverted in two ways. First, American soldiers are constantly prevented from action they believe is necessary or right by a ponderous military bureaucracy and repressive rules of engagement and combat. Second, the idea of proficiency is attributed to the VC and NVA. American characters are torn between their inherent cultural respect for anyone who performs with excellence and the fact that those performing with such excellence are the enemy.

In broad generalizations, the myth of the frontier hero is upheld in several novels but largely ignored in most of the sample. The myth of war as sacred and regenerative is addressed in most novels, with at least one character holding this opinion. However, the regeneration myth is strongly subverted in the majority of novels. As for the myth of technical proficiency, American soldiers (especially Green Berets) were proficient but would have been much more so had they not been constantly impeded by mountains of bureaucratic rules. The enemy is understood to be as or more proficient than the Americans.

The Warrior Myths of Militarism and Moralism

Two American cultural myths isolated by Karen Rasmussen and Sharon Downey (1991) and discussed in terms of Vietnam War films are militarism and moralism, which are both "central to [America's] image of the warrior" (p. 117). These two complementary myths can be situated within the framework of Stewart's (1986) proficiency myth.

> Militarism specifies the skills required of men as *soldiers*. The perspective is impersonal: order, efficiency, unity of purpose, and domination by a central authority are essential for survival. Affirming power and control, this stance advocates subordination of self to group norms. (p. 180)

This first part of our mythical image of the warrior relates almost solely to men's adherence to military precision and focus. Rasmussen and Downey conceptualize the subversion of militarism in terms of what they call "military psychosis," which is the result of militarism gone berserk (p. 181). Here the warrior becomes dispassionate, dehumanized, demented, or an arbitrary killer.

The second and complementary part of this myth cast our warrior as fundamentally a humane and benevolent person:

> Grounded in principled, compassionate action, moralism is personal rather than impersonal. . . . Moralism's portrayal of people as humane choice makers becomes the foundation for sanity and integrity in war. Moralism's recurrent emblems are companionship and compassion. (p. 180)

Central to our image of the frontier hero or warrior is the idea that, ultimately, his moralism will always allay or mollify his militarism. When the mythology of moralism is subverted, this doesn't happen. The subversion of the warrior myth or moralism results in what Rasmussen and Downey call a "moral psychosis" (p. 182). This subversion is manifested when moralism "degenerates into self-interest, apathy, and self-pity" (p. 182). It would seem, then, that these myths (if functioning properly), as Rasmussen and Downey interpret them, credit frontier heroes, or American soldiers and their awesome technology, as capable of dazzling battle performance, but held in check by their inherent morality. If, however, the myths are subverted, then this will not be the case. As Rasmussen and Downey conclude, "if militarism degenerates into military psychosis, moralism gives way to unprincipled action. The two values, which complement each other in a context of regeneration [the same regeneration myth discussed earlier], disintegrate when survival motivates all action" (p. 182). In other words, when the regeneration myth is violated and subverted, the myths of militarism and moralism are soon to follow.

What follows is an examination of the manifestation and possible subversions of the warrior myths of militarism and moralism in the sample of novels. As in the previous sections, the novels will be discussed in groups delineated by their narrative structures.

Combat Novels—Duty Subcategory

The Duty novels uphold both types of warrior myths. In *Special Forces Trooper* (1967), Stan reflects on the nature of war after a small firefight in which he has killed several people in hand-to-hand combat. "There could not be anything personal in a war, Stan realized as he slogged the rest of the way to Luc Co. Men killed each other on sight, neither aware that the other had ever existed before, and both believing their cause to be right" (p. 142). Through experience, Stan comes to understand the impersonal nature of the militarism myth. If soldiers stopped to think about the men that they were killing as human beings, perhaps less killing would be done.

The concept of moralism enjoys a prominent place in this book. The Green Berets are painted as a macho Peace Corps, a benevolent force, who have come to help all of the people of Vietnam. When a VC guerrilla is wounded and captured, he is immediately given compassionate medical treatment. In the section of the novel that details Special Forces training, the Green Berets are accorded pseudo-missionary status.

> The character of the men of the Special Forces, the know-how derived from their intensive training, prevented a complete take-over of the Montagnards by the Vietcong and a bloody revolt of these hill people against the South Vietnamese government. Instead, Special Forces detachments trained and equipped a force of 700 Montagnards to protect the outpost of Buon Brieng. They gave them food, schooling, and medical aid. In sharp contrast to the majority of the Vietnamese, the Americans showed them respect and refrained from calling them *Moi*, or savage. (p. 14)

Despite the fact that this passage seems to show the Americans in an especially moral and compassionate light, the next few pages go on to patronizingly describe the Montagnards as a quaint people who believe that many spirits control their world.

In the two novels by William Butterworth, *Orders to Vietnam: A Novel of Helicopter Warfare* (1968) and *Stop & Search: A Novel of Small*

Boat Warfare Off Vietnam (1969), the concept of militarism is disdained, but upheld. Both protagonists, Bill Byrnes and Eddie Czernik, are suspicious and resentful, if not openly insubordinate, to men that have less skill but more rank than they have. Any pilot or sailor that has attended West Point or Annapolis or goes too closely by the book is scorned. When Bill, a warrant officer, is complimented on his "snappy salute" by Lieutenant Halverson, Bill silently fumes, "I learned to play soldier the same place you did, you stuffy little jerk" (*Orders to Vietnam*, p. 49). Later another lieutenant tries to make Halverson more palatable to Bill, assuring him that "Halverson is all right, Byrnes. He goes by the book. Maybe a little too much. But he's a West Pointer, and that's the way they play the game, I guess" (p. 52).

Eddie Czernik has much the same complaint as Bill Byrnes—a contempt for military rules and courtesy and a feeling that many higher-ranking men should not have their rank. Eddie nearly subverts the myth of militarism when he grows to hate his new commanding officer, Lieutenant Potter. Potter has replaced the very relaxed Lieutenant Asher, who was killed when their boat was ambushed. Potter takes his militarism very seriously.

> "I also understand . . . from inquiring around that PCF-16 [Eddie's patrol boat] has earned itself sort of a reputation as a very loose ship. In fact, that you all have previously taken some sort of perverse pride in being as unmilitary as possible.
>
> Still Eddie said nothing.
>
> "That's all changed," Potter said. "I believe that old saw that a tight ship is a happy ship. Do I make myself clear?"
>
> "Yes, sir."
>
> "Then please do me the courtesy of standing up when you're talking to me," Potter said.
>
> Eddie stood up.
>
> In the next three days, Eddie learned not only to hate Lt. Potter, but the Navy generally for putting people like him in positions of authority simply because they had the rank. (pp. 138-139)

Both Eddie and Bill wish for a more egalitarian military where natural leaders emerge and are followed. Neither completely subvert the militarism portion of the warrior myth, because they both decide at the end of their respective novels to continue their military careers—both becoming commissioned officers and both upholding the concept of militarism.

The inherent morality of American soldiers (in this case, sailors) is succinctly demonstrated through a scene in *Stop & Search* (1969). Eddie's patrol boat has come across a Vietnamese junk that *may* be hauling supplies for the VC. The Vietnamese officer aboard Eddie's boat wants to sink the junk, but the Americans refuse without some proof of contraband. Subsequently, there is a firefight between the patrol boat and the junk in which two Americans and the entire junk crew is killed. The Vietnamese sailors callously throw the bodies of the VC into the river, but the Americans solemnly and gently clean up the bodies of their fallen comrades and quietly place them in body bags. While it is true that the Americans are taking care of their own and that the Vietnamese sailors are dealing with the bodies of their enemies, it is unlikely, given the previous action of the Americans, that they would have been shown tossing the VC bodies off the junk. This compassion for the dead would be an example of moralism.

The two final Duty novels are the stories of nurses, Joanna Shelton and Lisa Blake. In much the same way that Green Berets are almost automatically cast as frontier heroes, nurses are almost without exception seen as examples of American moralism. Rasmussen and Downey (1991) list "companionship and compassion" as moralism's "recurrent emblems" (p. 180). Who could more easily fit that role than an angel of mercy—a nurse? The two nurses in these novels take care of all the wounded that they encounter—American or Vietnamese. At various times the Green Berets in their lives, Captain Wayne Moore and Captain Mace Thomas, nurse alongside them showing their own compassion. In both novels, the highest ideals of the myth of militarism are upheld. Everyone who populates these novels has the greatest of respect for the military and military men. No one questions the purposes or actions of the military, and the military characters maintain the full warrior myth.

Combat Novels—Vietnamese Perspective Subcategory

The warrior myths of militarism and moralism do not play a pivotal role in the majority of novels in the Vietnamese Perspective subcategory.

This is perhaps because American military personnel play only secondary roles with only Vietnamese protagonists. As in *Special Forces Trooper* (1967), the Green Berets in *The Man in the Box* (1968) are presented as moral soldiers who have come to help and teach the Montagnards. They are compassionate and personally involved with Montagnard characters.

In *Cross-fire* (1972), Harry continually skitters between upholding and subverting the moralism component of the warrior myth. He is compassionate to the four Vietnamese children that he has with him—but only as long as they do what he expects of them. When he first comes across twelve-year-old Mi holding her infant baby brother, he distrusts them. When he hears noises in nearby bushes, he holds his M-16 to the baby's head screaming for Mi to tell those in the bushes to come out—a complete subversion of the moralism. When the children act appropriately grateful and friendly, Harry is the soul of moralism; otherwise, he is cruel and threatening—moralism is subverted. When contemplating what to do with the children, Harry thinks back to his military training.

> The first thing they taught you in survival school was this: Never take prisoners. They drummed it into you, again and again: Never take prisoners. The only good Vietnamese was a dead one. So what am I supposed to do? Harry asked himself wearily. Shoot them? Shoot a girl and two kids and a baby? He couldn't do it. He couldn't shoot kids . . . . hell, it would be like committing murder. (p. 37)

Harry obviously thinks of himself as a good guy—a moral man, but he fails to realize that shooting unarmed children *is* murder, not *like* murder. Later while Harry is sleeping, the children leave, taking his gun and some of his food, unsure of whether they can trust him. When he awakens, he immediately calls the children "ungrateful, thieving, slant-eyed gooks" thinking of how much he had grown to like them and that "he'd wanted to help them, too. And this was the thanks he got for being decent" (p. 54). Again, Harry thinks of himself as a moral man, but forgets that just hours earlier, he threatened to blow off a baby's head.

Continuing with Harry's contradictory (both supporting and subverting) portrayal of the moral warrior, Harry has a confrontation with Mi's younger brother, nine-year-old Ton. When Ton does something that Harry thinks is disrespectful of Mi (disregarding the fact that what would be considered disrespectful between genders in Vietnam is different than in America), Harry picks Ton up, shakes him, punches him in the face and holds him underwater long enough that Ton nearly loses consciousness. The internal narration describes Harry thinking of this incident as trying to teach Ton some manners. Just a few pages later, Harry thinks to himself that you just can't trust the Vietnamese—"no matter how nice you treated them" (p. 68). Does Harry think that he has treated these children nicely? When Mi is protective of the infant (that Harry has threatened to kill), Harry becomes embarrassed and irritated, saying, "Listen, I won't hurt you, if you're on the level. We don't go around killing kids, for God's sake" (p. 12). In a final gesture of moralism, Harry tries to save Ton from being killed by an American airplane by pulling him to cover. Harry is killed in the process. But in the final subversion of the moralism myth, these very children are killed by American soldiers for no other reason than they startled the soldiers.

Harry's character is an interesting and complex examination of the morality component of the warrior myth. In fact, he is almost symbolic of the entire American war effort in Vietnam. Harry continues to think of himself as a moral soldier, but his actions often subvert this idea.

Combat Novels—Platoon Subcategory

The warrior myths of militarism and moralism are of some significance in the Platoon novels. In *War Year* (1972, 1978), the concept of militarism characterized by "order, efficiency, unity of purpose, subordination to group purpose" (Rasmussen & Downey, 1991, p. 180) is almost completely subverted. Within the army, there is a great resentment between the men who actually fight the war and those that the combat soldiers refer to as REMFs (rear-echelon mother fuckers), and also between those young draftees who have little interest in being soldiers and older career soldiers known as "lifers." The low-ranking grunts and engineers almost think of the lifers as another enemy. When John gets pulled for sandbag detail, he and the other men have little use for military authority.

> "Yeah," said another guy with an Alabama drawl, "this fuckin' army—we gotta spend all day fillin' sandbags we'll never get t'use."
> "I don't know," I said. "We might be behind 'em tonight."

> "This goddamn fuckin' army. Charlie keeps ya awake all night and the fuckin' sergeants won't let ya catch up in the day." (p. 33)

In a pivotal scene at the Cam Rahn Bay convalescent center, John tries to explain to an older sergeant that he is being sent back to combat before he is physically ready because of a paperwork screw up (which is truly the case). The ensuing exchange is indicative of the breakdown of militarism:

> "Well, they put me on the shipping roster today—"
> "Congratulations."
> "Goddammit, Sarge, I can't half *walk* yet!"
> "Look, son, I get twenty guys come in here ev'ry morning trying to get off the shippin' roster. Tough shit, all of 'em. I ain't never let one through, never will."
> "Sarge. . ."
> "Yer all just a buncha chickenshits, don't wanna go back an' fight." He was shouting, and I could smell whiskey. "I was in Korea . . ."
> "Bet you were tough, Sarge." I'd rather have killed that motherfucker than all the VC in the world. I slammed the door good and hard on the way out.
> So at 9:00 I rode a bus to the airport and got on a C-130 to Pleiku. (p. 107)

When factions of a military are so at odds with other factions, there can be no unity of purpose, order, or efficiency.

Throughout *Fallen Angels* (1988) soldiers are presented as fundamentally moral. Being a group of young and inexperienced grunts, the moralism component of the warrior myth plays a more important role than the militarism component in the lives of Perry's squad. As is common in the Combat novels, there is a scene in *Fallen Angels* where American soldiers exhibit their inherent moralism only to be rewarded with Vietnamese brutality.

A Vietnamese woman and her two children approach an American and ARVN firebase where Perry's squad is resting. The ARVN soldiers start slapping the woman around, but the Americans stop them and take her to the headquarters tent. Peewee picks some long grass and begins to make the children little dolls. As she leaves, the American soldiers are polite and respectful, walking her to the edge of the camp.

> I thought it was cool when the woman stopped just before she reached the dikes and handed one of the kids to a guy from Charlie Company.
>
> The GI's arms and legs flung apart from the impact of the blast. The damn kid had been mined, had exploded in his arms.
>
> Guys not even near him, guys who had just been watching him take the kid into his arms, fell to the ground as if the very idea of a kid exploding in your arms had its own power, its own killing force.
>
> I saw the woman running across the paddy. I saw her fold backward as the automatic fire ripped her nearly apart. I saw part of her body move in one direction, and her legs in another.
>
> The woman's other child stood for a long moment, knee deep in water and mud, before it, too, was gunned down. (p. 230)

American soldiers are moral and compassionate in their original behavior toward the Vietnamese woman and children, but as the situation changes, their behavior becomes much less so. Killing the Vietnamese woman in retaliation for her actions is possibly justified, but in killing the other child, the Americans' behavior is just as horrific as that of the woman. No comment is made in the novel about the fact that the Americans have killed an innocent Vietnamese child.

The image of the Americans as inherently moral soldiers is displayed in minor scenes of grunts playing with Vietnamese children, giving them food and candy. Their morality is also shown in their respect for the (American) dead. After a joint American army/ARVN mission that ended in a brutal firefight in a hamlet, both groups of soldiers tended to their dead. Knowing that they must quickly pull out of the hamlet, the Americans gently gather their dead, collect dog tags, and prepare to burn the bodies (ostensibly to save them from mutilation at the hands of the VC). The ARVN, on the other hand, "watched us impassively. They didn't want any part of what we were doing. They left their dead where they were. They stripped them, took the ammo, and the supplies. They closed their eyes" (p. 254).

Even though Perry has openly thought that "maybe the time has passed when anybody could be a good guy" (p. 150), he resents the insinuation of a fellow grunt that as they enter a village on a pacification mission they aren't the "good guys" anymore.

> The M-16 I carried felt bigger than it usually did. We came into the village to pacify the people who lived there. Lobel found me and came alongside.
> "You know who we are?" he asked.
> "Who?"
> "You remember those cowboy movies when the bad guys ride into town? You know, the killers?"
> "Yeah?"
> "That's us," Lobel said.
> "I'm not a killer," I said.
> He looked at me and smiled. I hated him saying that. (p. 110)

At this point, Perry continues to cling to the idea that as soldiers, they are moral men. Lobel is not so sure.

When the Platoon's young and caring lieutenant is killed in a later firefight, Perry begins to have thoughts that subvert both the moralism and militarism components of the warrior myth. He becomes dispassionate and apathetic—numb.

> The war was different now. Nam was different. Jenkins had been outside of me, even the guys in Charlie Company had been outside [both references to characters killed earlier]. Lt. Carroll was inside of me, he was part of me. Part of me was dead with him. I wanted to be sad, to cry for him, maybe bang my fists against the sides of the hooch. But what I felt was numb. I just have these pictures of him walking along with us on patrol or sitting in the mess area, looking down into his coffee cup. It was what I was building in my mind, a series of pictures of things I had seen, they seemed more and more a part of me. (p. 136)

As the war continues, the men in *Fallen Angels* find it harder and harder to live up to either component of the warrior myth.

The *Echo Company* books (1991-1992) address both myths—frequently to subvert them. As a draftee, Michael is less than enthusiastic about his conscription into the army. He thinks or says "FTA—*Fuck the Army*" repeatedly in response to various situations in the four novels. On his first night of guard duty after arriving at the firebase, Michael reflects on his personal dislike of rules, bureaucracy, and teamwork and concludes that "the Army must be what teams are like in Hell" (*Echo #1*, p. 68). These pithy phrases hardly demonstrate Michael's commitment to upholding the warrior myth of militarism.

Michael is, however, reminded of military hierarchy and the order that comes with the idea of ranks after he has had a confrontation with a lieutenant.

> "I'm sorry, Sarge," Michael said. "I didn't mean to be disrespect-ful."
>
> Unexpectedly, Sergeant Hanson laughed.
>
> "You just spit at an officer back there, Mike. That's, uh, that's pretty disrespectful."
>
> "*He* doesn't deserve my respect," Michael said.
>
> Sergeant Hanson shrugged. "Maybe, maybe not. But, you're in the Army, and no matter who the man is, you have to respect the rank." (*Echo #2*, p. 14)

In this exchange, Hanson is exhorting Michael to accept the militarism aspect of the warrior myth. Later in the same book, Michael does briefly embrace the notion of putting a group purpose ahead of his own desires.

> One thing he was learning about the Army was that you could be tired, or sick, or in pain—and you did the job, anyway. You might gripe and groan a little—or even a lot—but you did what had to be done. If he were at home, and had blistered his hands this badly raking leaves, say, or shoveling snow, he would probably have quit, and gone inside the house to lie down. Here, he had to just grit his teeth, and get on with it.
>
> So, he was either building character, or else he had fallen so deep into the group mentality that he was incapable of making any sort of decision for himself. (*Echo #2*, p. 111)

Michael's tentative acceptance of militarism is quickly subverted when he begins to think that there is little unity of purpose between ranks. It is his idea that the grunts' purpose is to survive the war, but the officers' purpose is to further their own careers and to perhaps win the war—by requiring the grunts to risk their lives. This perception leads Michael to the conclusion that if not all soldiers were at equal risk, then officers and enlisted persons were at cross purposes. This resentment of central authority is a subversion of militarism. During a particularly fierce battle in which many Americans are being killed, Michael contemplates the fact that there are no officers in sight.

> There were helicopters cruising around in the sky—some were Cobra assault choppers and the like, but others were LOHs—[commonly known as "loaches"] light observational helicopters—and C & Cs, which were Command and Control. In other words, where generals and other Army brass sat to enjoy the show, and pretend that the blood and death was just one big chess game. (*Echo #2*, p. 208)

This subversion of the myth of militarism continues throughout the books because the lower-ranking men resent being expected to submit to a military authority that they don't respect. The grunts feel that the ranking officers don't share their purposes.

> As they waited to pull out, everyone around him was either dangerously silent—or bitching and moaning, and Michael was very glad that *he* wasn't in charge. Giving orders to a bunch of pissed-off guys, carrying loaded weapons, was a risk he wouldn't enjoy taking. (*Echo #4*, p. 93)

This near-mutinous subversion of militarism mythology shows the breakdown of "order" and "domination by a central authority" (Rasmussen & Downey, 1991, p. 180).

The moralism component of the warrior myth fares little better than its militarism counterpart in the *Echo* books. Upon arriving in Vietnam, Michael and the other soldiers are given a Military Assistance Command—Vietnam (MACV) book of rules for their behavior toward the Vietnamese. The rules sound mainly like a guide for moralism: "to treat the women with politeness and respect, to make personal friends among the soldiers and common people, to always give the Vietnamese the right of way. . ." (*Echo #1*, p. 25). The soldier who earnestly complied would be personally involved with the Vietnamese and act in a principled and polite manner. Michael never manages to display any real compassion or companionship toward any Vietnamese people, but he does befriend a stray Vietnamese dog, feeding and taking care of it for a time.

The concept of moralism does, however, take a beating as Michael and his squad become indifferent and only interested in themselves. After endless days of humping (generally defined as trudging through the jungle on patrol often carrying more than fifty pounds of gear), the men have become worn down and apathetic.

> Over the next couple of days, it rained and rained, and they walked and walked. Same old thing. Took some sniper fire. Tramped down into the valley and through a few rice paddies. Took a lot *more* sniper fire. Searched a pathetic little village. Rounded up two, probably harmless, old men as prisoners and sent them off on a chopper to face interrogations. Took still *more* sniper fire. Made an effort to give a damn. (*Echo #4*, p. 106)

The total exhaustion that soldiers endure in the *Echo* books was a significant contributor toward the subversion of both parts of the warrior myth. Lieutenant Rebecca Phillips understands how the general misery in Vietnam undermines the largest part of moralism when she says that "good intentions [are] worthless here" (*Echo #3*, p. 76)

Finally, the ultimate subversion of moralism comes at the hand of militarism. It is technically moralism's job to keep militarism in check, to make sure that America's military stays compassionate and humane—moral. After Michael has participated in his first "zippo raid" (burning down a Vietnamese hamlet), he questions the Platoon's lieutenant about the inherent immorality of the Americans' actions.

> "Things were getting out of control there today, sir," Michael said and looked back at him.
>
> Lieutenant Brady sighed. "SOP [standard operating procedure]. That's our *job*. That's why we're here."
>
> "Felt like a Nazi, sir."
>
> "It's a complicated war, Jennings. We're all just doing our best." Michael didn't say anything.
>
> "You and I are just part of the machine," Lt. Brady said.
>
> Michael shrugged. "Doesn't make it right, sir."

"Look—" Lt. Brady stopped. "What's your first name again?
Michael?"

Michael nodded.

"You're going to do so many wrong things in the next year,
Michael—God willing—that it's going to be hard to—" He stopped
again. "Well."

"I, uh—I'm having trouble understanding what's going on,"
Michael said. "It seems—I don't know."

Lt. Brady didn't answer right away. "The bottom line," he said,
after a pause, "out here, is that we all have to be able to depend on each
other. You have to be able to live with yourself, but the group is more
important. Not everything you do is going to be right, but most of the
time, you aren't going to have the luxury of stopping to figure that out."
(*Echo #1*, pp. 143-144)

In this bizarre exchange it seems as if Lieutenant Brady is instructing
Michael to check his moralism at the door, that militarism is far more
important.

There are several scenes in the unofficial continuation of the *Echo*
books, *The Road Home* (1995), that parallel the destruction of Vietnamese
hamlets in *Fallen Angels*. Michael's best friend, Snoopy, reports to
Lieutenant Rebecca Phillips that after some of the platoon's moral leaders
left the bush, things took a decided turn for the worse. There appeared to
be very little inherent moralism in the majority of the remaining soldiers.

"It got real bad out there," Snoopy said, both hands gripping his
chipped mug, "after we lost [Michael], and the Sarge. I mean, it's kind
of hard to explain, but they were like the *enforcers*. When they were
there, everyone *acted* right, you know? In the villages and all . . . .

"Things got *real* bad, ma'am. I mean mostly it wasn't fighting
anymore, it was *hurting* people. You know? Breaking the rules."

She nodded. There had been so many rumors about atrocities since
Tet that she had always known that some—maybe even *more* than
some—of them had to be true.

"I wasn't doing it, but—Meat [Michael] and the Sarge, they would
have *stopped* it, and—guys would've listened up. I just—I didn't have
any buddies left, and—there was this one guy, Mojo, and we'd just go
away, you know? Sit down in the road or something, like we didn't
know them." (p. 203, emphasis in original)

Even though there are moral characters in *The Road Home*, the myth of moralism is subverted more than it is upheld.

Response to the War Novels

The complementary and balanced warrior myths of militarism and moralism play little part in the novels of the Response to the War category. This is perhaps not so surprising given that no Vietnam vet characters populate this group. After forcing the entire family to watch LBJ's State of the Union Address (*And One for All,* 1989), Mr. Brennan, a World War II vet, tries to pass on to his son Wing and Wing's friend Sam the ultimate acceptance of the concept of militarism—unquestioning loyalty.

> Daddy shook his head. "The president's got the best military minds in the world advising him—we have to trust that they know more than we do, same as we had to trust our commanding officers in the Pacific, whether we understood or not."
> "But what if they'd been wrong, Mr. Brennan?" Sam asked quietly. "What if you'd been sure the officers were wrong—would you have followed their orders anyway?"
> Daddy never hesitated. "I'd have had no choice, son; it wasn't my place to pass judgements like that. A soldier has to follow orders, or there'd be chaos—you know that."
> Sam didn't reply.
> "You'd go again, wouldn't you, Dad?" Wing asked now. "If you were younger, I mean, and you got called up?"
> This time Daddy didn't answer right away. He looked hard at Wing and Sam both. "Yes," he said at last. "I would. And I know you boys would go too, if you were needed, if it had to be. But I hope to God it never comes to that." (p. 69)

Mr. Brennan is attempting to pass on to the younger males his conception of the myth of militarism—emphasizing "domination by a central authority" and "subordination of self to group purpose" (Rasmussen & Downey, 1991, p. 180).

Jonas Duncan, the seventeen-year-old son of a career marine officer (in Adrienne Jones's 1990 *Long Time Passing*), scorns his father's occupation as a professional soldier. He does not value militarism and helps to subvert it with his attitudes. After Jonas's mother's recent death, Lieutenant Colonel Hugh Duncan accepts an assignment in Vietnam that he could easily have declined—making Jonas resent both his father and the military all the more. Jonas thinks of his father as a man most interested in military destruction. Having lived all of his life on marine bases, Jonas has seen the transformation that takes place as young men become marines. He despairs about how the boys change from loving compassionate boys to hardened killers.

And in finally succumbing to militarism by joining the marines himself, Jonas tells his decision to Auleen, his girlfriend and an antiwar activist. She knows that the marines will change Duncan. He agrees that this is true and knows that the change will not be a positive one.

Returned Vet Novels

The final category of novels, the Returned Vet novels, does little to support or subvert the warrior myths of militarism or moralism. Militarism isn't addressed with significance in any of these novels. Only moralism becomes important here. Mitch Morgan (*Tough Choices: A Story of the Vietnam War*, 1993) exhibits Rasmussen and Downey's (1991) recurrent emblem of companionship when he decides to reenlist and return to Vietnam. He explains his decision to his younger sister, Sam:

> Sam, I learned a lot in Vietnam. Not just about how to fight, but about myself, too. War can bring out the worst in people, but it can also bring out the best. That's what it did for me. I made great friends in Vietnam. Better than any I'll ever have again. They were men I could count on for anything and everything. I like the way it feels to have friends like that. (p. 49)

This is a virtually incomprehensible sentiment—to want to return to war because it brings out the best in you and you make good friends. Mitch sounds as if he is describing summer camp.

During the height of Mr. Monroe's PTSD episode (*Pocket Change*, 1989), he tells Josie of an experience typical to his tour in Vietnam. This scene shows both Mr. Monroe's moralism and its systematic subversion.

He reports that the VC regularly gave young Vietnamese children disguised bombs and ordered them to deliver the packages to ranking American officers. Since the Americans knew of this possibility, it became a policy to shoot all Vietnamese children carrying packages near American firebases.

Even as Mr. Monroe realizes the inherent immorality of killing an innocent and unsuspecting child, he completes his task. This traumatic subversion of Mr. Monroe's moralism contributes to his eventual undoing.

Generalizations

The warrior myths of militarism and moralism play a less significant role in the sample of novels than do the myths of frontier heroes, regeneration scenarios, and technical proficiency. As before, the myths are more frequently addressed in all the Combat subcategories than in the Response to the War or Returned Vet novels. The Duty novels all support the myth of militarism. Even those novels (*Orders to Vietnam*, 1968; *Stop & Search*, 1969) whose protagonists initially question the value of aspects of militarism eventually embrace the myth as they choose to become warriors for life. In both of the nurse novels, all non-Green Beret characters demonstrate through speech and action their respect for and support of militarism in Green Beret characters.

While militarism does not play a significant role in the Vietnamese Perspective novels, it makes a strong reappearance in the Platoon subcategory. However, unlike the Duty novels, the Platoon novels are far more likely to subvert the myth of militarism. Each novel demonstrates, with varying intensity, the resentment and antagonism between combat troops and REMFs, between grunts and officers, and between draftees and lifers. When these conflicts are so open and apparent, there can be little unity of purpose, order, efficiency, or acceptance of domination by a central authority. Even though there are several episodes in the *Echo* books where an older or higher-ranking soldier is trying to convince a younger or lower-ranking soldier of the need for militarism, the younger lower-ranking soldiers always remain unmoved.

The myth of militarism is virtually ignored in the Returned Vet category and only briefly addressed in the Response to the War category.

As with the regeneration myth, the older male characters—fathers who are vets in both cases—try to pass on their beliefs in the necessity and worth of militarism, especially the need to obey a central authority. Consistent with the subversion of militarism in the Platoon novels, the young protagonists in the Response to the War novels remain unconvinced. The second component of the warrior myth—moralism—is addressed with considerably higher frequency in the novels of the sample. Moralism is upheld in the Duty books. The soldiers and sailors in these novels are portrayed as traditional warriors with both components of the warrior myth intact.

Within the Vietnamese Perspective subcategory, the myth of moralism is most strongly addressed in the novel *Cross-fire* (1972). Interestingly, Harry, a protagonist, comments throughout the novel about the inherent morality of the American military in general and himself in particular. Alternately, his actions both support and subvert the concept of moralism—although they subvert more often than they support.

The Platoon novels marginally support and significantly subvert the moralism myth. American soldiers are presented as inherently moral—at first. As the soldiers continue to experience combat and are exposed to brutality that grows both more frequent and more fearsome, moralism is steadily undermined. The more horrific the combat experience characters have, the more likely they are to become either vicious themselves or to become apathetic or numb.

In the Response to the War category, Jonas Duncan (*Long Time Passing*, 1990) concludes that militarism itself is what destroys the moralism of young men as they become soldiers. It is his opinion that these two concepts cannot exist together. Finally in the Returned Vet category, moralism is supported in one novel and subverted in another.

In broad generalizations, the warrior myth of militarism is upheld more often than it is subverted. Although there are fewer instances when militarism is subverted (especially in the Platoon and Vietnamese Perspective categories), it is subverted with more force and passion than the instances when it is supported. The warrior myth of moralism receives approximately equal time for its support and subversion. But similar to the treatment of the myth of militarism, when the myth of moralism is subverted, it is done with more vigor than when it is supported.

It is more than just a matter of academic interest that American cultural myths that surround war and warriors are repeatedly subverted in representations of the Vietnam War experience. Given that cultural myths constitute a significant influence on members of that culture's perceptions, it is a growing belief of anthropologists who study PTSD that at least a small part of the PTSD so commonly suffered by Vietnam vets is partially caused by the subversion of their cultural myths depicting war and warriors.

Cultural Myths as Related to Date of Publication

The combination of the date of publication and the narrative structure category of a novel is a relatively stable predictor of that novel's treatment of cultural myth. Bearing in mind for the purposes of this study that a novel's publication date may be significantly later than the actual time that the novel was written, the earlier the publication date of a novel, the more likely it is to uphold all of the myths—frontier heroes, regeneration, proficiency, militarism, and moralism. Of the six novels published in the 1960s, *Special Forces Trooper* (1967), *Orders to Vietnam* (1968), *Vietnam Nurse* (1968), *The Man in the Box* (1968), *Stop & Search* (1969), and *Nurse in Vietnam* (1969), only *The Man in the Box* is not part of the Duty subcategory of Combat novels.

The myth most often subverted in novels written in the 1960s is the regeneration myth. Given that these novels are fairly traditional and almost "G.I. Joe"-like portrayals of the military and combat in combination with the fact that they were written at a time of growing opposition to American involvement in Vietnam, it was perhaps safest not to present war as sacred or glorious in any way. The warrior myths of moralism and militarism are soundly supported during this time. This is perhaps an attempt to demonstrate that America's armed forces were fine upstanding young warriors.

The novels published in the early 1970s, as war protests reached a fever pitch and the war itself was still being fought but was beginning to wind down, are *One Day for Peace* (1971, Response to the War) *Crossfire* (1972, Vietnamese Perspective) *War Year* (1972—original edition,

Platoon) and *Children of the Dragon* (1974, Vietnamese Perspective). Without exception, these novels undermine the regeneration myth. No frontier hero characters are even peripherally included. When moralism or militarism is addressed, it is primarily in their subversion. The early 1970s appear to be a time in which representations of the war in Vietnam could not be presented in a mythologically positive light regardless of the narrative structure a novel may use.

From the late 1970s to the mid-1980s only two novels were published: *To Stand against the Wind* (1978, Vietnamese Perspective), and *Where the Elf King Sings* (1980, Returned Vet). These were the first novels to address the war after its unsuccessful conclusion. *Where the Elf King Sings* was the first attempt to show the effect the war had had on Vietnam veterans. Cultural mythology does not play a significant role in these novels. The myth of regeneration appears more frequently than other myths in these two novels; however, it does so in its subverted form.

Nineteen eighty-six marks a resurgence of Vietnam novel publication, with sixteen of the twenty-eight novels in the sample being published in the twelve years from 1985 to 1997, with one novel released nearly each year. The Platoon novels issued in this period—*Fallen Angels* (1988), *Echo Company #1-4* (1991-1992), and *The Road Home*, Part One (1995)—powerfully subvert the myths of regeneration, proficiency, militarism, and moralism. In some cases, the myths are briefly addressed in their positive form, but are eventually crushed under the weight of their negation.

The remaining novels published in the time period between 1985 and 1997 are *Caribou* (1984, Response to the War); *Travelers* (1986) and *Charlie Pippin* (1987, both Returned Vet); *The Best of Friends* (1989) and *And One for All* (1989, both Response to the War); *Pocket Change* (1989, Returned Vet); *Long Time Passing* (1990, Response to the War); *Tough Choices* (1993, Returned Vet); *Come in From the Cold* (1994, Response to the War); *The Road Home,* Part Two (1995, Returned Vet); and *Sing for Your Father, Su Phan* (1997, Vietnamese Perspective). These novels have a tendency to address the regeneration myth more frequently than the other myths, although the warrior myths of militarism and moralism are occasionally touched on. There appears to be an attempt on the part of these novels to "show both sides" of the myths addressed—although in the long run the myths are largely subverted in the Response to the War and Returned Vet books of the late 1980s and 1990s, they are not subverted with the overwhelming power of the subversions of those same myths in the Combat novels of the same time.

The earliest novels, published during the war but before 1970, most frequently support American cultural myth about war and warriors. As time passed through the 1970s and early 1980s, the cultural myths were blatantly subverted. The Platoon novels (1972, 1988, 1991, 1992, 1995) that contain predominantly combat scenes occasionally support, but overall most forcefully undermine all myths discussed. The final period of 1985 to 1997 appears in the non-Combat category novels mainly to subvert the war mythology.

Chapter Six

Representations of the Vietnamese and the Americans

This chapter will examine the representation of three major constituent groups surrounding the Vietnam War in this sample of novels: American military personnel, the antiwar movement, and the Vietnamese. By scrutinizing the depictions of each, we can distinguish the various ways in which the novels' characters and narration—the novels' content—represent each. It is important to establish these overall portraits of American soldiers, American antiwar protestors, and Vietnamese soldiers and civilians in order to gain a more refined perspective of how the war has been written for young adult readers.

Representations of American Soldiers

There are countless portrayals and descriptions of Americans in Vietnam in the myriad oral histories, personal narratives, films, and novels about the Vietnam War. These portrayals include a full range of representations—Americans are alternately presented as G.I. Joe figures, good guys, murderers, and rapists, and as being honorable, heroic, lazy, cruel, and vicious.

Combat Novels—Duty Subcategory

Twenty-one-year-old Green Beret Stan Rusat is the protagonist of *Special Forces Trooper* (1967), a novel whose Vietnamese section is set near the Cambodian border in the Central Highlands. Stan is part of a group of early American military advisors who supervise Army of the Republic of (South) Vietnam (ARVN) and Civilian Irregular Defense Group (CIDG—mainly Montagnard) troops. All of the American soldiers in this novel are Green Berets and are presented as G.I. Joe-like figures. They are tall, strong, brave, good-hearted, and extremely competent. They are committed to doing a good job, but have little to say about their feelings about that job. They have all enlisted—no draftees in the Special Forces.

Every American character is white except for "specialist 5 Pattison, the only Negro in the detachment" (p. 103). Pattison plays an extremely small part in the novel and is consistently referred to as "the Negro sergeant." There is no cursing, dialect, or military slang used in the novel. All Americans appear educated since none use anything other than standard English in dialogue.

William Butterworth's two novels, *Orders to Vietnam: A Novel of Helicopter Warfare* (1968) and *Stop & Search: A Novel of Small Boat Warfare Off Vietnam* (1969), represent Americans in Vietnam in approximately the same manner. Bill Byrnes, a helicopter pilot, and Eddie Czernik, a patrol boat pilot, are nonetheless ready to do their jobs. The pilots or sailors in these novels are committed to little but each other. They never mention or question their mission in Vietnam; their real concern is keeping each other alive. While never presented as victims, these young men are each aware that they are stuck in a lousy situation.

The army helicopter pilots in Bill's aviation company are all white. One maintenance sergeant is black. Bill's helicopter crew is white but ethnically diverse, including Sergeant Santos and Specialist Cohen. The sailors depicted in *Stop & Search* are all white. There is also a variety of ethnic backgrounds reflected in the names of the crew of Eddie's boat: Chernoff, Fineberg, Doud. All of the white soldiers and sailors use only standard English, but the black sergeant often uses non-standard English. There is no cursing and the men don't indulge in alcohol or drugs or talk about women.

Vietnam Nurse (1968) and *Nurse in Vietnam* (1969) provide the first opportunity in the Duty novels to examine gender relations in a wartime situation. While both of these novels could be considered romances set against the war, they do offer interesting representations of both soldiers and nurses. The Green Beret leaders, Captain Wayne Moore and Captain Mace Thomas, respectively, and their Green Beret units are presented as G.I. Joe-like figures. They are superhuman in their abilities, fearless, extraordinarily competent, polite, good-humored, tall, brave, and handsome. Discussing the men they've come to know in the hospital, the nurses in Vietnam consider them to be the epitome of American manhood. Wayne, Mace, and their men are all white with the exception of one "Negro" from Harlem who is a rifleman in Wayne's unit. Wayne's other men display the same ethnic diversity as the other groups of soldiers in this category. They are listed as Irish, German, Jewish, and, of course, Negro. None of the soldiers in the novels swear, drink, or speak in anything other than standard English. Ages are not given for the soldiers in *Nurse in Vietnam*, but Wayne Moore's men in *Vietnam Nurse* are all in their thirties—extremely uncommon given that the average soldier in the Vietnam War was a teenager.

Vietnam Nurse and *Nurse in Vietnam* are the only Duty novels that include women as protagonists or coprotagonists. Joanna Shelton and Lisa Blake, both nurses, are portrayed as the romantic interests of Green Berets. They have each come to Vietnam to help men. Joanna has come to help find her missionary/doctor father and Lisa to help the wounded soldiers. In *Vietnam Nurse*, Joanna is a stereotypical female who "blushes madly" when she meets Wayne Moore (p. 49). She is described in sexual terms as having a "tall, lithe body, short-cut black hair" and "refined, yet at the same time sensual features" (p. 40). We aren't given this sort of information about any of the male characters. Joanna realizes that the Green Berets who will escort her on her mission to find her father are annoyed by her presence and she understands their sentiment. "It was all very military and top-secret, and Joanna began to realize why the men resented her and disliked having to feel responsible for her. The jungle was no place for a woman at any time, especially during a war" (p. 63). She doesn't elaborate on why women shouldn't be in the jungle. On the first night of the mission, Joanna worries about the health and safety of her missing father. She stops herself from crying because "she didn't dare do anything so unforgivably feminine" in front of Wayne and his men (p. 74). When Joanna and the squad are captured by the VC, Joanna faints and has to be carried by the Americans. Gradually Joanna is accepted by Wayne and the other men. Finally Wayne pays her a compliment when he volunteers: "'I've said it before, but I'm about to say it again: you're a brave kid!' . . . Wayne's voice was so gentle it was as though he spoke to himself, 'nurses make swell wives. I'm beginning to see why'" (p. 172). He continues to refer to her as a kid throughout the novel.

Joanna's purpose in Vietnam finally focuses more on being Wayne's love interest than on finding her father. In the love declaration scene, obligatory in all romance novels, Joanna takes strength from Wayne:

> "You know what's happened, don't you, Joanna?" Wayne's voice was deep and vibrant as he held her in his arms. She could feel the strength of his shoulders as she stood there motionless and, somehow, strangely awkward. She did not reply. "I've fallen in love with you, Viet Cong, notwithstanding. It's a crazy time and a crazy place, but for me this is it, and, honey, this is something I've wanted to do for a very long time."
>
> Instinctively, Joanna moved closer to him. She felt his arms tighten and then begin to tremble slightly as he held her against him. This was it! She knew, she simply knew! . . .
>
> Wayne's lips sought her mouth and pressed down hungrily. Her arms reached upward and twined themselves around his neck, her hands on the broad shoulders; her nails dug into the fabric of his jungle suit. (pp. 174-175)

This unlikely exchange occurs while the squad is being held prisoner by the VC.

The women in *Nurse in Vietnam* (1969) fare little better than the same stereotypical representation as in *Vietnam Nurse* (1968). They are constantly referred to in diminutive terms: a trained nurse and military officer is a "girl" and a forty-year-old woman traveling abroad alone is "the little schoolteacher" (pp. 10, 11). The women in *Nurse in Vietnam* readily accept themselves as incompetent at anything other than nursing. A high-ranking head nurse, Colonel Phelps, says that she knows "positively nothing" about mechanics. "I can't even change a light fuse" (p. 36). Miss Lowry, the "little schoolteacher," doesn't want to know about the war, telling Lisa that "it's because I hate reading those grim newspaper accounts. I often skip over those stories in favor of the features and editorials and fashions" (p. 15).

We are given detailed physical descriptions of each female character as we meet her—i.e., "Lt. James, a very pretty girl with a bright smile and short-cut reddish-blonde hair . . ." (p. 26). Lisa and the other women are as concerned with how they look as they are with the conditions of the men they nurse. When Lisa is stranded at a field hospital, she moves in with the other nurses. A major laments the fact that they have to wash their own clothes, but

> the hardship did not dim the major's good humor. "If you think our living conditions are for the birds, you should see the time we have keeping ourselves looking halfway decent. Heaven help us! Just let us get our hair in rollers and an alert sounds." She laughed out loud. "And cramming a steel helmet down over those things *isn't* easy." (p. 129)

After a helicopter crash and a trek through the bush, Lisa's thoughts remain with her appearance.

> She smoothed the front of her crumpled uniform, touched her fingers to her damp black hair. Womanlike, she asked, "Do—do I look half way presentable?"
>
> He beamed at her. "Lieutenant," he announced, "you're the most."
>
> The expression on Mace's face when she appeared at the missionary's house indicated he did think she looked pretty. And when he whispered, "You're my Miss America," her heart raced. (p. 157)

Again "womanlike" Lisa is "sent into raptures" when she finds some charming linens at a local marketplace (p. 100). Lisa explains to a Filipino nurse, Erlinda, that a woman's natural role in life is to be a wife. Erlinda claims that no woman "escapes falling in love and wanting to get married." Lisa agrees that "women are meant to fall in love. And be loved" (p. 100).

Finally, Lisa refuses to take any responsibility for her own protection after the helicopter in which she is riding is shot down.

> Lisa felt Dr. Gregory's hand fold over hers. "Stay close to me, Lieutenant," he whispered in a hoarse paternal voice. "Everything will be all right."
> "Here, Nurse," Airman Jackson snapped. "Take my pistol."
> She winced, drew back. "No! I can't shoot."
> "You can if you gotta," and he shoved it into her hand. (p. 141)

While it is not customary for medical personnel to be armed, Lisa is a military officer in a combat situation and her behavior displays her readiness to be a victim.

Combat Novels—Vietnamese Perspective Subcategory

Since all of the protagonists (or coprotagonists) in the novels in the group are Asian, the representations of American military men carry an interesting twist—a supposedly Vietnamese perspective. However, since all but one of the novels are authorized by Americans, the closest that they can come is an American version of what a Vietnamese or Montagnard perspective on Americans might be. Only *Sing for Your Father, Su Phan* (1997) is co-authored by an Asian writer—in this case, Chinese.

The Man in the Box (1968) tells the story of the rescue of an imprisoned Green Beret by Chau Li, a young Montagnard boy. This is the only novel in the sample to have a Montagnard protagonist. The American soldier who Chau Li saves, David (whom Chau Li calls "Dah Vid"), and the other Green Beret advisors are all described as tall, brave, and tough—a "special kind of soldier" (p. 95). They've come to Vietnam to educate the Montagnards and to teach them to protect themselves from the VC. Everyone speaks standard English and there is no use of profanity, liquor, or drugs. All American soldiers are white except for one captain, who is black.

Harry is the only featured American soldier in *Cross-fire* (1972). As he travels through the jungle with the four Vietnamese children he has found, Harry is a classic "ugly American." He thinks that he is basically a decent and principled man, but his actions don't bear this out because he is frequently violent and derisive with the children. He makes little attempt to understand the Vietnamese children he is with. Harry, a draftee, uses some profanity in talking to and about the Vietnamese. In her article "Witness for the Innocent," Wendy Saul (1985) describes the Americans in *Cross-fire* (1972) claiming that "brave, intelligently cautious, selfless, and kind American soldiers are destroyed by their own similarly virtuous countrymen" (p. 190). Harry and the children are indeed killed by Americans whom they startle at the end of the novel, but there is little in the novel's content to suggest that Harry or the anonymous, unnamed soldiers deserved any of the accolades Saul uses.

To Stand against the Wind (1978) is the story of a young Vietnamese boy, Em, his family, and Sam, the American reporter that they befriend. Em's first impression of the American soldiers who visit his inexplicably unnamed hamlet is a very positive one.

> Soon Americans—big, noisy, friendly young men—came to the villages and the hamlets. In the beginning the people of Em's hamlet were afraid of the strangers. They were so big, so very big. The children were the first to make friends with them. Em could see that the Americans liked children and that the children knew it. They followed the men, and the men gave them chewing gum and candy and teased them and played ball with them and walked around, looking at everything and asking questions. (p. 34)

We cannot know of the American soldier's commitment to the war, but Sam has a driving personal reason for remaining in Vietnam. He is vehemently opposed to the American involvement and wants to make sure that someone is there to document what is being done in the name of the American people.

The Americans are represented as loyal and honorable to their Vietnamese allies. When a member of Em's family hears a rumor that Saigon is going to fall, she also hears that the "Americans had offered refuge to all who were loyal to their government and had been friendly and helpful to all the Americans" (p. 114). The same American captain who earlier accidentally killed Sam, arranges for Em's family to emigrate to America. While some Vietnamese were saved by the Americans and allowed to emigrate, many, if not most, Vietnamese who had worked for and with Americans were deserted by the very people who had promised them safety (Edison, 1994).

Combat Novels—Platoon Subcategory

Given that each of the Platoon novels centers around prolonged periods in the bush, on patrol, or in combat, as readers we are privy to an extended view of the men as they act in their capacity as soldiers. Vietnam vet Joe Haldeman's *War Year*'s (1972, 1978) protagonist, John Farmer, displays little commitment to the war and wishes only to be back home. Farmer and his squad of combat engineers (soldiers who deal with explosives), many of whom are also draftees, develop a deep devotion to each other. They do what they have to do to survive and freely admit how terrified they are in combat. As draftees, they are thrust into a situation that they openly resent and over which they have no control.

The named characters in *War Year* are all white with the exception of the medic, "Doc" Jones. In the first person internal narration, Farmer comments on the number of black soldiers as "a wiry little colored guy handed me a gray burlap sack. Seemed like every other guy in Vietnam was Negro" (p. 33).

The soldiers in *War Year* use nearly constant profanity and military slang. Only the older sergeants use nonstandard English. Drugs are plentiful in the rear, and beer is the most common beverage in the book. There is frequent mention of cases of beer being brought out to men in the bush on a resupply helicopter.

Women are often the topic of conversation in the bush—generally in terms of being sex objects. Wounded men are reassured by male corpsmen that there will be plenty of "Red Cross broads" and that they should feel free to "goose the pretty nurses as they go by" (pp. 42, 87). Even though he is speaking of an army officer, Farmer asks a nurse to come to his bedside for no other reason than to watch her walk away because her "white uniform was tight enough to give her a nice swivel" (p. 94).

Fallen Angels (1988) follows seventeen-year-old Richie Perry (the only black protagonist in any of the Combat novels) from his arrival in Saigon out to the bush and finally home after being wounded. The other grunts in Perry's squad are all young, poor, and have little formal education—often speaking nonstandard English. They develop a deep affection for each other and, like the men in *War Year* (1972), they display far more commitment to each other than to winning the war. The use of drugs and alcohol is rampant—although not specifically within Perry's squad.

Even though none joined the army for traditionally patriotic reasons, all of the men in Perry's squad enlisted. There are racial tensions in the army in general and occasional outbursts within the racially mixed squad (approximately five black and five white soldiers). Johnson, a large, quiet, black private makes the connection between racism and derisive names, regardless of which group is being scorned.

> "Those gooks will probably be having supper with the VC by the time we sit down to chow," Brunner said.
> "How come when you say gooks it sounds like nigger to me?" Johnson asked. (p. 54)

Sergeant Simpson attempts to quell any racial problems within his unit, although Perry acknowledges that on the whole, they tried to ignore the problem. "Back home the World seemed to be splitting up between people who wanted to make love and people who wanted to tear the cities down. A lot of it was blacks against white, and we didn't talk about that too much, but we felt it" (p. 152).

In one scene a new white squad leader, Sergeant Dongan, after having displayed some borderline racist attitudes, replaces white soldiers with black soldiers in all of the most dangerous positions when the squad goes on patrol. There is some resentment expressed by the grunts, but no one mentions the disproportionate number of black soldiers killed in combat in response to Dongan's actions. The actions of other men in charge are also called into question. Captain Stewart, the company leader, appeared to be willing to risk the lives of the men in order to obtain higher enemy body counts, which would increase his chances of being promoted to major. The men realize that Stewart is risking their lives to further his career and that Sergeant Simpson has confronted him with this information.

"[Simpson] found out that Captain Stewart is volunteering Alpha Company all over the place. He asked him what he's doing that for, and Captain Stewart said that if he didn't want to fight he shouldn't have extended."

What Jamal said went down hard. We didn't mind doing our part because it had to be done, even though we always didn't have an answer to why we were doing it.

But nobody wanted to go out and risk their lives so that Captain Stewart could make major. (p. 199)

Although not in this specific instance, in other scenes various squad members are shown to flatly disobey orders that they consider too dangerous and are absolutely ready to kill (frag) a higher-ranking soldier who puts their lives in jeopardy. When Lieutenant Gearhart accidently sets off a trip flare that gives away the squad's position during a firefight, Private Monaco lets Gearhart know that his incompetence will *not* be tolerated.

"Who set the first flare off?" Monaco asked. "We got somebody here working for Charlie?"

"It just . . . I made a mistake," Gearhart said.

"Don't be making no more mistakes, man, because I'll frag your ass in a hot damn minute!" Monaco spat on the ground. (p. 164)

In another example later in the novel, Captain Stewart is isolated with the squad out in the bush when they come upon a North Vietnamese Army (NVA) platoon out in the open. Since the NVA are retreating, the squad members know that this may be their only chance to escape detection. Captain Stewart, however, wants them to try to flank the withdrawing platoon.

"Get the perimeter!" Captain Stewart shouted. "You two men get to the other side of this clearing, the sixty [M-60, the large, belt-fed machine gun carried usually by only one man per squad] will cover you."

"Never happen!" Peewee dug in.

"Soldier!" Captain Stewart swung a forty-five on Peewee.

I didn't see the sixty move. I heard the impact of the bullets in the ground in front of Captain Stewart's feet, I saw him leap backward. I saw him dive for cover. The forty-five went back into its case. I looked over my shoulder. Johnson was on his knees, a menacing silhouette. (p. 259)

In general, grunts are represented as maintaining extremely cynical outlooks on the war. They do not trust their leaders to be competent or caring soldiers; they do not trust that anything good is coming of their efforts. They also no longer believe news stories about how well the war effort is going. "We heard all kinds of stories about how we were beating back the North Vietnamese. 'Somebody better send them a telegram so they know about it,' Peewee said" (p. 273). The grunts in Perry's squad are alienated from everyone and everything except each other; consequently they form a virtually impenetrable brotherhood.

The suggestion that the war in Vietnam will have a long-term effect on the men who fought is addressed at some length in *Fallen Angels* (1988). Perry tries throughout the novel to write home to his mother. He isn't ever able to tell her anything that has happened to him—hinting at the later potential uncommunicativeness of Vietnam vets about their Vietnam experiences. Perry realizes that the war has changed him and he wonders if he'll ever be "normal" again. "I knew Mama loved me, but I also knew when I got back, she would expect me to be the same person, but it could never happen. She hadn't been to Nam. She hadn't given her poncho to wrap a body in, or stepped over a dying kid" (p. 267). After Perry is wounded and is sent to a hospital, he tries to talk to a nurse whom he met on his flight to Vietnam. He speculates on how he changed in relation to the rest of the world. "I felt awkward talking to Judy. I was glad to see her, but I couldn't talk to her. The words didn't have the right proportion somehow. There was this feeling that everything I was going to say was either too loud or too strange for a world in which people did normal things" (p. 214). This uncommunicativeness about the Vietnam experience is one fact that vet counselors often cite as part of the cause of post-traumatic stress disorder (PTSD) (McCombs, 1994).

Perry also alludes to the beginnings of what many Vietnam vets call "survivor guilt." This is the feeling that regardless of how traumatic your personal experience may have been, there are others whose experiences were worse and that by comparison, you shouldn't complain. Perry gets his first taste of survivor guilt as he tries to write a letter to the widow of the squad's young lieutenant who had just been killed. "It took me three tries to get the letter even close to something worth saying, and then it was nothing special. In a way I felt real bad just being alive to write it. I could think of her wondering why I didn't do something, why I didn't save him" (p. 130). Regardless of the fact that Perry is not a medic, he still feels that he should have been able to do something to save Lieutenant Carroll's life. Near the end of the novel, Perry, Peewee, and Monaco are all wounded in an ambush. Perry and Peewee have both received "million dollar wounds" (serious enough to be shipped home, but not serious enough to cause any permanent damage), but Monaco is healthy enough to rejoin the unit. While most soldiers in Vietnam wanted desperately to go home, Monaco exhibits guilt about leaving friends in the bush. Perry, Peewee, and Monaco are conflicted about Monaco's having to return to the bush. "Me and Peewee didn't want Monaco to have to go back. Monaco didn't want to go, either. But he didn't feel it was right to leave the squad unless he had to" (p. 303). Survivor guilt was a reaction to the brotherhood that soldiers had formed. Vietnam vet Mike Viehman (1993) claims that guilt was one of the most prevalent emotions in his war experience—each time that someone he knew was killed or wounded, he felt more guilty about still being alive. Fellow vet John Provo (1994) summarizes the guilt surrounding the war and hinted at in *Fallen Angels*:

> If you were a civilian and you didn't get drafted or enlist, you felt guilty. If you went in but didn't go to Nam, you felt guilty. If you went to Nam but didn't serve in a combat unit, you felt guilty. If you were in combat, but didn't get hit, you felt guilty. If you got dinged but came out okay, you still felt guilty, 'cause some of your buddies got hurt a lot worse. Even if you got really fucked up, you still felt guilty, 'cause some of your buddies didn't come back. The only way to avoid the guilt was to not come back. So everyone who came back feels guilty. (p. 1)

The *Echo Company* (1991-1992) series centers on the experiences of eighteen-year-old draftee Michael Jennings as we follow him from his arrival in Saigon to joining Echo Company in the bush. The soldiers in Michael's squad closely resemble those in Perry's. They are young, scared, and want nothing more than to get home alive. As the squad's FNG (fuckin' new guy), author Zack Emerson (the pen name of Ellen

Emerson White) details Michael's initial treatment at the hands of the other grunts. Within the army's one-year rotation plan, replacements appeared in the bush one at a time—often with little training. More-experienced soldiers resented the presence of FNGs, who were often sent because a previous squad member had been killed or injured. The new man could also jeopardize a squad on patrol or ambush because of his inexperience. Only after Michael proves that he won't be a burden is he accepted by the squad.

The other grunts in Michael's squad are all young, poor, and uneducated, much like those in *Fallen Angels*. They speak a mix of standard and nonstandard English, with frequent and explicit profanity. They are evenly split racially, with black squad leaders but no black officers. There are potential racial troubles in the *Echo* books, but no major incidents occur. Shortly after arriving in Saigon, Michael senses undercurrents of racial hostility in an EM club (for enlisted soldiers) at Long Binh.

> So, no fight. In a way, he was sorry. He wasn't one to start fights, but he was generally pretty happy to hit back. Only, judging from the way everyone was split up in the place, this particular fight probably would've become a black/white thing—and he hated that stuff. Happened pretty damned often, too, in the Army. He'd kind of hoped that they'd be too busy with, you know, War, to bother with race garbage once he actually got over here, but—didn't look that way. (p. 19)

Racial tensions are acknowledged in the *Echo* series in much the same manner as in *Fallen Angels*. Squad leaders (black soldiers in both cases) attempt to deal quickly with racial incidents that higher-ranking officers appear uninterested in.

As was seen in *Fallen Angels* (1988), officers are shown blithely volunteering their men for extraordinarily dangerous missions in order to further their own careers. Also similar to Perry's experience is Michael's inability to write home about his experiences in the war. This uncom-municativeness sets the stage for potential PTSD. Later, when the company is finally on a stand down on a base in Pleiku, Michael and some of the other grunts decide that they can never talk about some of the things that they've seen and done.

> "What happens in the bush, stays in the bush," Michael said. Stiffly.
> "Yup," Finnegan said.
> Unbreakable grunt rule. (*Echo #4*, p. 22)

Lieutenant Rebecca Phillips who is featured in *Echo #3* and appears in *Echo #4* (and who is more fully examined in *The Road Home*, 1995), also notices the potentially permanent traumatic effect that the war has on some soldiers, commenting that "they were always disoriented when they came in from the field. Life, as they remembered it, seemed completely foreign" (*Echo #3*, p. 10).

Emerson movingly represents the camaraderie that Vietnam vets felt for each other in Vietnam and sets the stage for that relationship to be carried back to the World in this exchange between Michael and an unnamed grunt whom Michael has never met.

> "Nice try, man," a heavily bandaged guy lying in the bed behind him said. Bulky chest and stomach dressings, tubes everywhere—and no right arm. Looked like he might be missing part of his foot, too.
> "Guess I struck out," Michael said, trying hard *not* to look at the stump.
> The guy nodded. "The big whiff."
> Michael nodded, feeling guilty to be standing there with nothing more than a mildly gimpy knee. "How you doing, man?"
> The guy shrugged. "Don't mean nothin.'" [Common Vietnam slang used when a vet has decided to shut down an emotionally crippling reaction to a traumatic event.]
> Right. "Same old shit," Michael said. . . .
> They looked at each other. Not that Michael had ever met this guy, but anyone who had been out in the bush was a brother. Sort of this unspoken fraternity. (*Echo #4*, p. 219)

This feeling that no one except another "bro" could understand Vietnam experiences is also a major contributing factor in PTSD.

Only in *Echo #3* (and continued in *The Road Home*, Part One) are we given a realistic glimpse of what life for a nurse in Vietnam might have been like. Rebecca and the other nurses suffer the same emotional numbing and survivor guilt that the grunts in the field did. The nurses spend their nights drinking heavily to blot out any memories of the endless flow of young, mangled soldiers that they spend their days trying to save.

> [Rebecca] dragged herself off the bed and out to the common room, bringing back three Carling Black Labels. Enough to kill the caffeine, but not enough so that she'd wake up drunk. The balance she always tried to strike. . . . She gulped her first can in a few long swallows, then started in on her second. There was so much liquor in Vietnam, and it was so unbelievably cheap, that most of the people she knew seemed to be turning into borderline—or even beyond—alcoholics. Certainly, she had never thought that *she* would gulp the stuff down like there was no tomorrow. Then again, around here, tomorrow was a pretty uncertain commodity. (*The Road Home*, pp. 36-37)

The nurses and grunts are all traumatized by their war experiences.

Rebecca Phillips' story is continued in *The Road Home* (1995). The first half of the book, Part One: The War, describes her grisly work at an evac hospital in Vietnam. She's in a position to interact with soldiers and to be part of the military herself. Even being a nurse and a volunteer, she finds herself dealing with the cross-purposes of lifers and short-timers. When Rebecca is reprimanded by a superior officer and fellow nurse, Major Doyle, she exhibits the same reaction that grunts do in all of the Platoon novels.

> "My point exactly," Major Doyle said, sounding quiet and sad. "Second lieutenants don't *make* decisions—they follow orders."
>
> Lifer logic. Lifer *horseshit*, more accurately. Rebecca shook her head, but didn't say anything. (p. 53)

Rebecca also sees more than her share of the survivor guilt discussed earlier. Nursing soldiers who wouldn't be going back to the bush brought up these feelings daily. After Michael shoots Finnegan (characters in the *Echo* series who also appear in *The Road Home*) in order to get him out

out of the war, Finnegan reacts with the same survivor guilt that Peewee and Perry spoke of in *Fallen Angels* (1988).

> "I shouldn't have left 'em," Finnegan said. "They're gonna *need* me."
>
> Considering that he had a leg wound that might well be permanently crippling, he didn't have a whole lot of choice in the matter. "They'll be fine," [Rebecca] said, doing her best to sound soothing. "You just worry about getting better, okay?"
>
> He looked up at her, tears rolling down his cheeks. "Will I have to go back out there?" . . .
>
> He stared up at her, his expression twisted in that familiar combination of relief and guilt she saw on so many of them. Overjoyed to be out of the bush, but unable to bear the idea of leaving their friends out there. (*The Road Home*, p. 83)

This overwhelming guilt resurfaces in the Returned Vet books as a major contributing factor to the PTSD that many of the vets suffer.

Being a female in war certainly made Rebecca and her fellow nurses a minority. Unlike the "Vietnam nurses" of the two Duty novels, Rebecca and her colleagues didn't come to Vietnam to date Green Berets. Their predominant concern is not their appearance or their manly boyfriends. They also find themselves dealing with male expectations of their roles in Vietnam.

> Usually the general's aide was a tall, slim second lieutenant, but today's helper was a not-so-slim Red Cross worker. They were known as Donut Dollies, and had a reputation for being very promiscuous with field-grade officers, who, rumor had it, considered them to be their personal property. On the other hand, Army nurses had the exact same reputation, so Rebecca found the notion highly suspect, at best. (p. 158)

Rebecca is the only one to mention the troubles that American women in Vietnam may have had with American men.

Response to the War Novels

Given the narrative structures of the Response to the War novels and the fact that only one novel contains a character who is a soldier, there are only sketchy representations of American military personnel in this category. No American soldiers are included in *The Best of Friends* (1989), but toward the end of the novel, a character enlists and will be leaving in a matter of days for basic training and then Vietnam. Dan thinks that quiet, soft-spoken Will won't make a good soldier, because Dan envisions American soldiers as aggressive killers of Vietnamese civilians.

> In six months [Will] would be sitting in a chopper with a bunch of GIs, ready to pour out into a village already smoking from the bombs the jets had dropped. A village with all the huts on fire and old people trying to pull stuff out of the way and animals and kids running in circles, bellowing and screaming, trying to get away from the guns and the smoke and the explosions. And GIs tying up VC prisoners, twisting their arms back, pushing them down into the mud. Prisoners who looked like kids. . . . It sure wasn't going to be easy for [Will] to torch some old lady's house. All that awful sadness he'd been seeing for years was going to land on top of Will, and there wasn't a thing anyone could do to change it. Not Sarah with her peace pamphlets or Dad with his rah-rah for democracy. Nobody. (p. 166)

Dan's is the first implication by a character not in Vietnam that American soldiers might be all too destructive and vicious.

The one character in *And One for All* (1989) who joins the marines and goes to Vietnam is presented as someone who has given little thought to what his enlistment may mean. Wing Brennan drops out of high school and enlists in a fit of temper after not doing well on an English exam. Before Wing is killed in combat, his younger sister wonders if Wing is not truthfully sharing his war experiences.

Returned Vet Novels

The final category of novels in the sample are those in which Vietnam vets and their families attempt to come to terms with the vets' combat experiences in Vietnam. This attempt to understand the vets' experience takes place any time from immediately upon return from Vietnam in one novel (*Tough Choices*, 1993; *The Road Home*, 1995) up to sixteen years after Vietnam in another (*Pocket Change*, 1989).

The earliest adolescent novel that focuses on a Vietnam vet trying to deal with his experience in Vietnam is *Where the Elf King Sings* (1980). This story follows twelve-year-old Marcie Breckenridge, whose father Bill was an army captain in Vietnam six years prior to the setting of the novel. Bill is unable to hold a job and has bouts of alcoholism and depression. When he finally becomes physically destructive, Marcie's mother makes him leave. Through the help of a local vet counselor, Bill joins a vet "rap" group and eventually goes to a VA hospital for treatment.

In this novel, Vietnam vets are treated as true victims. They were sent into a hellish situation and their only hope was getting out alive. They are still plagued by the survivor guilt discussed in the Platoon novels. A vet counselor recounts some of his own war experiences for Bill's family, trying to explain survivor guilt—the idea that combat veterans feel guilty for surviving the war, when so many of their friends had died. Since returning to America both Bill and Kurt (the counselor) feel that they have been discriminated against in terms of employment. Bill tells Marcie that he's looked for a job, but every time a job looks promising, the opportunity disappears as soon as it becomes known that Bill is a Vietnam vet. Bill feels victimized by the attitudes that people hold about Vietnam vets being unstable and untrustworthy; however, he does suffer from flashbacks and alcoholism and until the end of the novel refuses to even talk about his war experiences.

The family tries to understand Bill's behavior, although they seem to have little interest in trying to understand the combat experiences that have caused Bill's PTSD. Bill's mother tries to explain to Marcie about her father's outbursts by explaining about flashbacks—something that she's read about in veteran publications. Marcie remembers a flashback that her father had had at a family picnic and is less forgiving about her father's behavior. Marcie's mother doesn't understand at all about PTSD and is tired of waiting for Bill to "get over" the war.

After a particularly traumatic anniversary of his best friend being killed in Vietnam, Bill checks himself into the PTSD unit of the local VA hospital. Expecting that he'll have to stay for some time, Marcie's mother tries to explain something about the PTSD clinic to Marcie and her brother. She tells the children that Bill will be with other men who have the same problems and that if he stays in the hospital, the problems will go away.

Many vets would find this notion of deciding to check oneself in for treatment and immediately being allowed to do so to be bitterly laughable. It is, in fact, the perception of many Vietnam vets that for financial reasons, the VA does everything in its power to avoid diagnosing or treating PTSD or PTSD-related disabilities (W. T. Edmonds, personal communication, March 1994).

The only other novel that addresses PTSD in such depth is *Pocket Change* (1989), the story of Josie Monroe and her father, who sixteen years after his return from Vietnam, begins to have violent flashbacks that endanger not only himself but his entire family. Jack Monroe was drafted and sent to Vietnam in 1970. He refuses to ever talk to Josie or any of the family about his experiences in Vietnam.

After Jack begins to react strangely to loud noises and eventually to flash back to a particularly traumatic event in Vietnam, Josie contacts a vet counselor, Dr. Whitehead. He explains to Josie some of the reasons that a soldier in Vietnam might end up with PTSD. Dr. Whitehead feels that most vets don't think that a non-vet could ever begin to understand what the war was like. This makes them feel very isolated—as if they had no one to talk to.

The only difference between Vietnam and other wars that Dr. White-head mentions is the rotation policy. He doesn't go on to discuss how Vietnam vets may have been treated differently by the American public nor does he mention the relative unpopularity of the war or the general social climate of the time—all of which could certainly affect how a vet perceived his or her experience. Dr. Whitehead explains a little about Jack's condition to Josie mentioning both survivor guilt and PTSD. PTSD is defined by the veterans of the Vietnam War (1993) as

> a set of disorders ranging from insomnia to depression to substance abuse to suicide, often found in people's reaction to severe stress—whether it be from war, a natural disaster, or victimization as in rape or abuse. PTSD pays no attention to education, intelligence, race, or socioeconomic background. (p. 3)

Jack has flashbacks that last for hours. Josie follows her father when he leaves the house believing that he is on patrol in Vietnam. She shakes and screams at her father until he recognizes where he is. Dr. Whitehead tells Josie that had she not startled Jack out of the flashback, it might have lasted for days. This idea of a flashback stands in complete contradiction to the description of an experience that lasts only seconds that many actual Vietnam vets give. PTSD-diagnosed Vietnam vet W. T. Edmonds (personal communication, March 1994) describes flashbacks as

> an instantaneous full body experience in personal time travel; here, there, and here again in the blink of an eye. It can be quite terrifying for the traveler; you think you're going round the twist. . . . You can visualize the process if you think of watching TV and then having a subliminal picture flashed on the screen for an instant in the middle of the program. You're watching Swan Lake and a picture of the kid from the fourth grade who stuck you with the pencil pops on the screen and is gone. . . . Now it can take several minutes or more to recover from your little trip and during that time you can revert to [a] survival mode; but this is the response to the flashback, not the flashback itself.

Regarding the idea of "startling" a PTSD sufferer out of a flashback, Edmonds states that "amateur intervention can be stupid and dangerous. You don't try to startle a vet out of a flashback, too short. You don't try to startle a vet out of the aftereffect of a flashback, too dangerous."

During a particularly vivid "flashback" (which Edmonds would call a hallucination), Jack imagines that VC guerrillas are approaching his home. With his three-year-old son in the house, Jack turns off the lights and starts shooting a rifle into the yard. After the police finally disarm him, Jack is sent to the VA where, like Bill in *Where the Elf King Sings* (1980), he is accepted without question.

Pocket Change (1989) is the only novel to mention the possible effect of the use of Agent Orange on Vietnam vets. Josie and a friend find a newspaper article in her father's bedroom. The article states that veterans' groups believe that soldiers who were exposed to Agent Orange were very likely to have medical problems. This is a very sketchy mention of the thousands of vets with Agent Orange poisoning and the more than 65,000 children of these vets born with moderate to severe birth defects. Also there is no indication of the lack of recognition by the VA and the EPA of the validity of Vietnam vets' claim of Agent Orange exposure (Veterans of the Vietnam War, correspondence, October 1993).

Charlie Pippin (1987) is the story of young Chartreuse "Charlie" Pippin's attempt to understand the war that so affected her veteran father and uncle. *Charlie Pippin* represents the only black protagonist in the sample other than Richie Perry in *Fallen Angels* (1988). Charlie's father Oscar doesn't suffer from any PTSD symptoms, but he, like Josie's father in *Pocket Change*, is uncommunicative about the war. Charlie is interested in his experiences and he angrily refuses to discuss them with her although he never gives any reason for his refusal. For her sixth-grade social studies project, Charlie decides to research the Vietnam War. Oscar resents her "nosiness."

Toward the end of the novel, Charlie and another vet, Uncle Ben, visit the Vietnam Memorial in Washington, D.C.—the Wall. Uncle Ben's sister, Charlie's Aunt Jessie, expresses real bitterness upon seeing the Wall for the first time. She feels that most of her generation were affected by the war and really questions the use of monuments when medical treatment and jobs were what was needed. At the novel's end, there is still no resolution of Oscar's refusal to talk about the war, nor is there any information given to imply that his experiences were significantly more traumatic than those of Uncle Ben or other soldiers who are less reticent.

Characters in *Charlie Pippin* (1987) do take the opportunity to express opinions about the extreme youth of many soldiers and about the special problems of black soldiers. Charlie's grandmother (Oscar's mother) is appalled that such young boys were sent to war and Mama Bliss has a point. The average age of soldiers in Vietnam, nineteen, was significantly lower than that of soldiers in World War II, twenty-six (Appy, 1993).

The unfair treatment that black soldiers received in Vietnam is one point on which Oscar and Ben can agree. They were of the opinion that black men were sent to fight in disproportionate number.

There are amazingly few statistics regarding a breakdown by race of combat assignments and numbers of soldiers killed or wounded. According to the Department of Defense (1985), as many as 20% of all combat deaths in 1965 and 1966 were black soldiers. There is also an indication that black soldiers were more likely to be assigned to combat infantry positions than white soldiers. In her research, Charlie finds a book about black veterans, but realizes that they're not acknowledged elsewhere. She is horrified to realizes that there was little mention and no pictures of black vets in the encyclopedias that she used. Because of her family's involvement in the war, Charlie knows that many black men died.

When interviewing her grandfather about black soldiers, Charlie finds that recognition is something that they've never received. He shares his experiences as a black soldier in World War II. Explaining how white German prisoners were better treated that black American soldiers, he can barely contain his bitterness.

Mama Bliss also mentions that Vietnam vets have received little recognition for their efforts in Vietnam claiming that they received no parades or thank yous. Neither Charlie nor Mama Bliss venture any opinion about why Vietnam vets may have been treated differently upon their return to America.

Tough Choices (1993) and *The Road Home* (1995) are the only novels that address the experiences of Vietnam vets *immediately* upon their return to the World. *Tough Choices* follows the Morgan family as they pick up Mitch at the airport returning from Vietnam. Mitch, much like the other vets in this category, is reluctant to talk about his experience in Vietnam. Mrs. Morgan tries to get Mitch's young sister, Sam, to pry some information out of him:

> "See if Mitch will talk to you about Vietnam," Mom said.
> "Why?"
> "Because he told me he wasn't ready to talk about it yet. Said he might never be ready," she said. "And then he said I wouldn't understand anyway. How could his mother not understand?"
> "I can't make him tell me stuff he doesn't want to," I said.
> "Try." (p. 18)

In this exchange Mrs. Morgan has practically proven that indeed she would not understand since she doesn't have any idea of why her son may not choose to confide in her.

As Mitch and Emmett argue about the war, Emmett suggests that American soldiers are perhaps every bit as brutal and destructive as they accuse the VC of being. This is not something that anyone else in the novel is even willing to consider.

When Sam accompanies Emmett to an antiwar rally, she meets a Vietnam vet in a wheelchair who gives her some insight into what Mitch might be feeling. He suggests that perhaps Mitch feels guilty for leaving his closest friends in combat. He also tells Sam that the war has probably changed Mitch so significantly that he will never be the same person. This anonymous vet's assessment of Mitch turns out to be correct. Given some overwhelming survivor guilt and citing his many friends still in Vietnam, Mitch decides to return to Vietnam for another tour.

When Rebecca returns from Vietnam to her parents' house (*The Road Home*, 1995), she returns as a reclusive alcoholic. She continues to have vivid nightmares of her time in Vietnam. She feels directionless and restless and is unwilling to talk about her experiences with both her parents and friends. When she and Michael (from the *Echo* series) reunite after the war, they both suffer from nightmares and refuse to talk about their experiences.

Generalizations

There are some real similarities within each narrative structure category regarding the representation of American GIs in Vietnam. In the Duty novels the soldiers show a great commitment to each other, but mention little in the way of commitment to the war effort. Everyone wants to perform well, but the satisfaction appears to be in the job well done alone. The Green Berets in *Special Forces Trooper* (1967), *Vietnam Nurse* (1968), and *Nurse in Vietnam* (1969) are all G.I. Joe-like figures. They are perfect soldiers and perfect specimens of American manhood—tall, brave, strong, competent, polite, and handsome. Racially, all but three characters in the five novels are white. The three black soldiers are given only a small part in the stories. The soldiers speak standard English and do not drink, take drugs, or talk about women.

The two "Vietnam nurses" featured in *Vietnam Nurse* and *Nurse in Vietnam* are stereotypical. They are physically weak and dependent and readily accept their role as the weaker sex. They blush, are more concerned with their appearance than their safety and refuse to do anything to protect themselves. Interestingly in a study of earlier adolescent war literature, Laubenfels (1975) comments on the treatment of female characters as role models in war literature, claiming that the "lack of positive female characters as role models may be partially responsible for the fact that war fiction is generally unpopular with high school girls" (p. 62).

In the Vietnamese Perspective novels, the one Green Beret (in *The Man in the Box*, 1968) follows the earlier pattern of the Green Berets. In *Cross-fire* (1972) Harry curses, brutalizes the children whom he imagines he's taking care of, and displays inappropriately sexual thoughts toward a twelve-year-old Vietnamese girl. The other unnamed soldiers indiscriminantly kill all of the featured characters (including Harry) at the end of the novel. The American soldiers in *To Stand against the Wind* (1978) are shown, on one hand, killing many innocent Vietnamese civilians, but, on the other, go out of their way to help a Vietnamese family emigrate to America.

The soldiers in the Platoon novels are represented differently than American soldiers in the other subcategories. They are most frequently draftees. None exhibit any real commitment to the war effort, although they *all* exhibit an intense bond and commitment to each other. In each of the Platoon novels nearly half of the soldiers are black, and there is some acknowledgment of potential racial problems in the army. There is extreme and constant use of profanity and military slang. The ubiquitous presence of liquor and drugs is acknowledged, but significantly never used by any of the characters (even peripherally) in the novels. This is perhaps unrealistic given Sheehan's assessment of the army at that time.

> The riflemen who had fought with Hal Moore in the valley of the [Ia] Drang and at Bong Son would not have recognized the U.S. Army of 1969. It was an Army in which men escaped into marijuana and heroin and other men died because their comrades were stoned on these drugs that profited the Chinese traffickers and Saigon generals. (p. 741)

The extreme youth of the soldiers (the three protagonists are seventeen, eighteen, and nineteen) is emphasized as is their likelihood to be drafted and from poor and uneducated backgrounds. Baritz (1985) confirms that it would have been likely to have huge groups of drafted soldiers from the lower socioeconomic classes.

The draft was biased by level of income. The higher the income, the less chance of being drafted, importantly but not exclusively because of educational deferments. Poor young Americans, white as well as black and Hispanic, were twice as likely to be drafted and twice as likely to be assigned to combat as wealthier draft-aged youth . . . . Poor black Americans were swept into the fighting war in disproportionate numbers. Economic class, even more than race, except that people of color were more likely to be poor, was what determined who fought and who died.

Education in this country is a badge of class. One study of Chicago neighborhoods found that kids from areas with low educational levels were four times as likely to be killed in Vietnam than those from more schooled neighborhoods. Two staff officials of President Ford's clemency board showed that a college graduate who enlisted had about a 40% chance of being sent to Vietnam, while a high school graduate's chance was about 65% and that of a high school dropout was 70%. (pp. 284, 285)

Appy (1993) concurs, claiming that

roughly 80% [of soldiers in Vietnam] came from working-class and poor backgrounds. Vietnam, more than any other American war in the 20th century, perhaps in our history, was a working-class war. The institutions most responsible for channeling men into the military—the draft, the schools, and the job market—directed working-class children to the armed forces and their wealthier peers toward college. (p. 6)

This information is not specifically stated in any of the Platoon novels, although it is implied by the fact that all of the grunts have little formal education and come from lower socioeconomic groups.

Many characters experience the beginnings of PTSD. They are unable to talk about their war experiences to anyone other than fellow vets, and they are plagued by survivor guilt. Officers are shown to volunteer their men for extremely dangerous missions in order to further their own careers. Men refuse direct orders and are not punished. Yet, despite all of this they do not appear demoralized. Sheehan (1988) might disagree, assessing the American army in 1969 as an

Army whose units in the field were on the edge of mutiny, whose soldiers rebelled against the senselessness of their sacrifice by assassinating officers and noncoms in "accidental" shootings and "fraggings" with grenades. The signs of demoralization were evident by the time of Westmoreland's departure in the mid-1960s. (p. 741)

Although the soldiers in Farmer's, Perry's, and Jennings's squads were upset by what they saw, none appeared to be more than temporarily traumatized. They were all represented as fundamentally moral men stuck in a horrific situation who had formed a close bond with the others. None of the soldiers in any of the novels are described as correspondent Michael Herr (1977) described the men that he saw in Vietnam.

He had one of those faces, I saw that face at least a thousand times at a hundred bases and camps, all the youth sucked out of the eyes, the color drawn from the skin, cold white lips, you knew he wouldn't wait for any of it to come back. Life had made him old, he'd live it out old. These were the faces of boys whose whole lives seemed to have backed up on them, they'd be a few feet away but they'd be looking back at you over a distance you knew you'd never really cross. (p. 16)

There were also no soldiers, even in peripheral positions, who were brutal or vicious or who had grown to love the killing. Herr reports the story that some reporters asked a helicopter door gunner, "How can you shoot women and children [from the helicopter]?" His answer had been, "It's easy, you just don't lead 'em so much" ("leading" is the term used to describe aiming your shot slightly in front of a moving target so that the round and the target arrive at the same place at the same time) (p. 35).

There are few representations of American soldiers in the Response to the War novels. Those that enlist in the army are presented as having done so with little thought regarding that decision; they're never shown to be patriotic or enthusiastic about winning the war. In the Response to the War novels in general and especially in *One Day for Peace* (1971), soldiers are shown to be victims of an uncaring government.

Finally, in the Returned Vet novels, issues of PTSD and Agent Orange poisoning are addressed. As in the Response to the War category, the vets are seen as victims. Their efforts are unappreciated by the American public; they are discriminated against in the job market; their traumatic war experiences have ruined (at least some) of their lives. Here is also seen the *only* representation of returned female Vietnam vets. Nearly eleven thousand American women served in the military in Vietnam and countless other American civilian women served in country as well. The problems of readjustment that these women may have faced are explored in only one novel, *The Road Home* (1995).

The representation of Vietnam vets as victims is an interesting diversion according to Appy (1993), who feels that this victim status protects vets from being asked larger questions.

> . . .Vietnam veterans [are] typically presented in ways akin to the hostages, as survivor-heroes. Indeed throughout the Reagan years, people who suffered terrible ordeals at the hands of foreigners or in the name of the U.S. were accorded the status of heroes. Victims and survivors of disasters . . . became the dominant models of heroism. Hostages, prisoners of war, the 241 marines in Lebanon killed by a car bomb, . . . were all treated as heroes by the media and by national politicians. By focusing on what people suffered or endured in foreign lands, you need not examine what they were doing there in the first place. By this standard, Vietnam vets seemed the ultimate survivor-heroes. After all, as the typical treatment went, these were men who had endured jungle rot, malaria, poisonous snakes, booby traps, invisible enemies, spitting war protestors, and other, unimaginable horrors. . . .
>
> The desire to offer veterans nonjudgmental acceptance has led many writers to avoid challenging these men to answer difficult questions about Vietnam, believing such inquiries might elicit further pain and grief. In much of the writing, veterans appear as victims and the writers as opinionless confessors. Like the title of *Newsweek*'s special feature on Vietnam vets, the accent is on "What Vietnam Did to Us." (pp. 4, 5)

In all but the Duty novels, American soldiers are presented in varying degrees as victims.

Representations of the Antiwar Movement

Every war in American history has been met with some opposition from the American people (Lens, 1990). Depending on the war, dissent has been everything from negligible to immense. Americans who protested their country's military and political intervention in Southeast Asia have been alternately vilified and valorized by the American public. They have been both accused of treason—providing aid and comfort to the enemy, thereby prolonging the war, and praised for standing up for the highest ideals of American democracy. The formal antiwar movement was situated within the larger youth culture of the 1960s. Civil rights, women's rights, and the free speech movement (among others) were intertwined yet competing interests within the counterculture of the times. Many of the disaffected youth of the 1960s did not begin as militant or politically sophisticated activists—they were often part of an alienated youth culture described by Sidney Lens (1990) as "expressing revulsion against conformity" (p. 44). Antiwar activist and eventual president of the Students for a Democratic Society (SDS), Todd Gitlin (1987) describes the estrangement that became a canyon-sized generation gap:

> Little by little, alienation from American life—contempt, even, for the conventions of flag, home, religion, suburbs, shopping, plain homely Norman Rockwell order—had become a rock-bottom prerequisite for membership in the movement core. The New Left felt its homelessness as a badge of identity . . . ; damned if it was going to love what it had spiritually left. (p. 271)

Out of this counterculture emerged groups such as the SDS, Committee for a Sane Nuclear Policy, the Black Panthers, the National Coordinating Committee to End the War in Vietnam, the Student Non-violent Coordinating Committee. Teach-ins, sit-ins, civil disobedience, strikes, protests, and rallies small and large were the tools of the New Left.

By 1965 the antiwar movement was gaining momentum and by 1966 and 1967 the war to end the war had become fierce. The Tet Offensive in the early months of 1968 and the riots at the Democratic convention later that summer pushed antiwar activity into fever pitch. Gitlin (1987) cites growing participation in "huge, orderly, antiwar mobilizations" as steadily influencing the American public.

> On April 26, 1968, up to a millon college and high school students took part in a national student strike. Profuse and varied were the efforts to give the antiwar movements a presence in common American life, from the tough-talking militance of draft-resistance organizers in working-class communities to the plainspoken antiwar workers in unions, town meetings, local party caucuses, and in the heart of the military itself. Truly the movement against the Vietnam War was a broad-based antiwar mobilization of a sort rarely if ever before seen in the blood-soaked history of the world. (p. 293)

By 1967 there were enough veterans of the Vietnam War who so opposed America's involvement in Southeast Asia that they formed a group—the Vietnam Veterans Against the War, Inc. (VVAW). The VVAW's original published objectives[1] included a demand to end the war, a demand to recognize the war as racist against nonwhite soldiers and the Vietnamese, support for active duty soldiers who refused to fight, and support for draft resistors (B. Chitty, personal communication, November 16, 1993). The VVAW was the first official group of veterans organized to oppose the war in which they had earlier participated.

Not all Americans, however, supported the efforts of antiwar activists and draft resistors. Many Americans who opposed the war in Vietnam objected even more strongly to the antiwar activists. Gitlin (1987) remarked that the

> dovishness that showed up in surveys coexisted with a moral panic against antiwar activists; the national pragmatism which thought the war ought to be liquidated as a bad investment, a "mistake," a "mess," was incensed at students who insisted that it was a crime. (p. 141)

Opposition to the antiwar movement grew more violent and harsh as the movement grew more widespread and militant. Protestors at antiwar rallies were often spit on and physically attacked by more conservative Americans. Police forces and National Guard units often attacked demonstrators for exercising the very free speech protected by the democracy that America was supposedly fighting in Vietnam to establish

(Lens, 1990). Gitlin (1987) recalls the amazement with which antiwar activists saw America's apathy toward police brutalization of the demonstrators.

> To our innocent eye, it defied common sense that people could watch even the sliver of onslaught [by policy against antiwar activists] that got onto television and sided with the cops—which in fact was precisely what polls showed. As unpopular as the war had become, the antiwar movement was detested still more—the most hated political group in America, disliked even by most of the people who supported immediate withdrawal from Vietnam. McGeorge Bundy had been right to tell Lyndon Johnson, in November, just after the Pentagon and Stop the Draft Week: "One of the few things that helps us right now is public distaste for the [antiwar protestors]. . . ." Apparently the majority agreed with Bundy that whoever swung the clubs, we were to blame. (p. 335)

After the murder of four antiwar protestors at Kent State University by Ohio National Guardsmen in 1970, the movement took on a more dire tone. "In the end, nothing intimidated like official violence. Once the initial shock and rage wore off, Kent State proclaimed to white activists nationwide what People's Park had said to Berkeley a year before: The government is willing to shoot you" (Gitlin, 1987, p. 414). The People's Park incident in Berkeley to which Gitlin refers in which students were fired on and killed by California National Guard troops was ordered by then Governor Ronald Reagan.

It is important to examine the representation of the antiwar movement in general and antiwar activists individually in these novels about the Vietnam War. Are activists portrayed as villainous or naive traitors or as the true patriots? Is the movement perceived as having had any influence on the war in Vietnam? For the purposes of this study, antiwar activists will be defined as those who formally engaged in activity specifically designed to end America's involvement in Vietnam.

Combat Novels—Duty Subcategory

One common thread within the narrative structure of the Duty novels is the notion that young men in America had an obligation to fight in the armed forces in wartime. While the war is occasionally referred to as "senseless" (although with no explanation), no military characters in the

Duty novels openly question the objectives or inherent morality of the war. Only in *Special Forces Trooper* (1967) is the antiwar movement even mentioned. During Green Beret training, Stan Rusat and fellow trainee Willie Ryall go to a movie. Before the movie, a newsreel containing footage of a protest was shown.

> They sat out the newsreel and ground their teeth when an anti-war demonstration was shown; beatniks for the most part, with their female counterparts, carrying signs that intimated that all servicemen serving in Vietnam were prime patsies. "I'd round them up," Willie said, "and drop them into a rice paddy and arm them with cap pistols. Maybe their smell would keep the Charlies away from them." (p. 22)

The misuse of the term "beatnik" and the implication that somehow only males could be "beatniks" demonstrates author Joe Archibald's lack of knowledge of the antiwar movement. Antiwar sentiments are not discussed and shown to be faulty; they are merely hinted at and then dismissed with an ad hominem attack on the protestors.

After arriving in Vietnam, Stan's mother sends him a letter expressing her worries about his safety. Even though she does not overtly question the war, Stan interprets her letter as antiwar propaganda.

> Tritely she informed him that she would rather have a live son than a dead hero, and that she was beginning to sympathize with the demonstrations against the war in Vietnam here at home. Kids that had grown up with him were making themselves secure in good jobs, and she would never understand the reason for his being where he was.
>
> His mother was an intelligent woman, but having already suffered one irreparable loss [her husband's death in the Korean War], she was vulnerable to irresponsible reporting on the part of journalistic "doves," and influenced by a confusion of opinion. (p. 153)

In this passage, the media is accused of "irresponsible reporting," which presumably means reporting the war in such a one-sided manner as to falsely present the war in a negative light. Given that the majority of the American press, both print and broadcast, were solidly behind the war effort, at least until Tet in early 1968, the press's dovish influence in or before 1967 (*Special Forces Trooper*'s publication date) is extremely unlikely (Sheehan, 1988). Again the antiwar position is not addressed and proven faulty, but is dismissed out of hand and irrational rage toward the protestors is demonstrated.

Combat Novels—Vietnamese Perspective Subcategory

Within the Vietnamese Perspective group, only one novel acknowledges the existence of a formal antiwar movement. In *Children of the Dragon* (1974), set in North Vietnam, school children in a country hamlet receive a letter from an American child who supports the antiwar movement. The letter is read aloud to the class:

> Viet Nam:
>> I hope you feel better. I hope the war ends. I hope our government lets you get the kind of government you want. I hope there is peace there. I hope people stop getting bombed. I hope there is peace there all the time.
>> Larry Jacobs, Age 8
>> Huong said softly to her daughter, "See Hoa, there are many people in the United States who don't want this war either. And they are our friends." That night Hoa lay in bed with her eyes wide open for a long time, thinking of her American friends who wanted peace. (p. 42)

Despite the implausibility of this scenario (Would mail to North Vietnam have been delivered from America? Do these Vietnamese children read English or has Larry Jacobs written his letter in Vietnamese?), this letter is taken to be representative of the attitudes of "many people in the United States" (p. 42). Since this story is told from a purportedly North Vietnamese perspective, the fact that antiwar protestors are considered "friends" of the North Vietnamese is perhaps a dubious compliment.

Combat Novels—Platoon Subcategory

Despite the fact that Joe Haldeman, the author of *War Year* (1972), attempted to register for conscientious objector status prior to his being drafted, he does not include any mention of the antiwar movement in *War Year* (McCloud, 1989). Burning draft cards is the antiwar activity discussed in *Fallen Angels* (1988). One of the members of the squad featured in the novel receives a newspaper from home containing several articles about war protestors:

> "What else you got in the mail?" Monaco asked.
> "A newspaper," Walowick said. "Only thing in it is the stuff about guys burning their draft cards."
> "Faggots and Commies," Brunner said. "Anybody who wouldn't stand up for their country is either a faggot or a Commie."
> "They're doing what they think is right," Monaco said. "Maybe they are right, who knows?"
> "That's why we got four and five-man squads [a squad should be nine soldiers]," Brunner said. "'Cause those jerks are home smoking dope and burning their draft cards. You get blown away because you don't have a full squad, you can thank those creeps." (p. 146)

In this exchange Brunner expresses a common opinion—anyone against the war must be anti-American. The "my country right or wrong" mentality that Brunner displays blames antiwar activists with endangering the lives of soldiers in combat—not the government that sent them and then refused to keep the proper numbers up.

The *Echo Company* series (1991-1992) does not mention the antiwar movement until the final novel, *Echo #4* (1992). There is a single mention of evading the draft by going to Canada in *Echo #1* (1991), which is dismissed as being a "gutless move" (p. 19). In discussing draft evaders, the men from Echo Company, much like those in *Fallen Angels*, perceive those who go to Canada as men who don't want to come to fight in Vietnam—not as antiwar activists. In *Echo #4* (1992) antiwar activists are described by the army brass to the grunts as "long-haired hippie scum demonstrating against you brave, patriotic boys fighting for freedom and democracy" (p. 23). Again we see purely ad hominem attacks. Obviously the irony of resenting antiwar demonstrators for exercising the very "freedom and democracy" that the "brave, patriotic boys" are fighting for is lost on these characters (p. 23).

Several times throughout *Echo #4*, Michael speaks or thinks derisively about protestors who have student deferments protecting them from the draft. Strangely, those who both had access to student deferments (which were pared down in 1966 and virtually eliminated later) and protested the war are especially scorned as cowards. This flies in the face of common sense. If an antiwar protestor did *not* have a student deferment, the charges of self-interest could be more easily leveled; e.g., he protested because he was afraid that *he* might have to go to Vietnam. However, if because of a student deferment a young man was exempt from the draft and still protested the war, it would seem that his motives would be above suspicion. Michael never explains what he means when he makes comments to the effect that anything would be "better than protesting with a deferment snug in your back pocket" (*Echo #4*, p. 274).

Response to the War Novels

One Day for Peace (1971) is the first novel in the sample to take antiwar activities as its main plot. After her friend Jeff is killed in Vietnam, junior high student Jane Simon organizes a peace march that will culminate in a downtown rally where a tree will be planted. Jane and her young group are the target of some resistance and resentment within the small community, but eventually many adults, including the mayor, agree to take part in the march.

After the peace committee is initially formed, Jane and her friends try to decide on an activity to attract attention. Donald explains to the committee how peace groups are often deviously broken up by the government through the use of *agent provocateurs*. This fairly sophisticated view of government interference in groups of whom they disapprove is reiterated throughout the novel.

As Jane becomes more and more involved in organizing the peace march, adults in positions of authority (e.g., the church pastor, the school's principal) challenge her. Jane is finally called into the principal's office, where he implicitly threatens her:

> "I am deeply concerned with this peace committee that you and Donald Lehman have organized. In the first place, it is very rash for young people of your age to pass judgement on our leaders in time of war.
>
> "In the second place, you may be doing serious injury to yourself. . . .
>
> "You see, Jane, many young people are endangering their careers by becoming known as activists. In this school, we would think twice before giving a high recommendation for college to an activist. And if

the student were admitted to a college, responsible employers might hesitate to hire him upon graduation. A responsible employer wants a responsible employee, not one who will stir up trouble. . . . . Your whole future could be in danger if you become known as a troublemaker." (p. 63)

This "permanent record" perspective toward antiwar activity is a strange addition. In no other novels are potential activists counseled against acting on their beliefs in order not to be labeled as troublemakers.

Once the mayor and his aides weigh the consequences of crossing the American Legion and other "professional patriots," the mayor issues a proclamation condemning the war and supporting Jane's march. Letters to the editor of the local newspaper both support and decry the antiwar activity. One states that the proclamation and the march are "giving a boost to morale in Hanoi" (p. 74). Another is from a Holocaust survivor who states that if people in Germany had protested their government when it was engaged in an immoral activity, then maybe the Holocaust would never have happened. The American Legion is again specifically named when they

passed a resolution that was really crazy. They wanted the district attorney to investigate us for communistic activities or something. The legion commander told a reporter for the *Gazette*, "If the authorities fail to meet the challenge of these juvenile radicals, we may wake up some morning to find that our schools have been burned in the night." (p. 75)

The school burning non sequitur notwithstanding, this letter implies that antiwar activity is perceived as anti-American by the American Legion.

On the morning of the march, Jane is concerned about those who resent any antiwar activity and wonders if there will be any violence toward the marchers. "I knew that peace demonstrators in New York City had been beaten up by construction workers in hardhats while the police just stood there. We have lots of people in Winchester who think the war is OK—like those four boys who went after Donald" (p. 92). Those who are against the antiwar movement are presented as small-minded, and the only violence in the novel is perpetrated by those against the antiwar movement and the antiwar folks.

Caribou (1984) centers on how the war affects the Silverman family. Nineteen-year-old Stevie Silverman's birthday is chosen first in the draft lottery in the summer of 1970. Stevie decides that he cannot go to Vietnam—but his motivation to avoid service has nothing to do with protesting American involvement in Vietnam. Stevie is afraid that he might be killed. He readily admits that he's never been interested in the antiwar movement and still isn't. After Stevie refuses to go to his pre-induction physical, he buys a one-way bus ticket to Montreal. Even though Stevie is evading the draft, he doesn't consider any real antiwar sentiment, given his professed apathy toward ending the war.

Similar to Michael Jennings's (from the *Echo Company* books) reaction to those with college deferments protesting the war, characters in *The Best of Friends* (1989) consider these same people suspect. When Dan begins to take a staunchly antiwar stand, friends who will not receive student deferments question his attitudes. Other characters' attitudes toward college-deferred protestors mirror Michael's, and thus seem backward. If young men who were at minimal risk of being drafted protested, then why wouldn't their motives be even less suspect?

Dan's younger sister Sarah and her friend Kris became involved with distributing antiwar material at the local college. The girls are referred to as "weird" and "peace freaks" (pp. 14, 15). More time is devoted to describing how freakishly Kris is dressed than telling what her antiwar pamphlets say. For the most part, Sarah's and Kris's efforts are ignored by the college students. Despite Dan's antiwar attitudes, he ridicules Sarah for not accomplishing anything. Sarah's father believes that people involved in the antiwar movement are dangerous and that American leaders should not be questioned.

> I see people like you up at the college every day, so sure they're right about things, so sure they know more than anyone in Washington. That kind of talk is dangerous. The government, President Nixon, the Congress, the military, they need the unconditional support of the American people if we are going to win this war. We can't have people questioning the government, running around second-guessing every decision. (p. 95)

What Mr. Ulvang describes as dangerous sounds much like the foundation of the very democracy that the United States ostensibly went to war to protect.

Sarah chides Dan for doing nothing to act on his belief that the war is fundamentally immoral. After much soul-searching, Dan rips up his draft card and gives it to his father who is the head of the local draft board. He tells his father that the war is immoral and that he will have no part of it. The novel ends with Dan's declaration, so the reader is not given any detail of Dan's potential antiwar activity.

Most of the characters in *And One for All* (1989) are vehemently opposed to the antiwar movement. This story follows friends Sam Daily and Wing Brennan from 1966 to 1968. Wing eventually enlists in the marines and goes to Vietnam; Sam becomes an antiwar activist. The entire Brennan family looks with disgust at what they consider treasonous antiwar activity.

> There was a [television news] story about a peace march in Washington on the screen. Demonstrators were waving signs and shouting in front of the White House. Some of them were burning draft cards, getting arrested. A man wrapped in a United States flag was lying in the grass, playing dead. Policemen were hauling him away somewhere.
>
> "Don't those people realize they're just dragging out the war with that rot?" Daddy said. These reports always got him stirred up. . . . "Can't they see they're hurting our own men?" (p. 17)

Much like the sentiment expressed in *Fallen Angels* (1988), the antiwar protestors are credited with harming American soldiers while no accusations are made toward the government responsible for sending soldiers to war in the first place.

After Wing has quit high school and joined the marines, the Brennan family comes across Sam passing out antiwar leaflets denouncing American involvement in Vietnam. Mr. Brennan is ready to end a ten-year friendship because of their differing opinions on the war. Young Geraldine tries to sort out her feelings about Sam and his antiwar activities.

> *Was Sam a traitor?*
> Daddy seemed to think so. He had always said that the protestors were not better than traitors, that they were really just prolonging the war with their yammering about peace. That was what General Westmoreland had said in the paper the other day. He claimed the antiwar people were aiding and abetting the enemy, encouraging them to keep fighting by making it look as if Americans didn't support their own soldiers. . . .
> *Sam a traitor?*
> "Surely Sam *means* well—just because he's against the war doesn't mean he's against Wing," Mama said finally.
> But Daddy said, "It all amounts to the same thing, Mother. Didn't you read what he's saying in that fool paper? Calling Americans murderers—that's what he's doing. The Communists couldn't have written better propaganda themselves!" (p. 133)

Mr. Brennan clearly cannot separate antiwar attitudes from antisoldier or anti-American attitudes. In *And One for All*, just as in the previous novels, there is no real attempt to examine the statements of antiwar activists and then renounce them as faulty. They are simply dismissed as seditious and anti-American.

After Wing is killed in Vietnam, Geraldine runs away to Washington, D.C., to find Sam. Inexplicably, she blames the antiwar protestors in general and Sam specifically for Wing's death—not the government that sent him to Vietnam or the Vietnamese who shot him. In an implausible plot twist, Geraldine gets off the bus at the station in Washington, walks to the Mall, and begins stopping anyone with long hair, asking them if they know Sam. As she moves through the growing crowd of protestors on the Mall, all of whom have been helpful and friendly, she "hardened her heart against their kindness; these were all the enemy, she told herself—Wing's enemies. They might look kind on the outside, but underneath they were cold-blooded killers, cowards" (p. 165). No explanation is given for this vitriolic non sequitur. How are these people killers? How are they Wing's enemies? Just as inexplicably, Geraldine later has an epiphany wherein she realizes that the antiwar activists are really just interested in ending the war so that no one else will be killed and that their purpose is not, in fact, solely to label American soldiers murderers.

Long Time Passing (1990) includes some antiwar activists among its minor characters. Set in 1969, the story follows the developing romance between Jonas Duncan and Auleen Delange. Jonas's mother has recently died, his marine father is in Vietnam, and he is temporarily living with an older aunt in northern California. Auleen has friends among what author Adrienne Jones calls the "commune kids"—college students who camp out together and are a far stretch from anything that could be legitimately called a commune. The "commune kids" are shown to frequently use drugs, specifically marijuana, LSD, and heroin, and to have open sex. Among the commune kids is Davey, who is an organizer of marches and demonstrations. Through Auleen's descriptions, the antiwar activists are presented as tough but brutally victimized by repressive authorities. Auleen, Jonas, and Gideon discuss the relative safety of antiwar activity when, as Todd Gitlin (1987) warns, "the government is willing to shoot you" (p. 414). Auleen specifically relates the story of "Bloody Tuesday," when California National Guard (called out by then Governor Ronald Reagan) troops teargassed and opened fire on unarmed protestors in People's Park. It was Auleen's opinion that demonstrating against the government was always dangerous work. She cites the voter registration drives in the South and the work of Dr. Martin Luther King, Jr. and claims that antiwar protestors put themselves in danger in much the same way that soldiers in Vietnam do.

After the "commune" moves to Berkeley, Davey organizes a "Ban the Draft" rally in Oakland. He plans to burn his draft card and then continue to protest as long as possible before eventually having to go to Canada. Auleen admires Davey for the personal sacrifices he's had to make as an antiwar activist. After he burns his draft card, Davey will have to leave the U.S. for Canada, thereby cutting himself off from everything he knows and loves. She believes that Davey is honoring soldiers by protesting the war. *Long Time Passing* is the first novel to explore, if briefly, the effect of being an antiwar activist on the lives of those who made that choice.

Twenty years later, Jonas and Auleen are reunited. She has spent the majority of that time in Canada with Davey. Auleen firmly believes that the antiwar protests were responsible for ending American involvement in Vietnam, although she gives no evidence to support her beliefs. She tells Jonas that the sacrifices that she and Davey made were worth it.

Later in the same discussion, Auleen reiterates her belief that the antiwar movement was largely responsible for bringing the war to an end. There is no ensuing discussion of if, in fact, the antiwar movement *did* have such an effect on ending the war or the dubious notion that "the people" had never ended wars. Jonas accepts Auleen's statement at face value.

Come in from the Cold (1994), much like *One Day for Peace* (1971), focuses predominantly on characters involved in antiwar activities. Maud's older sister, Lucy, an activist, has been accused of being involved in the killing of several secret service agents. As a result, Lucy lives "underground" for many months. She eventually resurfaces at the University of Minnesota to plant a bomb to destroy the physics building. Lucy herself is killed in the explosion. In a parallel situation, Jeff's (another antiwar activist) older brother Tom is killed in Vietnam. Maud and Jeff meet after their siblings' deaths and are drawn together in the antiwar movement.

Before Tom is killed, he confronts Jeff about antiwar activities. Tom, like many characters before, is completely unable to separate antiwar sentiment from antisoldier or anti-American sentiment.

> "It was a resolution condemning U.S. involvement in Vietnam." [Jeff had been involved in passing this through the high school's student council.]
> "Somehow that doesn't surprise me. Maybe it's time we do talk, about whether or not you think your brother is, oh, what is it they call us? Baby-killers? Why don't you say it?"
> "I don't think that about you, Tom. Tom, I don't want to fight about this. My argument with the war has nothing to do with you or any other guy in uniform."
> "That's crap. If you hate the war, you hate the guys who do the fighting. You can't separate us from the dirty deed, little brother." (p. 55)

This nonsensical position, that you couldn't be against a war without despising the poor men who were forced to fight it, is unfortunately common among the war-supporting characters in these novels.

Jeff, like Auleen (*Long Time Passing*, 1990), also believes that many antiwar activists sacrifice a great deal for their beliefs. These are the only two novels to explore the detrimental effect the war can have on those who were not soldiers. Jeff and Roger, a local minister involved in antiwar activities, discuss the hidden casualties of Vietnam:

> "Have you ever thought how many more casualties of war there are beyond the official numbers?"
>
> "Do you mean the Vietcong dead? They add those up, Roger. They brag about the numbers, in fact."
>
> He shook his head. "No, I mean like you. Others. Lives changed and destroyed." He shrugged. "Like me. Did I ever tell you that my father hasn't talked to me in two years? The first time I spoke out against the war was in an editorial in the seminary paper. He read it and ever since has refused to speak to me. If I call home and he answers instead of my mother, he just hangs up without a word. He was an army major in WWII. He lost an arm. My mother says he believes I'm dishonoring him by opposing the war." (p. 94)

Finally, there is the backward objection to war protesting by those with student deferments that is so frequently seen in other novels.

> "Tell me, when it's your turn, do you plan to go to Canada? No, you'll be safe. Another year of high school, four of college, and by then old Nixon's secret plan for peace will have worked and we'll be out. You're absolutely safe, Jeffie. That figures—you won't have to face it, so it's cool to be against it. What does Tom think about having a peacenik for a brother? Does he like having a traitor in the family? Does he mind you spitting in his face?
>
> "It's the chickens that squawk the loudest. . . . Chickens and girls—you ever noticed that, peacenik? It's chickens and girls that mouth off against the war. Like that one who got herself knocked up. You know what I think? I think when it comes to war, girls should keep their mouths shut. Especially the sluts." (p. 70)

This Neanderthal attitude is unfortunately common. Just as in the majority of the novels in the sample, antiwar attitudes and beliefs are dismissed without any discussion. Antiwar activists are the victims of ad hominem attacks and irrational rage.

Returned Vet Novels

The final category of novels addresses the postwar experiences of soldiers who were in Vietnam. Antiwar protestors figure most prominently in *Tough Choices* (1993) and *The Road Home* (Part Two, 1995), but this is perhaps because these novels are both set immediately upon the vets' return to America. *Tough Choices* is set in 1968 and begins as the Morgan family greets returning vet Mitch at the airport. Before Mitch gets off the airplane, his younger sister Samantha spots a group of "twenty teenagers wearing tie-dyed shirts and bell-bottom pants walking in a circle carrying home-made signs . . . chanting 'Hell no, we won't go!'" (p. 3). Even though the signs make no recriminations toward the soldiers, Sam and her family are enraged by their presence.

In this lengthy exchange, the protestors are presented very negatively when they approach Mitch and his family on the way to the car from the airport.

> "Hey, Baby Killer!"
> At first I didn't understand. Baby killer? Who could they be talking to? Then another protestor spoke up.
> "We're talking to you, soldier," she said. "How many babies did you murder in Vietnam?"
> She was talking to my brother. I couldn't believe it. How could she ask that? My brother went to Vietnam to fight the Communists. How could she think he killed babies?
> Mitch stared at the protestors. His face had gone pale. He looked confused.
> "You've got the wrong guy," he said. "I'm one of the good guys."
> The protestors laughed. One or two of them spit on the ground.
> "You're just a killer hired by Uncle Sam," one said.
> "Take that back!" Mom yelled. "You're nothing but a bunch of dirty hippies. You wouldn't know a decent person if you saw one." Mom started across the street toward the group. Her face was red and her fists were clenched. I couldn't wait to see her hit a few of those teenagers.
> Mitch grabbed Mom's shoulder.
> "Let it go, Mom," Mitch said. "I just want to go home."
> Lee Ann [Mitch's girlfriend] stood close to both of them. Two tears slid down her cheeks. Mitch rubbed his eyes and then put on his sunglasses.

> I looked at the protestors, who had started chanting, "Killer, killer, killer!"
>
> "I'll hit them," I said. "The police won't arrest me." . . .
>
> Splat! An egg landed on the ground in front of us. Then another. A beer bottle crashed on the sidewalk near us. . . .
>
> "I'm sorry those peaceniks ruined your homecoming," I said. (p. 11)

The inherent contradictions in this exchange aren't commented on in the dialogue or internal narration. Mitch was in Vietnam to fight for freedom, but the Morgan family isn't ready to extend that very freedom to the demonstrators to express their opinions. Also, Mama screams that the "dirty hippies" wouldn't know a decent person if they saw one as she prepares to physically assault them for holding opinions contrary to hers. While perhaps some events such as this did actually occur, there is little in this novel to suggest that the antiwar movement was ever actually antiwar and not merely antisoldier.

Those with antiwar attitudes fare little better in *The Road Home* (Part Two, 1995). This novel is relentless in its condemnation of the antiwar movement. When Rebecca returns home from her tour in Vietnam, she has the same stereotypical experience that appears in all the novels in this category. Having just landed in California from Vietnam,

> she fell asleep almost as soon as she sat down on the shuttle bus, waking up just in time to hear the end of a lecture a grouchy master sergeant gave them, with specific orders *not* to shame their uniforms by responding to provocation by yellow-bellied in-dee-vi-jwals of the hippie persuasion.
>
> The E-5 in the next seat—one of the many guys who had already changed into civilian clothes, although their haircuts were dead giveaways—told her that she had slept through the egg barrage by a motley little crew just outside the gates of the base.
>
> Somehow, she wasn't sorry she'd missed it. (p. 223, emphasis in original)

When they got [to the San Francisco airport], they were greeted by a few waving signs, and some "Hell, no, we won't go!" business, but it was early, and the group's energy level seemed sluggish. She ignored the taunts as she walked inside, although she happened to meet eyes

with one particularly grungy-looking man with hair past his shoulders,
who promptly scowled and flipped her off.

   Yes. It was *so* nice to be home. (p. 225, emphasis in original)

Here again, antiwar protestors are presented as having nothing to say
about the actual *war*, and focusing their entire efforts on maligning
returning soldiers. When written in this manner, protestors are easily
dismissed.

When Rebecca finally gets home to the airport in Boston, she has an
odd exchange with a stranger as she waits for her bags:

   "You know things are bad," he [a preppie stranger] said, "when a
   girl like you goes over to the enemy."
   Last she'd heard, *North Vietnam* was supposed to be the enemy.
   She glanced down at his bags—too long, the way he'd studied her
   chest. Goddamn bourgeois bags. "*Catcher in the Rye* go to your head?"
   she asked, and walked away.
   When she got over to her parents, her father nodded in the guy's
   general direction.
   "Nice to see a boy your age act like a gentleman," he said.
   She *couldn't* let that one go by, when it came right down the
   middle, all nice and fat like that. "Dad, right before you showed up, he
   was about to spit on my bag," she said. And then, who knew, maybe on
   her. As a smugly self-authorized booster of the heroic People's Army.
   (p. 242, emphasis in original)

This man wasn't presented as an antiwar protestor, but he obviously had
antiwar feelings. Inexplicably, Rebecca assumes that the man is about to
spit on her bags, although he has done nothing to make that a reasonable
assumption, regardless of their minor confrontation.

Only casual mention of antiwar protestors is made in the remaining
three Returned Vet novels. Toward the end of *Where the Elf King Sings*
(1980), after Bill (the returned vet) has committed himself to PTSD
treatment, vet counselor Kurt tells Bill's family about his experiences with
antiwar protestors upon returning from Vietnam. He describes antiwar
demonstrators waiting at the airport to scream accusations at returning
veterans. The portrayal of the antiwar movement in *Charlie Pippin* (1987)
is very similar. When young Charlie interviews her grandfather about her

father's experiences in Vietnam, the novel's only mention of the antiwar movement is made. Granddad describes something very close to Bill's experience. The same baby-killer and murderer accusations were screamed and the same spitting was detailed.

No attempt is made in either novel to show that the majority of antiwar activity was concerned with stopping the war and questioning both its purposes and values, not spitting and accusing returning veterans of murder. There is also no serious consideration or examination of the ideas of the antiwar movement. The only specific examples of antiwar activity in *Tough Choices* (1993), *The Road Home* (Part Two, 1995), *Where the Elf King Sings* (1980), and *Charlie Pippin* (1987) are extremely negative ones.

The final novel in the category, *Travelers* (1986), gives us the only mention of the organization, the VVAW. The novel follows Jack Karlstad as he seeks out his KIA father's military friends some fifteen years after their return from Vietnam. Ron Hopkins, a friend of Jack's father, A.J., was so turned against the war during his Vietnam experience that he "came back to the States and joined Vietnam Vets Against the War, marched, went to Washington and got arrested, the whole number" (p. 90). We are not really given any information about the organization or its objectives or about the antiwar movement in general. Later in the novel, Jack reads a letter that his father wrote to his mother from Vietnam. In it, A.J. blames the antiwar movement for prolonging the war, saying that "we'd be home already if it weren't for the hippie protestors and pussy congressmen who don't know what the hell's going on" (p. 98). This is quite contradictory to his later experience as one of those "hippie protestors" himself.

When Jack meets the wife of another of his father's friends, she tells him about her family's experience with antiwar activists after her husband's return from Vietnam, which includes the apparently obligatory "baby killer" comment. This example, just like the others in the Returned Vet category, portrays antiwar activists as vicious, accusatory, and self-righteous. No examination is made of the beliefs or motives of the activists.

Generalizations

Overall, the antiwar movement is not given much attention in this sample of twenty-eight novels. It is, in fact, not even mentioned in ten of the novels—at least one from every category and subcategory with the exception of the Response to the War novels. Those ten novels completely ignore the antiwar movement. One would never know that there were people organized to protest the war after reading these selections.

The three novels that predominantly and positively feature antiwar activists, *One Day for Peace* (1971), *Long Time Passing* (1990), and *Come in from the Cold* (1994), are all Response to the War novels. Quite opposite from the other novels, in these three stories, antiwar activists are presented as being victimized by violent and/or repressive authorities. The only violence in these novels is committed against protestors by those who would stifle the protestors' opinions. Antiwar activists are shown to be doing what they feel is right and making great personal sacrifice to do so. In *Long Time Passing*, there is the only mention of the notion that the antiwar movement was actually responsible for ending the war.

In the rest of the novels that mention antiwar activists, their views are never examined and found to be faulty; they are merely dismissed out of hand. Ad hominem attacks are constantly leveled at the protestors themselves. Within the Platoon novels, the GIs perceive antiwar demonstrators as the reason that they don't have enough soldiers to do their jobs properly—in other words, the antiwar movement endangers soldiers' lives.

Within the Response to the War category, the antiwar movement is viewed negatively in *And One for All* (1989). The Brennan family considers antiwar activists to be traitors who prolong the war and hurt soldiers. With no explanation, the Brennans blame the antiwar movement for their son's death in Vietnam.

Finally, in the Returned Vet novels, the antiwar movement is presented in the most consistently negative light. In the novels that mention antiwar protestors (all but *Pocket Change*, 1989), the antiwar movement is first mentioned in a neutral or noncommittal manner. Then, when a returned vet in the novel tells of his or her specific experiences with antiwar protestors, it is always in terms of a nasty confrontation. Returning vets are called murderers and/or baby-killers and are spit at in *each* of the novels. If these representations were accurate, America would still be standing knee-deep in spit. Even though this may have indeed happened on occasion as vets returned from Vietnam, the novels portray only these incidents and exclude any mention of the larger purposes of the antiwar movement. Also, as in earlier categories, the views of antiwar activists are dismissed out of hand in the Returned Vet novels. There is never an attempt to explore and then discredit the beliefs of the antiwar movement. Also consistent with earlier categories, the dismissal of antiwar views is generally accompanied by ad hominem attacks on the protestors themselves.

Representations of the Vietnamese

Perhaps the most underincluded group in novels that depict the Vietnam War are the Vietnamese themselves. In discussing the representations of the Vietnamese in cinematic depictions of the Vietnam War, Ringnalda (1990) claims that the war in Vietnam is presented as "an *American* tragedy, virtually ignoring America's racist actions toward the Vietnamese people" (p. 66). Despite the fact that all of the novels in the sample address some aspect of America's involvement in Vietnam, the majority of the novels contain not even one named Vietnamese character. For the purposes of this analysis, representations of the Vietnamese will be divided into three groups: Vietnamese civilians (including the Montagnards), the South Vietnamese military (the ARVN), and the North Vietnamese army and Viet Cong guerrillas (NVA and VC).

Combat Novels—Duty Subcategory

Since all of the Combat novels are set in Vietnam, it would seem likely that Vietnamese characters would be included—but this is not necessarily the case. Only two of the five Duty novels contain named Vietnamese characters. *Special Forces Trooper* (1967) tells the story of a group of American advisors and the ARVN and CIDG forces whom they "advise." Throughout the novel, derisive comments are made about the Vietnamese and Montagnards. There are many mentions of the "impassiveness of their race" (p. 106) and their extremely small size: "the smiling little Montagnard" (p. 104), "a little Vietnamese radio operator" (p. 113), "the little native trooper" (p. 113). In *Special Forces Trooper* (1967), Vietnamese geographical names are incorrectly run together as if they were one word: Vietcong, Iadrang, Danang.

The ARVN soldiers are shown to be lazy, cowardly, and uncooperative and good fighters only if forced by the Americans. An American sergeant laments having to prod them into fighting: "The ARVN won't hunt out the enemy, for they have no stomach at all for hand-to-hand fighting, and the Cong know it. Viet airmen haven't the guts for low-altitude flying . . ." (p. 124). On several other occasions, American advisors recount instances of ARVN cowardice and instances where ARVN soldiers would not fight unless American soldiers physically forced them to do so. ARVN soldiers are shown to have racist attitudes toward the Montagnards, and the Americans have difficulty preventing violence between the ARVN and CIDG. "Captain Luy [ARVN commander], in fractured English, reminded Martsell [American commander] that the Montagnards were untrustworthy. They were *moi*, savages, and he believed at least half a dozen of the tribesmen were Viet Cong that had infiltrated the camp" (p. 123). ARVN Captain Luy's English is described as "fractured," but we aren't given any indication of how well the American characters speak Vietnamese.

The CIDG or Montagnard troops are accorded more respect by the American advisors. They are presented as somewhat primitive, competent fighters, although unstable and likely to start fights. Protagonist Stan Rusat describes the CIDG: "the native strike-force soldiers looked even smaller than he had heard they were, but there was a fierceness in their eyes and general bearing that compensated for a lack of stature and plainly spoke of more than brief skirmishes with the VC" (p. 99).

The VC are presented as "fanatical and suicidal" (p. 5) vicious, but respected, "hard core" soldiers (p. 106). When the Americans capture a Vietnamese soldier whom they initially assume is VC, they quickly change their minds when the prisoner appears frightened. The implication being that no real VC would ever be afraid. The VC are often described in animal-like terms. They "disappear like so many rats" (p. 100), they "scurr[y] through the undergrowth" (p. 116), and they have "glittering eyes" and "bared teeth" (p. 173).

Neither *Orders to Vietnam* (1968) nor *Stop & Search* (1969) contain any named Vietnamese characters. Only the VC are mentioned in *Orders to Vietnam* and those instances portray a ruthless group of people. VC guerrillas are accused of mutilating the bodies of U.S. Air Force prisoners (no details given) and of shooting down a dustoff—a helicopter picking up wounded Americans. This same idea of the VC purposely killing medical "noncombatants" is also included in *Stop & Search*, when an American doctor is described as wearing "no red cross. He was also carrying a .45 automatic in a holster. The Viet Cong paid little attention to the age-old tradition of regarding medical personnel as noncombatants" (p. 132). One could argue, however, that if the doctor were carrying a .45 it would be hard to classify him as a noncombatant.

None of the Vietnamese in *Stop & Search* (1969) are presented in a positive light. Protagonist and river boat pilot Eddie Czernik, constantly comments on the stench of the Vietnamese river boats, called junks. The American sailors' mission is to stop all junks on the river to be certain that none are hauling supplies for the VC. The Vietnamese civilians who pilot these junks are perceived by the Americans to be victims of the VC. Finding no contraband after having searched a junk, Eddie and Lieutenant Russell discuss how the families of the junk pilots are kidnapped by the VC in order to assure their cooperation. They imply that Vietnamese civilians would not choose to help the VC of their own free will.

Nurse Joanna Shelton of *Vietnam Nurse* (1968) freely admits that she despises Vietnam—the country in which she grew up with her missionary/physician father. When she remembers the countryside itself, her description is of an "ugly," "primeval," and "slime"-covered "semi-aquatic world" permeated by an incredible "stench" (p. 28). The countryside is "primitive" (p. 91) and the people (military, civilian, and VC) are both primitive and brutal. When Joanna describes the Vietnamese to Green Beret Captain Wayne Moore, she further displays these astoundingly racist attitudes:

> I know these people, Captain; the family ties are strong, but not that strong. I've known them to desert old people because they were too much of a liability. I've known them to carry old people off into the jungle and leave them to die; and I've seen them do the same things with their babies, two and three-year-olds. Life in Vietnam is very

>cheap. . . . You yourself said this was a tough country, a cruel country.
>Such a country breeds cruel people, some of them unbelievably cruel
>. . . . (pp. 107, 109)

Not only is this an astoundingly inaccurate assessment of Vietnamese attitudes toward family, but it's a racist assumption. Worse yet, no one questions Joanna's unbelievable statements. Vietnamese characters are considered inscrutable. When Joanna asks a VC leader a question that he doesn't wish to answer, he "pull[s] the Oriental curtain down over his emotions, successfully screening the truth from Joanna" (p. 161). The Vietnamese language is referred to as "singsong sounds" (p. 169).

As Joanna and her Green Beret escorts move through the jungle looking for Joanna's missing father, Dr. Shelton, they come upon a Montagnard village where they stop to offer medical aid. The Vietnamese often refer to Montagnards as *moi*, a derogatory term meaning savage. Joanna describes the villagers to the Green Berets as "the Churu, an offshoot of the *Moi* tribe. . ." (p. 56, my emphasis). Joanna is not being derisive in this passage, so it can only be assumed that author Ellen Elliott did not understand in her own research that there was *no* Moi tribe and that, in fact, Moi is a term akin to our own "redskin" or "nigger."

The VC are represented as cruel and vicious people in *Vietnam Nurse*. When Joanna learns that her father may have been captured by the VC, she immediately assumes that they would kill him. After Joanna and the Green Berets are themselves captured by the VC, they learn that the VC are also holding Dr. Shelton. The captives realize that they must fully cooperate with the VC in order to ensure Dr. Shelton's survival.

>"Either we do as they want or your father dies."
>"And they're cruel enough to do exactly that," Joanna whispered,
>shivering. "They're primitive as savages; they'd be capable of
>anything." (p. 73)

Despite Joanna's characterizations of the VC, they treat the captured party fairly well, with the exception of Dr. Steve Donovan, whom they kill (although he is shown to have largely brought this on himself). The VC reunite Joanna with her father and eventually release the Sheltons and the Green Berets unharmed.

Finally there are no named Vietnamese characters in *Nurse in Vietnam*. There are, however, constant slurs made against Asians of several nationalities. On the ship to Clark Air Force Base in the Philippines (where Lieutenant Lisa Blake is to be stationed), one Korean passenger becomes ill, prompting the ship's captain to remark that "Asiatics are bum seamen" (p. 11). After arriving at Clark, Lisa is warned by her roommate to be on guard against the Filipinos, who are prone to thievery:

> "We have to be on watch every minute to keep from being robbed blind."
> "You're kidding."
> "Kidding nothing! This apartment is guarded around the clock. Otherwise you wouldn't have a possession left by the time you returned."
> "You mean they really burglarize these apartments!"
> "And are these Filipinos clever thieves! They make a hole in the fence and before you know it, they can break into an apartment and strip it clean." (p. 29)

> "Nancy's parents sent her a box of goodies months ago, and she hasn't received them yet. Those Filipino postal clerks have very sticky fingers. They even steal money from personal letters." (p. 62)

When Lisa first ventures into downtown Saigon, she is appalled by what she sees.

> No sooner had she started down the street of ornate fussy buildings, gaudy little shops and strange smells. . . . With each step she became increasingly aware of the countless pungent odors that surrounded her. The stench of rotting garbage, the smell of gutter pools filled with floating swill that was sickening.
> Squalor was every place, and it was readily obvious that children were the most pitiful victims of the poverty. But for all their malnutrition and open sores on their small, scrawny bodies, there was a certain resilience about them as they romped around like rabbits in and out of the pedestrians, begging or trying to peddle black market cigarettes. Adolescent girls, garbed in dirty dresses, played hopscotch or chuck-a-luck in front of store entrances.

> The Vietnamese women whom Lisa passed looked much alike with their black hair and light olive skin. All wore their Ao-dais—native costumes—patterned with loose-fitting pantaloons and tight-fitting tunics, separated into two panels, one in front, one in back, which dropped almost to their ankles. Some of them looked too pretty to be a part of the filth and misery.
>
> Suddenly Lisa thought, This isn't the way Clint described Saigon. It's bedlam. It's old and shabby and in need of repairs. And it's rampant with greed and corruption and clogged with refugees. (p. 74)

In this one passage Lisa thinks of Vietnamese children as pitiful animals with mothers who look alike. One wonders how Lisa concludes that Saigon is "rampant with greed and corruption" by merely walking the streets. As her visit continues, each merchant that Lisa deals with attempts to take advantage of her. Lisa comments to herself about the "constant babble of Oriental tongues" (p. 19).

There are no VC actually shown in this novel, but they are mentioned when Lisa talks to a reporter in the hospital at Clark Air Force Base. The reporter tells Lisa that the VC are "brave" and "sophisticated," but also "ruthless" (p. 64). The reporter gives evidence to back up his claims of VC ruthlessness when he tells Lisa of an American airplane shot down by the VC. The survivors were shot as soon as they stepped from the wreckage. There is an implication here that there are "rules" for appropriate wartime behavior and that the VC violate them, although it's difficult to imagine how shooting at enemy soldiers during a war could be legitimately called cold-blooded.

Combat Novels—Vietnamese Perspective Subcategory

Since each of the five novels in this group has a Vietnamese or Montagnard protagonist or coprotagonist, it is here that the most information about Vietnamese life during the war is given. *The Man in the Box* (1968) follows a young Montagnard boy, Chau Li, as he rescues a captured Green Beret, David Lee, and returns him to a temporary American/ARVN base in a nearby Montagnard village. The VC in this novel are vicious and cruel. They have brutalized David by beating him, breaking the bones in his feet, burning the inside of his mouth, and forcing him into a bamboo cage with sides of only a few square feet. Previously, the VC had cut off the hand of the Montagnard village's teacher who had tried to help a man earlier imprisoned by the VC. The VC are also shown to victimize the Montagnards—stealing food and murdering anyone who crosses them.

The ARVN are thought to be racist by the Montagnards and cowardly by the Americans. Chau Li thinks of how poorly the Vietnamese have treated his own Montagnard people. "The lowlanders [Vietnamese] came with their heads high and haughtily called the Montagnards *Mois-*—savages" (p. 75). While Chau Li still has David hidden in a mountain cave, he meets a small group of Green Berets and ARVN soldiers. The men stop Chau Li and the ARVN accuse him of being a VC. They are ready to kill a Montagnard boy with no proof of his guilt, but the Americans won't let them.

Eventually, Chau Li brings David into the temporary camp the Americans and ARVN have set up in another Montagnard village. The Americans call for a medevac (medical evacuation helicopter) to pick up David. When the Americans realize that the helicopter is Vietnamese, they express doubt about the pilot.

> "The copter is coming, but not flown by an American. It is a Vietnamese copter."
> "Is the machine not as good?" Chau Li asked anxiously. He did not want Dah Vid flying through the air in an unreliable machine.
> "The machine is all right. If we can get the courageous pilot to land." The way he said "courageous," Chau Li did not think the Captain meant brave. The Captain could see the concern in his face. "Well, I guess anything is better than nothing at all. It'll be OK, boy. Let's get moving. . . . Throw your smoke. That dustoff will go right back down the valley if he doesn't spot us at once." (pp. 131, 132)

The Americans expect the ARVN pilot to be cowardly, even before they know specifically who he is.

It has been agreed among the Americans that Chau Li would accompany David to the hospital in Da Nang and then on to America. After David is loaded into the helicopter, Chau Li attempts to get in as well when "the [ARVN] medic in the copter looked at the mountain boy for a stunned moment and then shouted 'No *Mois* in the copter,' and shoved him out the door with both hands" (p. 134, emphasis in original).

In *The Man in the Box*, the Montagnards are portrayed as victims of both the Vietnamese and the VC.

Lost American soldier Harry and orphaned twelve-year-old Vietnamese girl Mi are the coprotagonists in *Cross-fire* (1972), a novel that shifts its limited third person narration between Harry and Mi in alternating chapters. This interesting technique gives readers a chance to see how both characters think. Throughout the novel, Harry continues to demonstrate racist and condescending attitudes toward the Vietnamese characters. He thinks of the Vietnamese language as "sing-song gibberish that meant nothing" and is completely surprised when Mi doesn't speak English (p. 10). Even after he knows that neither Mi nor her younger siblings speak any English, he continues to question them and then becomes irritated when they cannot answer. "Useless. Might just as well talk to a bunch of statues" (p. 14). When Mi finally manages to decipher something that Harry says to her, he still ridicules her language. "She turned to the others and said something, fast and sing-song, in Vietnamese. What a crazy mixed-up language! It wasn't any wonder that he couldn't speak it, with all that singing up and down every time you tried to say something" (p. 32). The derision continues as Harry thinks, "Damned Vietnamese . . . the least they could do is to learn how to speak English" (p. 108). Harry refers to the Vietnamese clothes as "pajamas" (p. 14) and the Vietnamese themselves as "ungrateful, thieving, slant-eyed gooks" (p. 54).

Harry thinks of the Vietnamese as primitive. When he gives Mi a book and she doesn't immediately open it, he assumes that "maybe she'd never seen a book before. This was pretty far out in the country, and most of the people were as poor as mud hens. Ignorant, too. No schools or anything like that. Like savages, almost" (p. 27).

> Man, it was hard to believe that people could live in the 20th century and still be as backward and ignorant as the average Vietnamese peasant, with his bullock and his wooden plow. They were still in the Dark Ages, except for a few of the educated ones who lived in the cities. (p. 57)

Finally, Harry can only interpret the Vietnamese children's behavior in terms of what would be expected of American children—whose behavior he sees as "normal." Mi's infant brother dies approximately halfway through the novel. Harry and the children bury the baby, but Harry doesn't think that the children mourn properly. "You'd think that they'd cry or something. White people would have cried. Or cursed. Or said something. But not these people, not the Vietnamese. It puzzled him, the way these people hid their feelings. It wasn't natural" (p. 133).

To Stand against the Wind (1978) tells the story of young Em, a Vietnamese boy whose family have been rice farmers in the Mekong Delta for centuries. The war gradually encroaches on their lives and after most of Em's family is killed when Americans bomb their village, Em and his few remaining relatives emigrate to America. For most of the novel, life in Em's unnamed hamlet is peaceful and idyllic. Em describes the South Vietnamese as having "great family love and loyalty; kin ties were very strong, and so were ties with the extended family, which reached beyond the kinship bond. Strangers, however, or foreigners—people one did not know or trust—were treated with fear and suspicion" (p. 13). The novel shows the love that Em and his family demonstrate for each other as they go about their daily lives, prepare for Tet, and prepare for Chi-Bah's (Em's oldest sister) wedding.

The people of Em's village appear to be caught between the VC and the Americans. Em ponders how the villagers react to the VC.

> At night there were flares dropped by parachutes to show the Americans where the enemy was, for the Vietcong seemed to be everywhere.
>
> The people of Em's hamlet knew this. They knew that some of those who lived among them were Vietcong, and they suspected others were. The South Vietnamese feared the VC's, as the Americans called them, but for that very reason they often befriended them, although some did so through loyalty or out of confusion, not knowing what else to do. (p. 41)

No reason is given as an explanation of why "the South Vietnamese feared the VC's" although American soldiers say that the villagers "know the VC's will torture them and eventually kill them, and yet they feed them. They shelter them" (p. 121). In the end, however, the only villagers killed are killed by Americans. No VC are shown in the novel.

Em's father, older brother, and brother-in-law are all loyal to the South Vietnamese government and are eager to join the ARVN to protect their country from the VC. Since no specific time is given for the setting of this novel, we cannot know to which Saigon government Em's father refers when he says "we who love our government must help in any way we can" (p. 72). But given the extreme unpopularity of the corrupt Diem and successive administrations with the peasants, this sentiment seems unlikely.

Children of the Dragon (1974) and *Sing for Your Father, Su Phan* (1997) are the only novels set in North Vietnam and including North Vietnamese characters. In *Children of the Dragon*, young Tri has been sent into the North Vietnamese countryside from his home in Hanoi to be safe from the nearly constant American bombing. Life in Dai Lai, Tri's grandmother's village, is idyllic and pastoral. Tri and his young cousin Hoa speak lovingly of Ho Chi Minh. They quote his poetry, and Hoa tells Tri of a time when Ho visited Dai Lai and danced with all the children.

Examples are given of how life is better now that the northern part of Vietnam has won its independence. "Communism" is never mentioned in *Children of the Dragon*, but the children discuss how life is much happier now that the villages are organized into "cooperatives." When Hoa's Aunt Ly visits from a neighboring village, Hoa's mother, Huong, questions her about fishing (Ly's job):

> "Are you catching enough fish to feed your village?" asked Huong.
> "Yes, now that our village is a cooperative," answered Ly. "We catch fish together, sharing our nets and boats. This way we catch more fish than anyone could do alone."
> "Our village is a cooperative, too." Hoa said proudly. "We own the lands, the animals, and our farm tools together. We can grow more food this way. And everyone helps." (p. 19)

Apparently conditions are much improved for North Vietnamese women under the new collective system. When Grandmother Te learns that Huong is to head the village plowing team, she

> beamed at her daughter. "When I was a child, we women were not allowed to be leaders. We worked hard and were treated badly." A look

of sadness and anger filled her eyes for just a moment. "But things have changed since we won our independence in the North." (p. 19)

When Hoa and Tri visit Kim in the hospital, after he is burned in an American bombing raid, it turns out that Kim's doctor is a woman.

Grandmother Te tells Tri about the village's theater group that performs at Tet and on other special occasions.

> Our village group is one of the best theater groups in all of Viet Nam. They have given plays in hospitals and in jungles with bombs falling all around. Today they will do a theater-of-laughter play. These plays are written by villagers just like us throughout our history. They talk about planting rice and building the dikes. Sometimes they tell about our wars against invaders. (p. 44)

Even though there again was no mention of communism, this proletariat theater group performing works about planting rice written by villagers would seem to be an example of what Marxist critics refer to as politic artistic commitment (Eagleton, 1976). The North Vietnamese in *Children of the Dragon* are represented as a peaceful, devoted, political, smart, and cooperative people who are thriving under a communist system and just want peace so that they can go back to being even happier.

Life in North Vietnam is hard for Su Phan (*Sing for Your Father, Su Phan*, 1997) and her Chinese immigrant family after Chung Bo, her father, is arrested for not becoming a communist. The NVA military police viciously ransack the family's home and destroy all their property.

> "But what has my husband done?" Voong Nhi Mui wailed as Chung Bo was dragged out the door by the rope around his wrists. "What has he done?"
>
> "It's what he has not done," the leader shouted. "He has not become a Communist, as everyone should. It's wrong for one person to have so much when others have so little. We'll keep him in prison until he learns the ways of Communism."
>
> "When will you let him return?" Mother cried out.
>
> "In two or three years, if he learns his lessons well," the policeman answered. (p. 42)

Chung Bo is not released from a reeducation camp for nearly seven years. There is no description of this treatment there.

The same devotion to Ho Chi Minh witnessed in *Children of the Dragon* is just as evident in *Sing for Your Father, Su Phan*. When Ho Chi Minh dies in 1969, a local official comes to the school to inform the teachers of Ho's death. All adults break into sobs. School is dismissed for the day and all the children are instructed to go home to mourn with their parents.

Combat Novels—Platoon Subcategory

The first of the Platoon novels, *War Year* (1972, 1978), focuses almost exclusively on the experiences of John Farmer and the other American soldiers. There isn't a single named Vietnamese character in the novel. John's first impression of the Vietnamese civilians he sees on his way to the base at Pleiku is that they are "skinny little Orientals" (p. 11), to whom he later refers as "gooks" (p. 125).

No VC are shown in the 1972 edition of *War Year*. In fact, when John's company is ambushed, not a single VC is seen or described. It's as if the bullets fly out of the jungle on their own. A small group of VC are shown in the last few pages of the 1978 edition as they come out in the open. While we don't see the VC themselves (with the exception of the end of the second edition), we are shown the results of their actions. John and the other engineers must search the bodies of dead VC after a firefight, because it is assumed that the VC would booby-trap the bodies. Vietnamese civilians are brought to the hospital where John is recuperating from a battle wound.

> The VC had attacked a bunch of people on their way to the voting booths in Tuy Hoa, and the hospital was suddenly very overcrowded. Waiting for the bus that would take us to the airstrip, I saw helicopters unloading the casualties. Horrible, mostly women and children. There was a little baby crying with an eerie scream, high-pitched as a whistle; you could even hear it over the roar of the helicopter. When two medics ran by with the baby balanced in the middle of their stretcher, I saw that both his arms had been blown off at the shoulder. (p. 100)

Here the VC are shown to have attacked civilians, not soldiers or Americans. There is some question as to which voting booths Vietnamese peasants would have been going, as there were certainly no elected governments in South Vietnam.

When John first arrives at the hospital, there is a wounded NVA soldier there. The NVA soldier has been shot in the arm and is screaming even though he has been given pain killers. The hospital orderly tells John that the NVA soldier probably thinks that he will be tortured. Both Americans promptly dismiss this idea, but in fact, both North Vietnamese and suspected VC report, in recent oral histories, systematic and extensive torture at the hands of their American captors (Hess, 1993).

The Vietnamese characters in *Fallen Angels* (1988) are nameless and virtually faceless. Called "gooks," "dinks," and "slants," the South Vietnamese peasants are presented as constant victims—brutalized by the ARVN, by the VC, and even if unintentionally, by the Americans.

The ARVN are represented in a consistently negative fashion. ARVN soldiers are shown to beat a VC prisoner and a civilian woman and her children. Otherwise, ARVN troops are thought to be fundamentally inept, dishonest, and cowardly by the American forces. When American and ARVN troops operate out of the same firebase, the American troops don't believe that the ARVN are actually completing their patrols.

> Most of the patrols going out were Vietnamese, and Johnson said that he didn't think most of them were really patrolling. "They ain't out a kilometer before you hear popping," he said. He was right. Half the time the ARVNs would go out, especially at night, they would be back within a half hour saying that they had been hit by a company of Charlies. (p. 198)

The Americans' fundamental distrust of the ARVN is demonstrated throughout *Fallen Angels*. On joint missions, American leaders want ARVN troops to approach a dangerous sight first—fearing that if they were in the rear that they would flee. When ARVN troops move out on an operation, the American grunts recognize their lack of military aptitude. Perry recounts that they "sat and watched as what looked like almost a full company of little soldiers moved out. They were bunched too tightly, and they were moving too quickly" (p. 243). The lack of respect and

camaraderie between the Americans and their ARVN allies is demonstrated in a scene following a particularly horrific firefight in which many
Americans and ARVN have been killed. The American and Vietnamese
troops have gathered at a landing zone to await the helicopters that will
lift them out of the danger of the approaching NVA troops. The ARVN
commander orders his men to encircle the Americans so that the
remainder of the ARVN can be picked up first. When the helicopters
come, the ranking American officer has his men wave their hands over
their heads so that the helicopter crews can see what is happening. The
helicopters' door gunners fire on the ARVN as do the Americans on the
ground. The Americans are picked up, shooting at any ARVN who tries
to board a helicopter.

The VC and NVA, quite opposite from the ARVN, are represented
as beyond human in both their abilities and their viciousness. Several
specific instances are recounted illustrating their cruelty to Vietnamese
civilians.

> "[The VC] messed up at least one person from each hut," Peewee
> said.
> "They cut a baby's head off." Monaco spoke slowly. His face was
> dark, his mouth quivered between words. "How the hell do you kill a
> friggin' baby?"
> "Like the major say," Peewee said. "They showin' the people we
> can't protect them so they might as well be on Charlie's side." (p. 178)

American soldiers are also shown to be the target of VC cruelty.

> "They found some tortured marines up near the demilitarized
> zone," the orderly said. . . .
> "Tortured?"
> "[The VC] tie them to trees and pull their guts out," the orderly
> said. "Then they just leave them there alive. That marine colonel said
> when they found them they were still alive and begging for somebody
> to kill them." (p. 135)

Perry remembers this information later in the novel when he and Peewee
are separated from the rest of the squad after dark far from the firebase.
"I touched the safety [of the M-16]. Changed clips. I put a frag grenade

in front of me. I had three. I'd use two and save one for myself if it came to that. I remember hearing stories about what the Congs did to prisoners" (p. 285). In another scene, a Vietnamese woman brings two children into an American firebase. One of the children is booby-trapped so that it explodes, killing several Americans.

Following the tradition of *War Year* and *Fallen Angels*, there are no named Vietnamese characters in any of the four *Echo Company* novels. Protagonist Michael Jennings travels by truck toward the DMZ to join his company. During this trip Michael sees the Vietnamese populace for the first time. He expresses his doubts as to the trustworthiness of any Vietnamese. The internal narration reveals Michael's thoughts about the people in general.

> . . . they were so goddamn small. Even the buildings seemed small, and rickety. Primitive. Apparently, there was no such thing as indoor plumbing, because he could see people stopping—like it was a normal thing to do—right by the side of the road, right in the middle of everything, to go to the bathroom. Jesus. On the drunkest night of his life, he'd still known enough to go behind a tree or something. Anyway, it kind of explained why this stupid country smelled so awful. . . .
>
> He had managed to catch the fact that they'd been riding on Route 316. Which sounded awfully civilized and American for an outdoor latrine surrounded by palm trees and rice paddies and masses of expressionless, tiny, black-haired people. (*Echo #1*, pp. 10, 13)

During his first visit to a Vietnamese village, Michael observes what he considers to be a typical Vietnamese scene.

> There were about twelve little huts, a couple of rickety wooden pens with skinny chickens and a pig, a battered wooden well, a building that looked sort of like a church. A lot of empty-eyed children came running out, kind of swarming around. There were women, who didn't even look up from underneath those scary conical hats, and a couple of old men, feebly doing chores. These people didn't look dangerous; they looked *pathetic*. Poor, and beaten down.
>
> And it smelled awful. No septic tanks around *here*. (*Echo #1*, p. 129)

Michael's attitude toward Vietnamese civilians is one of mixed pity and contempt—they're shown to be victimized by both VC and Americans.

As in *Fallen Angels* (1988), the VC in the *Echo* books are sadistic, but invested with superhuman qualities. No VC troops are ever shown, but Michael and the other grunts believe the VC to be wholly fearless and nearly magic—they can do anything, appear from nowhere, disappear into nothingness, remain virtually invisible, and survive anything. In a scene similar to the one in which *Fallen Angels*'s Perry and Peewee are separated from their squad, Rebecca is the only survivor of the helicopter crash. She, like Perry, decides, given her knowledge of the cruelty of the VC, that she would kill herself rather than be captured.

> She cocked it—the gun was *heavy*—and held it with both hands, her arms trembling, ready to fire at the first thing that moved. If it was only a couple of them, she would shoot them. Payback. If there were more than two or three, she would shoot herself. Because, she had seen too many mutilations—prisoners, from both sides—come through the ER [emergency room]. And *heard* too many stories about what the VC would do if they ever took an American woman prisoner. She would *not* let them take her alive.
>
> Not a chance. (*Echo #3*, p. 128)

Rebecca later remarks on what she considers to be conscription by virtual kidnapping of young men by the VC. Rebecca makes no mention of the similarity of American conscription practices, even though we later find out that her brother has gone to Canada to avoid the draft and protest American involvement in Vietnam.

The ARVN are only occasionally included in the *Echo* books, but those few mentions carry much the same tone as those in *Fallen Angels* (1988). When Echo Company and the rest of the battalion are planning an assault on VC-held Hill 568 in *Echo #2* (1991) and are concerned that there aren't enough soldiers, Michael thinks, "hey—there were always the ARVNs—Army of the Republic of Vietnam—not that any of them had much faith in the South Vietnamese soldiers" (p. 159). No previous incident in the series explains this lack of faith.

Rebecca Phillips (from both the *Echo* series and *The Road Home*, 1995) maintains some very derogatory attitudes toward the Vietnamese workers at the base where she is stationed. After the helicopter crash incident in *Echo #3*, her aversion to the Vietnamese increases. In *The Road Home*, Rebecca contemptuously considers the Vietnamese woman who works in the nurses' quarters.

> Before the crash, she had always tried to greet Truong with Vietnamese and be guiltily respectful, but these days—she mostly just said hi. Avoided her. Truong appeared to be in her forties, which meant that she probably had children Rebecca's age. Sons, maybe. If she *did* have a son, he was almost certainly a soldier, and as likely to be VC as ARVN. Maybe even more likely. After all, the day Tet started, Truong and most of the other civilian workers hadn't shown up at all. Suggesting that they concealed even more than she might have suspected behind those empty smiles. (p. 133)

As Rebecca prepares to leave Vietnam at the end of her tour, she inexplicably becomes even more racist and aggressive.

> [Rebecca's] balance was so unwieldy that she managed to bang into Truong, who was just coming out of Pat's cubby with an armload of crumpled sheets. Predictably, Truong did a lot of apologetic bowing and scraping—which kind of bugged her.
> "No, it's *my* fault," she said. "*I'm* the ugly American here, not you."
> Some of the sheets had spilled onto the floor, and she picked them up, almost toppling over in the process, Truong still jabbering on and bobbing her head, and—this woman was her mother's age, why didn't she just yell at her for not looking where she was going? Christ, she had really *had* it with Vietnam. (p. 175)

Rebecca's attitudes toward the Vietnamese stay with her after she returns to America.

Response to the War Novels

Given the narrative structure of the Response to the War novels, none of the protagonists included here have any direct experience with any Vietnamese. All of the protagonists' information about and impressions of the Vietnamese are gleaned from the media, both print and broadcast.

In *One Day for Peace* (1971) and *Caribou* (1984), the Vietnamese are only briefly mentioned. In both cases, the Vietnamese people are perceived as constant victims. *One Day for Peace* specifically indicts American soldiers for killing the Vietnamese; *Caribou* merely mentions that the Vietnamese were being killed—no recriminations made.

The notion of the Vietnamese as victims is carried over into *The Best of Friends* (1989). Vietnamese civilians are attacked by both the Americans and the VC. Sarah, a young antiwar activist, tries to convince Will, a potential draftee, of American policy toward the Vietnamese.

> "I'm thinking about all the people over in Vietnam being blown up and burned with the napalm from American jets. Do you know that one hundred thousand Vietnamese are killed every year? Mostly by us? By Americans?"
> "That's what happens in a war," Will said. "People get killed."
> "A lot of the people we're killing are civilians." She turned toward him. "Not soldiers." (p. 36)

Sarah recognizes the extent to which the war is being presented as an "American tragedy" when she comes across a *Life* magazine that contains, as a tribute, a picture of each man killed in Vietnam in a week's worth of fighting. Of course, no pictures of Vietnamese dead are included. Sarah asks, "What about all the Vietnamese who die every week? . . . Or don't they count?" (p. 90).

The only mention of the VC in *And One for All* (1989) is when Geraldine reads in the newspaper that they had burned down a church full of people. Antiwar activist, Sam, claims that "thousands of innocent men, women, and children are being needlessly slaughtered, day after day" in Vietnam by American soldiers (p. 111). Vietnamese civilians are again presented as the victims of both the Americans and the VC.

Returned Vet Novels

Other than to be called dinks and gooks, the Vietnamese are not mentioned in *Where the Elf King Sings* (1980). Vet characters in *Travelers* (1986) regard the Vietnamese as anonymous victims of American violence. One minor character recounts a Halloween party in Vietnam where he wore a Vietnamese peasant costume, saying that the pilots attending the party ought to have an idea of what the people they kill might look like.

In her attempt to find out more about the war in which her father and uncle fought, *Charlie Pippin* (1987) comes across the only statistic given in any of the novels that approximates the number of Vietnamese dead. Presenting her findings to her class, Charlie states that about 200,000 South Vietnamese soldiers were killed and that several times that number were wounded.

There are currently no definitive statistics on Vietnamese (North or South, military or civilian) killed, wounded, or missing, and attempts to estimate these figures continue to be a matter of some contention within the historical community (E. E. Moise, personal communication, 1994). The majority of Charlie's report, however, addresses American soldiers and American issues.

Josie Monroe, the returned vet's daughter in *Pocket Change* (1989), has to be reminded when reading an article about the war that the Vietnamese were affected too.

In the middle of a long PTSD episode, Josie's vet father tells her about a particularly heinous method the VC had used to kill American soldiers. He claims that the VC would give wrapped bombs to Vietnamese children and instruct the children to give the package to an American soldier. American soldiers justified shooting Vietnamese children carrying packages because of this risk. This story illustrates the victimization of Vietnamese civilians, the cruelty of the VC, and the potentially vicious assumptions of the Americans.

Mitch Morgan in *Tough Choices* (1993) has just returned from duty in Vietnam. He tells his younger brother and sister of the brutality of the VC, saying that "the Viet Cong kill any villagers who won't help them. Sometimes they wipe out whole villages—women, children, everyone. Even the pets" (p. 20). There is no mention that "whole villages" are also "wiped out" by American soldiers as well. Mitch's younger brother, Emmett, perceives the Vietnamese civilians as the victims of Americans' inability to distinguish VC from non-VC.

Generalizations

The Vietnamese are not significantly represented in this sample of twenty-eight novels that address the war in Vietnam. There are only named Vietnamese characters in seven of the novels. Five of those seven are in the Vietnamese Perspective novels. Most Vietnamese and Montagnard villages and hamlets are also unnamed. While it is perhaps understandable that American GIs traveling through a Vietnamese village may not know its name, it seems unlikely that in a novel like *To Stand against the Wind* (1978) or *Sing for Your Father, Su Phan* (1997) set in a Vietnamese village and told by a Vietnamese (or Vietnamese immigrant) that no village name would be mentioned.

The representation of the three groups examined in this section—Vietnamese civilians (including the Montagnards), the South Vietnamese military (the ARVN), and the North Vietnamese military and Viet Cong guerrillas (NVA and VC)—are remarkably consistent across the novels regardless of their narrative structure. Frequent comments are made regarding the literal smell of Vietnam. The Vietnamese language is referred to as "sing-song" and "gibberish." The Vietnamese themselves are inscrutable, primitive, and extraordinarily small.

Almost without exception the ARVN are represented as inept cowards. They won't fight and if they are forced to fight, they aren't good at it. Perhaps the ARVN are portrayed in this negative light in order to justify the "Americanization" of the *Vietnam* War. In other words, if it is taken as an accepted fact that communism must be stopped and that the incompetent ARVN can't protect their own country, then American troops *must* do it.

The NVA and VC guerrillas are unrelentingly demonized as ruthlessly vicious and exceedingly cruel soldiers. No one is spared their wrath—Vietnamese civilians and American GIs alike. They are willing to do whatever they have to do to win the war. American soldiers are genuinely afraid of the VC and resent the fact that the VC refuse the "play by the rules" of warfare that Americans believe are appropriate, e.g., not shooting at medical personnel. Despite their consistent brutality, American soldiers respect the VC's military talent and discipline. Perhaps not surprisingly, the political opinions of the NVA or the VC (in essence the North Vietnamese position) are never acknowledged. The NVA aren't protecting their country—they seem to exist only to kill Americans and terrorize the South Vietnamese.

The Vietnamese and Montagnard civilians alike are represented as victims. They are without exception the victims of the VC. The civilian populace is also portrayed as the victim of American aggression. Occasionally, as in *Fallen Angels* (1988), this aggression is portrayed as unintentional—a pacification mission gone horribly wrong—or the Vietnamese civilians are victims of Americans' inability to distinguish VC from non-VC.

None of these twenty-eight novels contain any real discussion of the impact that this war (that the Vietnamese call "the American war") had on the Vietnamese or of the role that the Vietnamese governments, military, or civilians played. Also no mention is made of the strategic hamlet program wherein rural Vietnamese civilians were forcibly removed by Americans from their ancestral land and driven into fortified camps in order to deprive the VC of any base of support. Also absent is any mention of American-established free-fire zones in which it was "legal" and requisite for any American to shoot any Vietnamese (whether or not the Vietnamese were aware of the zone).

Representations as Related to Date of Publication

There are a number of changes in the novels' representations of the American military, the antiwar movement, and the Vietnamese related to the novels' publication dates. The six novels published during the 1960s, *Special Forces Trooper* (1967), *Orders to Vietnam* (1968), *The Man in the Box* (1968), *Vietnam Nurse* (1968), *Stop & Search* (1969), and *Nurse in Vietnam* (1969), are remarkably similar in their representations of American military personnel and the Vietnamese. The antiwar movement is only mentioned in *Special Forces Trooper*, where it enrages soldiers who never examine any antiwar principles. American military personnel—Green Berets, sailors, pilots, and nurses—often appear to be at least as committed to each other as to stopping communism, although they never directly question the validity of prosecuting a war in order to stop communism. With the exception of *Orders to Vietnam* and *Stop &*

Search, which are about helicopter pilots and sailors, respectively, all of the novels published during the 1960s feature Green Berets, never regular army "grunts." Three of these novels contain one black character each; three contain only white Americans. The soldiers all speak standard English, use little if any profanity or military slang, and do not talk about women. There is no mention of drugs and only occasional mention of alcohol. Nurses in the 1960s novels are stereotypical characters—weak, silly, racist, and more concerned with their appearance than with their safety.

The only three novels in the sample that contain Montagnard characters were published in this early group: *Special Forces Trooper*, *The Man in the Box*, and *Vietnam Nurse*. The representation of all groups of Vietnamese changes little relative to publication date. Even in these novels, the ARVN are thought to be cowardly, and the VC vicious. There is less emphasis on the notion of Vietnamese civilians being victimized by the VC and almost none on the notion of Vietnamese civilians being victimized by Americans.

As novels are published in the early 1970s, there begin to be some real changes. *One Day for Peace* (1971), the first in the group of novels from the 1970s, details a small antiwar group's activities and portrays the group's detractors as small-minded and potentially vicious. Again and again, the idea that antiwar is not anti-American is stressed. This is the first novel to address the larger political issues of the war and to blatantly state that the war was immoral. American soldiers are presented as the victims of an uncaring government.

The other novels of the early 1970s, *Cross-fire* (1972) and *War Year* (1972), take a different angle on the war and the men who fought than the 1960s novels. Harry and John, the respective protagonists, were both draftees, neither of whom wanted to be in Vietnam. In *Cross-fire,* Harry is shown to hold racist attitudes and we see the first use in the sample of the term "gook." Vietnamese civilians are shown as victims of both VC and American aggression, and in the end all of the characters, including Harry, are killed by frightened and/or overzealous Americans. *War Year*, the only novel in the sample to be written by a Vietnam vet, appears to be more like recent portrayals of Vietnam than the 1960s portrayals, to which it is closer in publication date. This is the first novel to indict the army as a ponderous and inefficient bureaucracy. Soldiers drink heavily and use extreme and near-constant profanity (including the first use in the sample of the word *fuck*). Many of the featured soldiers are black and none, including the protagonist, appear to be educated. The representation of the Vietnamese is consistent with earlier novels. The antiwar movement is mentioned in neither *Cross-fire* nor *War Year*.

Children of the Dragon (1974) stands alone by virtue of both its publication date and its content. This is the first and only novel to contain North Vietnamese characters who are represented neither as victims nor as aggressors, but as peaceful people trying to help their fellow Vietnamese in the South win their independence.

Moving into the 1980s, *Where the Elf King Sings* (1980) was the first attempt in the sample to show the lingering effects of the war on veterans and their families. Despite the fact that the term "PTSD" is never used, the returned vet in this novel is the first to have flashbacks and battle with alcoholism as a result of his combat experiences. Vietnam vets are seen as having been victimized by the government who sent them, the protestors who attacked them, and the employers who refused to hire them after the war.

Caribou (1984) is the first novel of those from the 1980s to show a draft evader, albeit one who is not interested in protesting the war. *Travelers* (1986) gives the first mention of the VVAW and the murders at Kent State. The Vietnamese are only casually mentioned in these novels—in both instances as victims. *Charlie Pippin*'s (1987) father, Oscar, is the first black Vietnam vet in the sample. Vets are again represented as victims of both the government and the antiwar movement. Oscar Pippin is the first returned vet who flatly refuses to discuss his painful memories of the war. *Charlie Pippin* is the first and only novel to directly, if briefly, address the special plight of black combat soldiers and also the only novel in which characters visit the Vietnam Memorial in Washington, D.C.

The most complex novel of the sample, *Fallen Angels*, was published in 1988. *Fallen Angels* and the *Echo Company* (1991-1992) series brought a new realism to the representation of the Vietnam War. Combat squads were composed of teenage draftees, many of whom were black and almost all of whom were uneducated. The men in these novels form a deep brotherhood and care far more about each other than stopping the spread of communism. Soldiers here wonder about, if not directly question, their purpose for being in Vietnam. There are liquor, drugs, profanity, and so much military slang that the *Echo* books have a lengthy glossary. The first mentions of racial problems in the army are here. Ranking officers are shown to be incompetent and willing to risk the lives of their men for promotions, and in response, grunts appear to be willing to "frag" (or kill) anyone who recklessly endangers them. The GIs are unable to write home about their ordeal and experience survivor guilt, which lays the groundwork for later PTSD.

Fallen Angels contains the first mention of blatantly and dishonestly inflated body counts and also the first mention of the fact that lower-ranking soldiers did not believe what officers were claiming had been accomplished. The Vietnamese civilians are shown to be the pathetic victims both of American brutality and ignorance and of VC ruthlessness. A scene in which American troops massacre the inhabitants of a hamlet is first shown here. In all of these novels, the portrayal of the Vietnamese is consistent. The ARVN are inept, the VC are superhuman and vicious, and the Vietnamese civilians are victimized by both the Americans and the VC.

In *Echo #3* (1991) we see a "Vietnam nurse" who breaks the stereotype established in the earlier novels. Lieutenant Rebecca Phillips is smart, tough, pragmatic, and sufficiently traumatized by her work to need nightly to drink herself into oblivion.

The three Response to the War novels from the late 1980s to the early 1990s are *And One for All* (1989), *The Best of Friends* (1989), and *Long Time Passing* (1990). In all three novels, boys who join the military are shown to do so without having given the decision much thought. When mentioned, Vietnamese civilians are shown to be the victims of American aggression. In *And One for All* and *The Best of Friends*, many characters view the antiwar movement as traitorous. *Long Time Passing* valorizes the antiwar movement and, like *One Day for Peace*, views the protestors as victims of a brutal and repressive government. *Long Time Passing* (1990) is the first novel to state that pressure from the antiwar movement helped end the Vietnam War.

The four novels from the mid-1990s represent each of the three major categories. *Tough Choices* (1993) and *The Road Home* (1995) both explore the readjustment problems of Vietnam vets immediately upon their return from the war. Both books suggest that some vets may actually miss the war, and *The Road Home* is the sole examination of the experiences of returned female vets. In both of these novels, vets are portrayed as victims of the antiwar movement. Protestors are shown to be at least as antisoldier as they are antiwar. The VC are vicious and the Vietnamese civilians are victims of both the VC and the Americans.

Come in from the Cold (1994) follows in the tradition of *One Day for Peace* (1971) and *Long Time Passing* in its celebration of antiwar sentiment and questioning of government war policies. Finally, *Sing for Your Father, Su Phan* (1997) is the most recent work of adolescent fiction that addresses the war in Vietnam and the only novel to be written by someone who lived in North Vietnam during the war. Fay Tang was a Chinese immigrant who lived in North Vietnam, and this novel is largely based on her family's experiences during the war. Here these Chinese immigrants, if not North Vietnamese civilians, are shown as the victims of the "communists."

Overall, representations of the Vietnamese are remarkably consistent. However, Vietnamese civilians' victimization at the hands of American soldiers becomes more prevalent in later books. The ARVN were consistently inept and despised by the Americans; the VC were always vicious, but were more graphically vicious in the later books, and always respected and feared by the Americans. With the exceptions of *One Day for Peace*, *Long Time Passing*, and *Come in from the Cold*, the antiwar movement is represented as victimizing American GIs. All other novels that contain a scene with protestors also include instances of vets being called "baby-killers" and being spat at. Soldiers were never shown to be enthusiastically committed to stopping the spread of communism in Southeast Asia, and in the later books seem to be committed only to each other. The later books represent the veterans of the Vietnam War as the biggest victims of all—sent to Vietnam by a government that didn't care about them, led in Vietnam by men who were more interested in their careers than their troops' safety, vilified by the antiwar movement, and finally returned to a country that didn't want to hear about their experiences or care about their hardships.

Note

1. The original published objectives of the VVAW, Inc. are:
   - To demand an immediate cessation of fighting and the withdrawal of all American troops from Indochina; we cannot allow one more human being to die senselessly in Indochina.
   - To demonstrate that our military tactics dehumanize soldiers and civilians, and to make clear the underlying governmental policies of the U.S. military and the Nixon administration in prosecuting an unjust and immoral war can effectively voice their opinions.
   - To bring together a national coalition of veterans, National Guard and reservists, and active-duty servicemen and women for peace, so that the men and women who have first-hand knowledge of the military and the Indochina war can effectively voice their opinions.
   - To show that opposition to the war does not stem from cowardice or disloyalty; the best way to keep faith with our fighting men is to BRING THEM BACK ALIVE—NOW!!
   - To show that Americans allow their society to be pervaded by a racism which lets us view Asians and our own minorities as less-than-human. This racism pushes our minorities through inferior schools and into the combat arms. Thus, we send our minorities off to die in disproportionately high numbers while we kill Asians indiscriminately. We demand that the military recognized its complicity in America's domestic and international racism.
   - To demand an immediate increase in Veteran's Administration funds to correct the deplorably inhumane conditions that prevail in VA hospitals, and to facilitate the initiation of rehabilitative programs responsive to the needs of all veterans.
   - To make clear that the U.S. has never undertaken an extensive, open investigation of American war crimes in Indochina. We demand that the U.S. government, in its war in Indochina, affirm the responsibility of the individual soldier to refrain from committing war crimes. We also recognize that the ultimate and primary responsibility and guilt of American war crimes lies with our policy makers at all levels.
   - To demand that all active-duty servicemen and women be afforded the same rights that are guaranteed by the U.S. Constitution and Bill of Rights that are presently denied by the Uniform Code of Military Justice. We demand the immediate reform of the UCMJ. We endorse the efforts of the American Servicemen's Union to win a Bill of Rights for servicemen.

- To support active-duty GIs refusing orders to fight in Southeast Asia. We support all Americans refusing to be drafted.
- To deplore inhumane treatment of all persons imprisoned as a result of the Indochina conflict.

Chapter Seven

Conclusions

This study began with the assertion that there is currently a "culture war" raging in America and that this war is "ultimately about the struggle for domination"—"a struggle to achieve or maintain the power to define reality" (Hunter, 1991, p. 52). Hunter maintains that "whether about foreign affairs or domestic politics, . . . public debate in America has never been framed merely in terms of a competition of different interest but as a struggle between good and evil" (p. 62). This "public debate" includes a myriad of domestic and foreign issues—NAFTA, Bosnia, Iraq, abortion rights, affirmative action, multicultural education, the expanding literary canon, among others—all of which involve traditional and progressive factions battling for the position to disseminate their views and interpretations of these situations.

One part of this cultural struggle consists of varying interpretations of what actually happened in Vietnam, why it happened, and what it means to us as Americans today. Cultural critics Louvre and Walsh (1988) summarize this struggle to "interpret Vietnam" in the introduction to their book, which analyzes attempts by different groups to appropriate the meaning of the war.

> More than a decade after the end of hostilities, the Vietnam War continues to be a crucial litmus of American values. The war of interpretation, the battle for ideological appropriation of the war, continues unabated, fueled at one level perhaps by personal guilts and obsessions, at another by the need to promote versions of America's past that enhance its present status and—not least—by the promise of commercial gain. Vietnam is enduring trauma, opportunity for political image-making and good box-office all rolled into one. (p. xi)

Despite Louvre and Walsh's later argument that the "second phase of America's Indochina war is being fought, this time not in jungles or on paddy fields but on cinema screens and in the pages of comics and pulp novels," very few of the studies of Vietnam film or adult fiction frame their analysis from this perspective (p. 1). This study, however, does situate the analysis of adolescent Vietnam War fiction within the context of an ideological culture war. I maintain that historiographically, a very narrow range of perspective is presented in the novels, and that, in fact, as a group, they tend to be both ahistorical and apolitical.

Vietnam scholar and historian John Clark Pratt (1987) advises analysts of Vietnam literature to establish as part of a frame of reference both the "approximate place and time period of the books' internal action" (quoted in Lomperis, 1987, p. 124). This is virtually impossible in eight of the Combat novels and two of the Response to the War novels as no setting date is given. Only vague place names are given for the majority of the Combat novels—e.g., south of Saigon, the Mekong Delta, the Central Highlands. In the *Echo Company* series, the date is only obliquely given (as a reference to being five years after JFK's assassination), and not even that until nearly the end of the second book in the series. This lack of specificity is perhaps an attempt on the part of the authors to make their stories seem more universal, or perhaps a result of a lack of author research. But whatever the reason, the lack of specificity contributes to the ahistorical nature of the novels. When readers know neither specifically where nor when events in historical fiction occur, it is difficult for them to assess authenticity.

Another factor that significantly contributes toward the ahistorical nature of these novels is the fact that the novels focus almost exclusively on the individuals who fought the war in Vietnam, rather than on any larger issues (Dittmar & Michaud, 1990). Taxel (1980) also came to the same conclusion in his study of adolescent fiction of the American Revolution, claiming that "many of the books . . . display an increased preoccupation with the psychological state of the protagonist, a concern which leads, in some cases, to a deemphasis of the importance given to discussion of the issues involved in the conflict" (p. 117). In this instance, Taxel was referring to adolescent American Revolution novels that had been written between 1967 and 1975. It would seem, then, that the war novels studied, written during or after America's involvement in Vietnam, tend to examine individuals rather than larger issues. Novels as a literary form do, by their very nature, traditionally focus on the experiences of individuals. However, some novels situate narratives about individuals within a larger political, social, or historical context. The adolescent novel *Across Five Aprils* (Hunt, 1964) carefully tells Jethro's story set against his family's involvement in both sides of the War Between the States. Author Irene Hunt gives a moving personal account of a boy's experience during a time of war while also presenting, in meticulous detail, the historical and political context of the war itself. Authors of the Vietnam War novels used in this study chose to focus their collective narrative lens on the experiences of individuals to the exclusion of larger issues.

Referring to Vietnam War films, Dittmar and Michaud (1990) again comment on the lack of attempt to explain the historical or political context in which the Vietnam War was situated. The same generalization can be made about adolescent fiction about the Vietnam War.

> Several of the standard war-movie plots are missing from the Vietnam canon. These include the "command-level" films that were especially popular in the late 1940s. . . . These films were intent on explaining "The Big Picture" to American audiences; their task was to help the audience understand and come to terms with the sacrifices of individual men and women within the larger context of defeating the global territorial and political aspirations of America's enemies. (p. 5)

None of the novels in the sample were found to operate on this "command-level" and, in fact, low-ranking soldiers were by far the most frequent type of protagonist.

When Vietnam narratives (adolescent or adult, literary or cinematic) consistently do not ask larger political questions (e.g., what was America's real purpose in Vietnam? were these purposes moral, valid, or even feasible?), the idea of questioning becomes marginalized through its constant absence. In his evaluation of the representations of Christopher Columbus in children's books, Meltzer (1992) urged the asking of larger political questions, warning that "if we do not learn how to ask probing questions about the past, how will we meet the challenges of the present?" (p. 2). Writing specifically about the Vietnam movie *Platoon*, Porteous (1989) reiterates this notion of marginalization, which applies equally to adolescent novels as to this particular film.

> [*Platoon*] ignores the issues of political and military responsibility altogether. Above all, by dwelling, like many other veterans' accounts, on America's lost innocence, the film, like them, pays strikingly little attention to the far greater suffering of the Vietnamese, including those for whose freedom the U.S. ostensibly fought. It says nothing, either, about the political dimensions of the struggle. By these silences it perpetuates the kind of thinking, or lack of it, that made the war possible in the first place. (p. 158)

These consistent textual silences to which Porteous refers reinforce the lack of political and historical questioning of America's involvement in Vietnam.

If these novels focus only on the horror of war and the extreme terror that soldiers endured, they may serve to demythologize the perception of war as a glorious undertaking. This continual concentration on the misery of those involved in war can actually serve to co-opt antiwar sentiment. If we believe, as General Sherman stated regarding the War Between the States, that war is hell, then these novels can be said to advance the notion that a guerrilla war in the jungles of Southeast Asia is really, *really* hell. This concept, which on the surface appears to be critical of the war, is in fact only a commiseration with the plight of the combat soldier. Sympathizing with the extraordinary torment of soldiers who were in combat is not the same as questioning why they were in Vietnam in the first place.

In chapter 2 I examined several studies of the discussion of the Vietnam War in adolescent history textbook series. The original discussion was framed by the conclusion drawn by Anyon (1979) in her study of U.S. history texts:

> The school curriculum has contributed to the formation of attitudes that make it easier for powerful groups, those whose knowledge is legitimized by school studies, to manage and control society. Textbooks not only express the dominant groups' ideologies, but also help to form attitudes in support of their position. (p. 382)

This general idea of the selective tradition operating in history texts was specifically illustrated by studies that examined the discussion of the Vietnam War in history texts. Many of the conclusions drawn in those studies can be extended to the novels in this study. FitzGerald (1979) states that the "majority of the best-selling texts still have no firm grip on Vietnam geography or nomenclature" and that the texts are full of "inaccuracies and misspellings" (p. 124). She also found that the texts she examined contained "no reference, or almost none, to the peace movement or to any of the political turmoil of the late 1960s and early 1970s" (p. 127). Claiming that history texts are full of "distortion[s] and omissions" and "do not call into question any of the major premises of American foreign policy . . . that formed the foundation of the Vietnam War," Griffen and Marciano (1979) believe that these factors contribute to a lack of critical questioning of the Vietnam War (pp. xvii, 168).

> The treatment of the Vietnam War in American textbooks serves as one of the means by which schools perform their larger social functions. Their most basic function is to obtain an uncritical *acceptance* of the present society, thus hindering rational analyses of conflicts such as Vietnam. . . . It is not surprising that textbooks have served this role, in that they must reinforce, not critically question, the larger political goals of the educational system. There is no conspiracy at work; it is merely that the texts must serve the more primary purpose—which is to have students support U.S. foreign policies rather than consider them critically and possibly reject them. (pp. 164-165)

Given that the novels in this study could be considered part of a school's informal curriculum and that the readers of adolescent Vietnam fiction are the next generation of potential soldiers and war supporters, this assessment takes on a rather alarming tone. While textbooks and trade books are not equivalent and maintain different purposes and functions, novels do serve as a means of communicating historical knowledge (Brown, 1986; Taxel, 1989; Vandell, 1991). One novel in the sample does, however, seem to blur the line between trade book and textbook. *Tough Choices: A Story of the Vietnam War* (1993) is part of the "Once upon America" series of books written for young adults that address issues of historical fiction. The advertising blurbs from the book jacket indicate that the reviewers believe that *Tough Choices* will be used as part of a school social studies curriculum. Some examples include

> "Performs a valuable service for young readers. . . . Purposeful stories
>   that work as entertainment."—*Booklist*
> "Breathes color and life into a social studies curriculum."—*Publishers
>   Weekly*
> "Effective snapshots of the past."—*School Library Journal*

Tough Choices presents a very conservative and narrow view of the war and an extremely negative view of the antiwar movement. These review comments all imply that the information in the book is factual and that it is actually just an interesting textbook—not a work of fiction. The jacket blurbs are included here because I feel that they imply that "Once upon America" novels are in fact to be used as the equivalent of history textbooks—a manner in which novels do serve as a means through which to communicate historical knowledge.

Previous research on the selective tradition in adolescent fiction (Luke, Cook, & Luke, 1986; Meltzer, 1992; Taxel, 1980, 1981, 1989, 1992) has examined how adolescent fiction and curricular materials have traditionally and consistently marginalized and/or excluded certain groups and views and that, in turn, these texts can serve to reinforce and reproduce the existing hegemony of ideas and relations within our society. This study's examination of adolescent Vietnam War fiction fits squarely within that tradition. The parallel reinforcement of some information and exclusion of others is found in this sample. Three basic concepts are frequently reinforced: first, the equation of antiwar sentiments and activities with antisoldier and anti-American sentiments and activities; second, the notion that only those men who have served in Vietnam have any right to express anything other than a pro-war opinion; and third, the nonquestioning attitude of American soldiers and civilians toward the government's war policies. This last point can help to reproduce a citizen/government relationship in which citizens (whether military or civilian) do not question their leaders' decisions and policies or at least a relationship in which citizens carry out government policies without significant resistance.

This sample of twenty-eight novels regularly excludes or marginalizes certain groups and views. Only five of the twenty-eight novels have Vietnamese or Montagnard protagonists or coprotagonists. Very little is mentioned or examined with regard to the people for whose supposed benefit and in whose country this war was fought. None of the novels were authored by Vietnamese or Montagnard writers, so no true Vietnamese or Montagnard is shown. Only Fay Tang, (*Sing for Your Father, Su Phan*, 1997), who is Chinese but lived in North Vietnam during the war, comes close. I do not mean to imply that authors from one ethnic or cultural group cannot successfully or authentically write about members of another ethnic or cultural group, merely that in this sample there are no Vietnamese or Montagnard authors to represent the perspectives of their group.

Antiwar attitudes are consistently marginalized, if not outrightly excluded from the novels. The experiences of American women (military and civilian) in Vietnam are often trivialized on the few occasions that they're even mentioned. Their experiences as returned veterans are only mentioned in one novel. Twenty-four novels make absolutely no mention of American female involvement in Vietnam. Minority and working-class characters are numerically well represented in the Platoon novels—perhaps the most realistic of the Combat novels. The other categories contain few, if any, characters from racial or ethnic minorities.

Not only are certain groups and opinions marginalized or excluded from these novels, vast and important pieces of historical information are nowhere to be found. Vital information regarding events in Vietnam are never mentioned in the sample. The corrupt American-supported Diem government in Saigon, with its oppressive policies toward the Buddhists and the South Vietnamese peasantry, is mentioned in only one novel. The fact that Diem was killed in an American-acknowledged coup and that each replacement regime was ousted by a violent coup is never discussed (Sheehan, 1988). The Hue massacre and its various interpretations are never mentioned. The My Lai massacre is only referred to in passing in one Returned Vet novel. Neither the strategic hamlet program (an American policy that forced Vietnamese civilians off their ancestral lands and into prison-like reservations) nor the desertion of American allies (both Vietnamese and Montagnard) by American troops when leaving Vietnam are even alluded to. The list could go on and on. What remains is a relatively homogeneous representation of the American experience in Vietnam.

None of the novels articulated a specific historiographical interpretation of the war consistent with one of the positions held by Vietnam War historians—whether quagmire, revisionist, or radical. The novels as a group can be considered ahistorical when the only reason given for the war is the containment of communist expansion coupled with the domino theory. This is an underlying cause or purpose of the war in both quagmire and revisionist historiographies, but the novels rarely contain any further analysis. Sam in *To Stand against the Wind* (1978) is the only character to interpret the war in terms of a quagmire. Uncle Ben in *Charlie Pippin* (1987) interprets the war in revisionist terms. Mr. Simon in *One Day for Peace* (1971) and Dan in *The Best of Friends* (1989) both suggest a radical interpretation of the war as imperialist meddling in a sovereign state's internal affairs.

Interestingly, while many studies of adult Vietnam narratives (novels and films) comment on the fact that the narratives are apolitical and/or ahistorical, none really venture a hypothesis to explain this situation. While any idea could be only speculative, my conjecture includes a combination of the following three points. First, more "neutral" narratives are perhaps more likely to be marketable. Given the economically driven nature of the publishing industry, a novel that takes a strong political stand on a potentially divisive issue such as the Vietnam War risks alienating certain readers, thereby chipping away at a broad consumer base. Second, it is possible that authors are unwilling or unable to do the sort of research necessary to place a narrative in a more specific historical and/or political context. Given the recent interest in Vietnam, authors may choose to set a combat story in that war as opposed, for example, to World War II or the American Revolution. Third, if authors are not clear about their own historiographical stance on Vietnam, then it would surely be difficult for them to create a narrative with a consistent historiography.

American cultural myths are a significant means of reproducing American national identity. As James Hunter (1991) reminds us, cultural myths are "constructed through a selective interpretation of our national history"; they also "articulate the precedents and ideals for the nation's future" and "set out the national priorities" (p. 55). Cultural myths resonate through our perceptions of people and situations; they provide a framework through which to interpret the past while suggesting action for the future. They are an immensely powerful, though largely hidden, force that influences our understanding of ourselves, both nationally and individually, and the world around us. The first set of American cultural myths examined were those of the frontier hero, the regeneration scenario, and technical proficiency. Earlier Combat novels tended to contain characters who embodied the qualities of frontier heroes and who were more than likely Green Berets—a group with strong ties to American mythology. Later Combat novels occasionally attributed frontier qualities to characters, while novels in other groups did not.

The regeneration myth was frequently supported in the Duty novels. It was consistently contradicted in the Vietnamese Perspective and Platoon subcategories. The war is presented as something only to survive, not to win, and the defense of the Vietnamese is presented as so destructive that as many civilians are killed by the attacking enemy as by the defending Americans. Each Response to the War novel contains a character who casts the war in regenerative and sacred terms and one who questions the accuracy of this belief—subverting the regeneration myth.

The myth of technical proficiency is only significantly addressed in the Duty and Platoon novels. The Duty novels all attribute complete technical proficiency to American GIs. While soldiers in the Platoon books are not incompetent, they hardly take on the superhuman proficiency of the Duty soldiers. The proficiency myth is subverted in two ways: American soldiers in each category are prevented from prosecuting the war to the fullest extent of their capabilities because of government bureaucracy, and ultimately the VC are equally, if not more, proficient than the Americans. Given the inherent respect Americans have for skill, the myth is subverted when those that are most skillful and proficient are the enemy.

The second set of American cultural myths discussed were the complementary myths of militarism and moralism. Militarism addressed the skills required of men as soldiers, while moralism addressed the soldier's innate morality, which serves as a check on his militarism. As before, the myths were most frequently addressed in the Combat novels, although less frequently than the myths previously discussed. They myth of militarism is upheld in the Duty novels even when briefly questioned by an occasional character. Militarism is, however, consistently contradicted in the Platoon novels. The GIs in the Platoon novels question the value of militarism and neither accept nor display its characteristics. The actions they perform as soldiers function mainly to protect their lives and the lives of their friends—not to further a military goal.

As with militarism, the moralism myth is consistently supported in the Duty novels and nearly always subverted in the Platoon novels. There are, however, instances in the Platoon novels that marginally support the notion of an inherent moralism in American soldiers. GIs begin the Platoon novels as relatively moral soldiers, but as they experience more and more combat they become less and less moral. One character in the Response to the War novel *Long Time Passing* (1990) questions whether militarism and moralism are in fact complementary and, finally, concludes that it is actually militarism that destroys moralism. Overall, the myth of militarism is roughly subverted more vehemently than it is ever supported.

This frequent subversion or contradiction of American cultural myths addressing war cannot necessarily be assumed to indicate an antiwar stance. Cultural myths, when not teased out and examined, exist largely below surface. They resonate with us as Americans because they are an embedded part of our culture—not because we have learned to recognize and isolate them. I would argue that the subversion of cultural war myths found especially in the Platoon novels has perhaps become something of a "genre convention" in regard to representations (particularly of combat) in the Vietnam War. By a genre convention, I mean a narrative tradition, whether written or cinematic, in which certain situations, events, or characters have come to be commonly portrayed within a larger sphere of possibilities. For example, in either suspense or horror narratives, the protagonist/victim is very likely to be a female (Overstreet, 1994). Using female characters as victims in suspense or horror narratives is a genre convention. By that same token, consistently representing American soldiers in Vietnam in situations that subvert American cultural myths has perhaps become a genre convention as authors emulate those authors who have gone before. After Vietnam vet author Joe Haldeman first published the semiautobiographical *War Year* in 1972, subverting the myths, the other Platoon novels followed suit. Given that the most frequently seen soldiers and situations subvert these myths (Rasmussen & Downey, 1991), perhaps this has become the "standard" manner of envisioning war in Vietnam. In essence, the fact that American cultural myths have been consistently subverted in Vietnam narratives is not necessarily indicative of the fact that our cultural myths are, in fact, changing, but that perhaps this is the manner in which the war in Vietnam has conventionally come to be represented. I would speculate that there is something of a circular relation between the subversion of cultural myths and the fact that the war was lost—i.e., the war was lost because American soldiers' myth-influenced beliefs about war were contradicted (subverted) by their experiences in Vietnam, *and* in turn, the myths continue to be subverted in narratives because the war was lost. My notion that American cultural war myths are not actually changing might be tested by evaluating the treatment of these same myths in any narratives addressing America's involvement in the Persian Gulf War—a war that President Bush claimed ended the "Vietnam syndrome" once and for all.

The antiwar movement and the Vietnamese were represented with real consistency in the novels about the Vietnam War. Considering the extent of these two groups' involvement in the war and events surrounding the war, the antiwar movement and the Vietnamese are regularly underrepresented in the adolescent fiction examined—not even mentioned in many of the novels. The tenets of the antiwar movement are most often treated dismissively and are accompanied by ad hominem attacks on antiwar activists. In various novels, the antiwar movement is blamed for harming soldiers both psychologically and physically. Anti-antiwar characters in the novels appear to have great difficulty in separating antiwar sentiment from antisoldier or anti-American ideas. The novels in the Returned Vet category consistently represent the antiwar activists spitting and calling Vietnam veterans murderers and/or baby-killers.

While this sort of exchange may have occasionally taken place, the novels contain only these types of incidents and exclude any mention of the larger purposes of the antiwar movement. In the entire sample, only *Long Time Passing* (1990) advances the idea that the antiwar movement may, in fact, have significantly contributed to ending American involvement in Vietnam.

The Vietnamese are also consistently represented in the novels regardless of their date of publication or narrative structure. Characters in the novels have a tendency to perceive all Vietnamese in a racist manner. The Vietnamese themselves are small, primitive, and inscrutable and their language is sing-song. ARVN soldiers are inept and cowardly. The NVA and VC are demonized as inhumanly vicious, but respected by the Americans for their military skill. The VC and the NVA are repeatedly referred to as "communists" and this makes a significant contribution to their demonization. Given that "communist" and "communism" are such loaded terms in our society, calling a whole group "communist" immediately makes them an enemy. The Vietnamese and Montagnard civilians are consistently represented as pathetic victims. These civilians are purposely the victims of VC cruelty, and occasionally the accidental victims of American ignorance and an inability to distinguish civilians from VC.

The representation of American soldiers displays the widest range of variation of the three groups examined, with both publication date and narrative structure contributing to the variation. The earlier books in the Duty and Vietnamese Perspective novels have a tendency to portray soldiers in a G.I. Joe-like fashion. They are tall, strong, brave, clean-cut, white supermen. The Vietnam nurses are stereotypically presented as weak, silly, and more concerned with their appearances and their Green Beret boyfriends than with their own safety. Soldiers in the Platoon novels take on a wholly different perspective in that GIs are often draftees who resent their forced participation in the war. GIs in the Platoon novels are extremely young (protagonists are seventeen, eighteen, and nineteen), regularly use strong profanity, drink, and talk about women. Soldiers are split evenly along racial lines and racial tensions within the military are acknowledged. The Platoon soldiers show the beginning of PTSD and uncommunicativeness on the part of combatants, which is later manifested in the Returned Vet novels. Finally, in both the Platoon and Returned Vet novels, Vietnam vets are represented as victims of an uncaring government, an unappreciative American public, and a malicious and treasonous antiwar movement. And as Appy (1993) reminds us, when the focus is on Vietnam vets as victims, then larger political questions are less likely to be asked because of the compassion we feel for them as victims. If we truly perceive Vietnam vets as victims, then we may feel that probing questions (about, e.g., the morality of American actions in Vietnam) would cause vets unnecessary pain and continue their victimization.

A Few Limitations

One of my primary goals in doing this research was to determine the versions of the Vietnam War that have been written for young adult readers. An immediate limitation of the study rests in the fact that readers of the ages intended for these books were not consulted for the meaning they may make from these texts.

I would make no claim that every reader would perceive these twenty-eight adolescent novels in precisely the same manner that I have. I am only one adult reader examining this adolescent fiction through a very specific and particular lens—that of a political and historical critic who makes no claim that adolescent readers would necessarily make the same meanings as I have with these same texts. Despite these caveats, I feel that my interpretations of these texts are defensible in light of the fact that they have been situated within a larger body of research exploring the history, cultural mythology, and scholarly representations examined here on a smaller scale. Rosenblatt (1978) argues that while different readers make different meanings with the same text and that even the same reader makes different meanings with the same texts at different times, readings are constrained by the text. Rosenblatt asserts that "two prime criteria of validity [of interpretation] . . . are that the reader's interpretation not be contradicted by any element of the text, and that nothing be projected for which there is no verbal basis" (p. 115). I feel that I have provided textual support for my interpretations. Despite my critical view of these twenty-eight novels, it is not my intention to either discourage or recommend the reading of these books by any age reader. It is also not my intention to imply that I believe that authors *should* have addressed larger political and/or historical issues through their fiction, only that I believe they did not. By that same token, I would also state that I do not believe that the novels in this sample would have been better or more desirable had their authors included these larger issues, only different. In much the same manner that Irene Hunt tells a family's story set against the larger social, political, and historical issues of the War Between the States in *Across Five Aprils* (1964), it would be wonderful if there were some adolescent novels that treated the Vietnam War similarly.

Despite the fact that I have situated my analysis of adolescent Vietnam War novels within a larger theoretical framework that recognizes the influence of a conservative selective tradition, I would point out that I do not believe that there is a great conspiracy at work in the world of adolescent fiction. By this I mean that I do not believe that authors have conspired to create novels that continue to present information about the Vietnam War in a conservative manner in order to prepare the next generation of potential soldiers. However, regardless of authorial intent, the novels continue to privilege certain views (often, although not always, conservative) on the Vietnam War while marginalizing or excluding others. Even if authors feel that they are just telling a story, the theoretical framework of this study posits that no literature is "devoid of ideological content" (Eagleton, 1976, p. 17) and that all authors represent some ideology in their writing (Christian, 1984; Hunt, 1991; Leeson, 1977; Taxel, 1980).

A final issue that should be addressed is the possible implication that this research may have for classroom teachers. Regardless of the fact that I believe that all literature advances an ideological position, whether blatant or subtle, I would hope that teachers, librarians, and those who choose literature for young readers do not take this sort of information and create a type of censorship. Students do not necessarily need to be protected from literature whose ideology is not consistent with our own. Students should be taught to examine these issues critically, both independently and in a classroom context. Of course, this should be extended to all reading, fiction and nonfiction, not just literature that addresses politically sensitive issues.

A critical examination of adolescent Vietnam novels by students might serve as an informative base from which to study the war or to study the way in which historical information and perceptions can be included in fiction. All of the Platoon novels skillfully present the gritty and miserable reality of the experience of combat soldiers in Vietnam. These engrossing descriptions could lend a more personal or human face to a historical study of the war in Vietnam. Students could benefit from studying the varying historiographical perspectives on the war in order to understand that there is not necessarily a "true history" and that, as Edward Carr reminds us, "history means interpretation" (1961, p. 26).

Bibliography

Anyon, J. (1979). Ideology and United States history textbooks. *Harvard Educational Review, 49*, 361-386.

Appy, C. G. (1993). *Working-class war: American combat soldiers and Vietnam.* Chapel Hill: University of North Carolina Press.

Auster, A., & Quart, L. (1988). *How the war was remembered: Hollywood and Vietnam.* New York: Praeger.

Banfield, B. (1985). Racism in children's books: An Afro-American perspective. In D. MacCann and G. Woodard (Eds.), *The black American in books for children: Readings in racism* (pp. 23-38), (2nd ed.). Metuchen, NJ: Scarecrow Press.

Baritz, L. (1985). *Backfire: A history of how American culture led us into Vietnam and made us fight the way we did.* New York: W. Morrow.

Benjamin, W. (1979). Theories of German Fascism: On the collection of essays *War and warrior*, edited by Ernst Jünger (J. Wikoff Trans.). *New German Critique, 17*, 120-128. (Original work published in 1930).

Brown, J. (1986). Into the minds of babes: Children's books and the past. In S. P. Benson, S. Brier, & R. Rosenzweig (Eds.), *Presenting the past: Essays on history and the public* (pp. 67-84). Philadelphia: Temple University Press.

Burd, S. (1992, September 30). Humanities chief assails politicization of classrooms. *The Chronicle of Higher Education*, pp. A21-22.

Capps, W. H. (1990). *The unfinished war: Vietnam and the American conscious.* Boston: Beacon Press.

Carr, E. H. (1961). *What is history?* New York: Vintage Books.

Cheney, L. V. (1987). *American memory: A report on the humanities in the nation's public schools.* Washington, DC: National Endowment for the Humanities.

Christian, L. K. (1984). *Becoming a woman through romance: Adolescent novels and the ideology of femininity.* Unpublished doctoral dissertation, University of Wisconsin, Madison.

deBenedetti, C. (1990). *An American ordeal: The antiwar movement of the Vietnam era.* Syracuse: Syracuse University Press.

Department of Defense. (1985). *U.S. casualties in Southeast Asia: Statistics as of April 30, 1985.* Washington, DC: Directorate for Information, Operations, and Reports.

Dittmar, L., & Michaud, G. (1990). America's Vietnam war films: Marching toward denial. In L. Dittmar & G. Michaud (Eds.), *From Hanoi to Hollywood: The Vietnam war in American film* (pp. 1-15). New Brunswick, NJ: Rutgers University Press.

Divine, R. A. (Winter 1988). Vietnam reconsidered. *Diplomatic History*, 79-93.

Eagleton, T. (1976). *Marxism and literature.* Berkeley: University of California Press.

Eagleton, T. (1983). *Literary theory.* Minneapolis: University of Minnesota Press.

Edison, R. B. (1994). *It hurt then and it still hurts now!* Unpublished manuscript.

Elson, R. M. (1964). *Guardians of tradition: American schoolbooks of the nineteenth century.* Lincoln: University of Nebraska Press.

FitzGerald, F. (1972). *Fire in the lake: The Vietnamese and the Americans in Vietnam.* Boston: Little, Brown.

FitzGerald, F. (1979). *America revised: History schoolbooks in the twentieth century.* Boston: Little, Brown.

Fleming, D. B., & Nurse, R. (1982). Vietnam revised: Are our textbooks changing? *Social Education, 46*, 338-343.

Foner, E., & Wiener, J. (1991, July 29/August 5). Fighting for the West. *The Nation*, 163-166.

Frisch, M. H. (1986). The memory of history. In S. P. Benson, S. Brier, & R. Rosenzweig (Eds.), *Presenting the past: Essays on history and the public* (pp. 5-17). Philadelphia: Temple University Press.

Fromkin, D., & Chace, J. (1985). What *are* the lessons of Vietnam? *Foreign Affairs, 63*, 722-746.

Gitlin, T. (1987). *The sixties: Years of hope, days of rage*. New York: Bantam.

Griffen, W. L., & Marciano, J. (1979). *Teaching the Vietnam War: A critical examination of school texts and an interpretive comparative history utilizing* The Pentagon Papers *and other documents*. Montclair, NJ: Allanheld, Osmun & Co.

Halberstam, D. (1965). *The making of a quagmire*. New York: Random House.

Hellmann, J. (1986). *American myth and the legacy of Vietnam*. New York: Columbia University Press.

Herr, M. (1977). *Dispatches*. New York: Alfred A. Knopf.

Hess, M. (1993). *Then the Americans came: Voices from Vietnam*. New York: Four Walls Eight Windows.

Holland, N. N. (1975). Unity identity text self. In J. P. Thompkins (Ed.), *Reader-response criticism* (pp. 118-133). Baltimore: Johns Hopkins University Press.

Holsti, O. R., & Rosenau, J. N. (1986). Consensus lost, consensus regained?: Foreign policy beliefs of American leaders, 1976-1980. *International Studies Quarterly, 30*, 393.

Hunt, I. (1964). *Across five Aprils*. Chicago: Follett.

Hunt, P. L. (1991). *Criticism, theory, and children's literature*. Cambridge, MA: Basil Blackwell.

Hunter, J. D. (1991). *Culture wars: The struggle to redefine America*. New York: Basic Books.

Iser, W. (1974). The reading process: A phenomenological approach. In J. P. Thompkins (Ed.), *Reader-response criticism* (pp. 50-69). Baltimore: Johns Hopkins University Press.

Jameson, F. (1972). The great American hunter, or, ideological content in the novel. *College English, 34,* 180-199.

Johannessen, L. R. (1992). *Illumination rounds: Teaching the literature of the Vietnam War.* Urbana, IL: National Council of Teachers of English.

Kelly, R. G. (1974, May). Literature and the historian. *American Quarterly,* pp. 141-159.

Klein, M. (1990). Historical memory, film, and the Vietnam era. In L. Dittmar & G. Michaud (Eds.), *From Hanoi to Hollywood: The Vietnam War in American film* (pp. 19-40). New Brunswick, NJ: Rutgers University Press.

Kolko, G. (1969). *The roots of American foreign policy: An analysis of power and purpose.* Boston: Beacon Press.

Kroll, B. M. (1992). *Teaching hearts and minds: College students reflect on the Vietnam War in literature.* Carbondale: Southern Illinois University Press.

Leeson, R. (1977). *Children's books and class society: Past and present.* London: Writers and Readers Publishing Cooperative.

Lens, S. (1990). *Vietnam: A war on two fronts.* New York: Lodestar Books.

Lewy, G. (1978). *America in Vietnam.* New York: Oxford University Press.

Logan, W. C., & Needham, R. L. (1985). What elementary school social studies textbooks tell about the Vietnam War. *The Social Studies, 76*(5), 207-211.

Lomperis, T. J. (1987). *"Reading the wind": The literature of the Vietnam War.* Durham, NC: Duke University Press.

Louvre, A., & Walsh, J. (Eds.). (1988). *Tell me lies about Vietnam: Cultural battles for the meaning of the war.* Philadelphia: Open University Press.

Luke, A., Cooke, J., & Luke, C. (1986). The selective tradition in action: Gender bias in student teachers' selections of children's literature. *English Education, 18,* 209-219.

Martin, A. V. (1987). Critical approaches to American cultural studies: The Vietnam War in history, literature, and film (Doctoral dissertation, The University of Iowa). *Dissertation Abstracts International, 49,* 856A.

McCloud, B. (1989). *What should we tell our children about Vietnam?* Norman: University of Oklahoma Press.

McCombs, M. (1994). *Good times.* Unpublished manuscript.

McKeever, R. J. (1989). American myths and the impact of the Vietnam War: Revisionism in foreign policy and popular cinema of the 1980s. In J. Walsh & J. Aulick (Eds.) *Vietnam images: War and representation* (pp. 43-56). New York: St. Martin's Press.

Meltzer, M. (1992). Selective forgetfulness: Christopher Columbus reconsidered. *The New Advocate, 5,* 1-9.

National Center for History in the Schools. (1996). *National standards for history, basic edition.* Los Angeles: UCLA.

National Center for History in the Schools. (1994). *National standards for United States history: Exploring the American experience, expanded edition.* Los Angeles: UCLA.

Newman, J., & Hilfinger, A. (1988). *Vietnam War literature: An annotated bibliography of imaginative works about Americans fighting in Vietnam.* (2nd ed.). Metuchen, NJ: Scarecrow Press.

Nixon, R. M. (1985). *No more Vietnams.* New York: Arbor House.

Orwell, G. (1949). *1984.* New York: Harcourt, Brace, Jovanovich.

Overstreet, D. W. (1994). Help! Help!: A study of female victims in the novels of Lois Duncan. *ALAN Review, 21*(3) 43-45.

Paterson, T. G. (1988, Winter). Historical memory and illusive victories: Vietnam and Central America. *Diplomatic History,* 1-18.

Pelz, S. (1990, Winter). Vietnam: Another stroll down alibi alley. *Diplomatic History,* 123-130.

Peshkin, A. (1988). In search of subjectivity: One's own. *Educational Researcher, 17*(7), 17-21.

Podhoretz, N. (1982). *Why we were in Vietnam.* New York: Simon & Schuster.

Porteous, K. (1989). History lessons: *Platoon.* In J. Walsh & J. Aulick (Eds.), *Vietnam images: War and representation* (pp. 153-159). New York: St. Martin's Press.

Pratt, J. C. (1987). *Vietnam voices: Perspectives on the war years, 1941-1982.* New York: Viking.

Provo, J. (1994). *Guilt/Bros.* Unpublished manuscript.

Quivey, J. (1988) When buffaloes fight it is the grass that suffers: Narrative distance in Asa Barber's *Land of a million elephants.* In W.

J. Searle (Ed.), *Search and clear: Literature and films of the Vietnam War* (pp. 95-104). Bowling Green, OH: Bowling Green State University Popular Press.

Rasmussen, K., & Downey, S. D. (1991). Dialectical disorientation in Vietnam War films: Subversion of the mythology of war. *Quarterly Journal of Speech, 77*, 176-195.

Ringnalda, D. (1990). Unlearning to remember Vietnam. In O. W. Gilman & L. Smith (Eds.), *America rediscovered: Critical essays on literature and film of the Vietnam War.* New York: Garland Publishing.

Robbins, C. (1988). *Air America: The true story of the CIA's mercenary fliers in covert operations from pre-war China to the present day.* London: Corgi.

Rosenblatt, L. (1978). *The reader, the text, the poem.* Carbondale: Southern Illinois University Press.

Saul, E. W. (1985). Witness for the innocent: Children's literature and the Vietnam War. *Issues in Education, 3*(3), 185-197.

Schlesinger, A. M., Jr. (1992). *The disuniting of America.* New York: W. W. Morton & Co.

Scott, J. W. (1992). The campaign against political correctness: What's really at stake. *Radical History Review, 54*, 59-79.

Sheehan, N. (1988). *A bright, shining lie: John Paul Vann and America in Vietnam.* New York: Random House.

Sims Bishop, R. (1990). Fifty years of exploring children's books. In E. J. Farrell and J. R. Squire (Eds.), *Transactions with literature: A fifty year perspective.* Urbana, IL: National Council of Teachers of English.

Spradley, J. P., & McCurdy, D. W. (1980). *Anthropology: The cultural perspective* (2nd ed.). Prospect Heights, IL: Waveland Press.

Stewart, M. E. (1986). *Ambiguous violence: Myths of regeneration and proficiency in U.S. novels about the war.* Madison, WI: Center for Southeast Asian Studies.

Stromberg, P. L. (1974). *A long war's writing: American novels about the fighting in Vietnam written while Americans fought.* Unpublished doctoral dissertation, Cornell University, Ithaca, NY.

Taxel, J. A. (1980). *The depiction of the American Revolution in children's fiction: A study in the sociology of school knowledge.*

Unpublished doctoral dissertation, University of Wisconsin, Madison.

Taxel, J. A. (1981). The outsiders of the American Revolution: The selective tradition in children's fiction. *Interchange on Educational Policy, 12*, 206-228.

Taxel, J. A. (1986). The black experience in children's fiction: Controversies surrounding award winning books. *Curriculum Inquiry, 16*, 245-280.

Taxel, J. A. (1989). Children's literature: A research proposal from the perspective of the sociology of school knowledge. In S. de Castell, A. Luke, and C. Luke (Eds.), *Language, authority, and criticism: Readings on the school textbook* (pp. 32-42). New York: Falmer Press.

Taxel, J. A. (1992). The politics of children's literature: Reflections of multiculturalism, political correctness, and Christopher Columbus. In V. J. Harris (Ed.), *Teaching multicultural literature in grades K-8*, (pp. 1-36). Norwood, MA: Christopher-Gordon Publishers.

Taxel, J. A. (1995). Cultural politics and writing for young people. In S. S. Lehr (Ed.), *Battling dragons: Issues and controversy in children's literature*. Portsmouth, NH: Heinemann.

Tuchman, B. W. (1985). *The march of folly: From Troy to Vietnam*. New York: Knopf.

Vandell, K. S. (1991). *The everlasting if: American cultural identity in children's historical fiction, 1865-1965*. Unpublished doctoral dissertation. University of Maryland, College Park.

Viehman, M. (1993). *Survivor guilt*. Unpublished manuscript.

Wheeler, J. (1985). Coming to grips with Vietnam. *Foreign Affairs, 63*, 747-758.

Williams, R. (1977). *Marxism and literature*. London: Oxford University Press.

Williams, W. A. (1980). *Empire as a way of life: An essay on the causes and character of America's present predicament along with a few thoughts about an alternative*. New York: Oxford University Press.

Wittman, S. M. (1989). *Writing about Vietnam: A bibliography of the literature of the Vietnam conflict*. Boston: G. K. Hall & Co.

Appendix A

The Sample

Combat Novels—Duty Subcategory

Archibald, Joe. (1967). *Special Forces Trooper*. New York: McKay.
Butterworth, William E. (1968). *Orders to Vietnam: A Novel of Helicopter Warfare*. Boston: Little, Brown.
Butterworth, William E. (1969). *Stop & Search: A Novel of Small Boat Warfare Off Vietnam*. Boston: Little, Brown.
Dean, Nell M. (1969). *Nurse in Vietnam*. New York: Julian Messner.
Elliott, Ellen. (1968). *Vietnam Nurse*. USA: Arcadia House.

Combat Novels—Vietnamese Perspective Subcategory

Clark, Ann Nolan. (1978). *To Stand against the Wind*. New York: Viking.
Dunn, Mary Lois. (1968). *The Man in the Box*. New York: McGraw-Hill.
Graham, Gail. (1972). *Cross-fire*. New York: Pantheon.

Pevsner, Stella, and Tang, Fay. (1997). *Sing for Your Father, Su Phan*. New York: Clarion Books.

Terry, Karl. (1974). *Children of the Dragon*. San Francisco: People's Press.

Combat Novels—Platoon Subcategory

Emerson, Zack. (1991). *Echo Company #1—Welcome to Vietnam*. New York: Scholastic.

———. (1991). *Echo Company #2—Hill 568*. New York: Scholastic.

———. (1991). *Echo Company #3—'Tis the Season*. New York: Scholastic.

———. (1992). *Echo Company #4—Stand Down*. New York: Scholastic.

Haldeman, Joe. (1972). *War Year*. New York: Winston. 2nd ed. (1978). New York: Pocket Books.

Myers, Walter Dean. (1988). *Fallen Angels*. New York: Scholastic.

White, Ellen Emerson. (1995). *The Road Home*. New York: Scholastic. (Part 1)

Response to the War Novels

Crosby, Alexander. (1971). *One Day for Peace*. Boston: Little, Brown.

Jones, Adrienne. (1990). *Long Time Passing*. New York: Harper.

Nelson, Theresa. (1989). *And One for All*. New York: Orchard Books.

Qualey, Marsha. (1994). *Come in from the Cold*. Boston: Houghton Mifflin.

Rostkowski, Margaret. (1989). *The Best of Friends*. New York: Harper

Wolitzer, Meg. (1984). *Caribou*. New York: Greenwillow.

Returned Vet Novels

Antle, Nancy. (1993). *Tough Choices: A Story of the Vietnam War*. New York: Viking.

Bograd, Larry. (1986). *Travelers*. New York: Lippincott.

Boyd, Candy Dawson. (1987). *Charlie Pippin*. New York: Macmillan.

Jensen, Kathryn. (1989). *Pocket Change*. New York: Macmillan.

White, Ellen Emerson. (1995). *The Road Home*. New York: Scholastic. (Part 2)

Wolkoff, Judie. (1980). *Where the Elf King Sings*. New York: Bradbury Press.

Appendix B

Young Adult Novels about the Vietnam War

Combat Novels: The novels in this category are all set in Vietnam during the war and contain some combat.

Duty Subcategory: Novels all begin in America (one in Australia) and detail the protagonists' training before coming to the war. All characters, despite their personal feelings toward the war in Vietnam, have a great sense of duty about serving their country. All protagonists are American or Australian, and although important to the story, only a few scenes of combat are included.

Archibald, Joe. (1967). *Special Forces Trooper.*

Butterworth, William. (1968). *Orders to Vietnam: A Novel of Helicopter Warfare.*

Butterworth, William. (1969). *Stop & Search: A Novel of Small Boat Warfare off Vietnam.*

Dean, Nell. (1969). *Nurse in Vietnam.*

Elliott, Ellen. (1968). *Vietnam Nurse.*

Vietnamese Perspective Subcategory: Novels all have Vietnamese or Montagnard protagonists, and Vietnamese or Montagnard characters try to come to terms with combat, American characters, and America's involvement in their country.

Clark, Ann Nolan. (1978). *To Stand against the Wind.*

Dunn, Mary Lois. (1968). *The Man in the Box.*

Graham, Gail. (1972). *Cross-fire.*

Pevsner, Stella, and Tang, Fay. (1997). *Sing for Your Father, Su Phan.*

Terry, Karl. (1974). *Children of the Dragon.*

Platoon Subcategory: Novels begin as protagonists arrive in Vietnam. They are comprised predominantly of combat action.

Emerson, Zack. (1991). *Echo Company #1—Welcome to Vietnam.*

———. (1991). *Echo Company #2—Hill 568.*

———. (1991). *Echo Company #3—'Tis the Season.*

———. (1992). *Echo Company #4—Stand Down.*

Haldeman, Joe. (1972, 1978). *War Year.*

Myers, Walter Dean. (1988). *Fallen Angels.*

White, Ellen Emerson. (1995). *The Road Home.* (Part 1)

Response to the War Novels: The six novels that make up this category are all set in America during the war. In each novel, the protagonists struggle to make sense of the war and the effect that it has on their lives. Characters choosing to join the antiwar movement, evade the draft, or enlist and go to war in Vietnam are all profiled here, as well as the events that lead up to these important life-altering decisions.

Crosby, Alexander. (1971). *One Day for Peace.*

Jones, Adrienne. (1990). *Long Time Passing.*

Nelson, Theresa. (1989). *And One for All.*

Qualey, Marsha. (1994). *Come in from the Cold.*

Rostkowski, Margaret. (1989). *The Best of Friends.*
Wolitzer, Meg. (1984). *Caribou.*

Returned Vet Novels: The final category of novels in the sample are all set in America and all feature someone who served in Vietnam. In each case, Vietnam vets and/or their families try to understand the meaning of the war in both personal and national terms. This struggle by the vets and/or their families to comprehend the meaning of the war and the effect it continues to have on the vets and everyone who loves them comprise the overall narrative structure of the novels in this category.

Antle, Nancy. (1993). *Tough Choices: A Story of the Vietnam War.*
Bograd, Larry. (1986). *Travelers.*
Boyd, Candy Dawson. (1987). *Charlie Pippin.*
Jensen, Kathryn. (1989). *Pocket Change.*
White, Ellen Emerson. (1995). *The Road Home.* (Part 2)
Wolkoff, Judie. (1980). *Where the Elf King Sings.*

Appendix C

Summary of Novels in the Sample

Combat Novels—Duty Subcategory

Archibald, Joe. (1967). *Special Forces Trooper*. New York: McKay.

This story details Green Beret training. As the novel opens, a practice patrol wanders lackadaisically through the woods in North Carolina. We see that this is a demonstration for other Special Forces officers, VIPs, and the press. Flashbacks explain how Stan Rusat came to be in Green Beret/Special Forces training at Fort Bragg—including his father's death in Korea and his own dismissal from West Point.

Periodically in training, Stan is disappointed that the pre-Green Berets are taught so much about what he thinks of as being Peace Corps information. He wonders about the Green Beret image as a warrior.

Stan decides to try HALO school along with regular Green Beret training. HALO is a method of parachuting from an extremely high altitude and free falling for several minutes. Many pages and minute detail are devoted to what the trainees are learning in their MOS (military occupational specialty) and cross training.

After an extended training exercise, Willie, Stan, and Ackerman are shipped out to Vietnam early to join another team already there. They are sent to Luc Co on the Cambodian border, where there has been a lot of activity. There is discussion of the frustration of not being able to pursue the VC into Cambodia and of training the "native strike-forces" (p. 99).

The attack on Luc Co comes in a few days at dawn. A strike-force of forty-five Vietnamese and three Americans goes out to look for the VC. They find the VC and take a few prisoner. As the group searches for more, they are ambushed. Because of the brilliant actions of operations Sergeant Cantenbine, who countermanded a Vietnamese commander's orders, the group was saved—except for a few Vietnamese casualties.

Captain Martsell is notified that the Montagnards are "demonstrating" against the South Vietnamese again and is concerned about the mix at Luc Co. He thinks about disarming the one hundred Montagnards there, but decides that Captain Luy has enough strikers to keep them in line.

In order to distract the building tension between the Montagnards and strikers, Martsell orders Luy to take some of his men and Montagnards and four Americans and check on the hamlet of Buong Da for possible VC activity. While there they meet some of the villagers and interrogate some Montagnards who had come from a hamlet that had been overrun. They all report on the cowardice of the ARVN in the area.

The Green Berets go to Dong Ha to check out the story of the Montagnards. On the way back to Luc Co, the chopper that is carrying them is hit and doesn't crash-land, but does have to emergency land far from Luc Co. They are spotted leaving the helicopter by the VC and are followed. The three Green Berets are able to ambush eight VCs, killing seven and taking one prisoner.

The next morning, the prisoner is interrogated. The Green Berets threaten him with no food or water for days if he doesn't talk. The Vietnamese captors and the Green Berets act menacingly and imply threats more than they actually speak them.

In the meanwhile, three or four strikers are caught as VC infiltrators. They are interrogated and threatened and one of them talks, naming many others as VC. Not everyone is convinced that the strikers are telling the truth about a planned attack on Luc Co by the VC. Willie sets up a machine that he tells the strikers is a lie detector, but in actuality it will just electrocute them.

Things are tense in Luc Co as the Green Berets wait for the VC attack. Everyone is skeptical about the potential performance of the strikers. When the anticipated attack finally comes, the VC are fierce and break into the perimeter of the camp. Willie is wounded in the shoulder and the communications bunker is destroyed. The compound is nearly overrun many times.

Stan is wounded, but is shortly back in action. The attack continues for hours. Willie had called in air reinforcements as the attack began, but no one has come. Finally the air strike arrives and drops napalm carefully on only the VC, although the VC are in the perimeter. All the VC are killed and only a few Green Berets are wounded.

Butterworth, William E. (1968). *Orders to Vietnam: A Novel of Helicopter Warfare.* Boston: Little, Brown.

The story begins with Bill Byrnes' graduation from aviation school and his commission as a warrant officer. We find that he is the descendant of seven generations of army officers, but that he was drafted after quitting West Point after only two months. We also are told that Bill has grown up on army posts practically as a soldier and has an immense and natural ability with weapons. Through memories, we learn that Bill went to college after West Point, but couldn't afford it on his own, dropped out, and was drafted. Also, his father, the general, disowned him when he refused to join the military. Bill is presented as someone who is not intimidated by his father.

Bill arrives in Vietnam and is sent the next day to Pleiku. Major Kramer tells Bill and seven other new pilots about the aviation company to which they've been assigned. They're billeted in relatively comfortable and permanent "tents."

When Bill goes on his first mission with the group, Lieutenant Halverson is a "by the book" pain. The mission is a huge assault with many helicopters, infantry, and jets—all described in numbing detail. The movement of troops and supplies lasts all afternoon. The last run is a personnel pickup that includes several VC prisoners who demand to be treated according to the Geneva Convention. They fly much more that day and in many other missions—all described in too much detail and not enough drama.

At a barbecue one night, Major Kramer announces that there is a large tactical evacuation that needs to be flown immediately. Six helicopters will go, along with jets and bombers. Major Kramer's Huey crashes because it's overloaded. Halverson is hit and killed and Bill's leg is injured by flying debris. His instruments are damaged, it's dark, and he doesn't know what to do. He manages to find another chopper to follow back to Pleiku, but then goes on to An Khe to take the wounded to the hospital there.

Kramer and Gowald come to get Bill at An Khe. Kramer is upset because of Bill's foolish (and unauthorized) decision to fly on to An Khe. He demands that Bill come back and fly immediately and that he write a sympathy letter to Halverson's wife. Kramer tells Bill that he has called Bill's father, who is also in Vietnam, to tell him about Bill's injury.

After another mission, Bill packs up Halverson's things, and even though Bill was supposed to write it, Major Kramer writes a letter to Halverson's wife. Kramer sends it over for Bill to look at. Bill reacts angrily, saying that his family would rather have him alive and promptly receives a lecture on communist expansion. Hawker tells him that he has been promoted and that Kramer is leaving.

About the same time, twenty-three new pilots from Rucker come in. Bill is certified for flight duty and is sent to "try out" on a gunship. The next day Bill is surprised to find that his post-grounding check flight, his gun-instruction ride, and his gunship check ride are all going to be the same thing—and not just a practice, but flying support in a real mission. Bill proves himself to be a capable pilot and a good shot. Everyone is impressed.

There is a ceremony for all the men to receive decorations. People pass out from the heat. The next day, Bill realizes that he has been made a pilot (as opposed to a copilot) on a gunship and an instructor for the new guys. He is skeptical about his qualifications. His first job is to train the new Lieutenant Rodgers to be certified on the gunship and to head the platoon. Rodgers isn't a good pilot, but Bill doesn't know what to do because Major Hawker can't continue to fill in a gunship platoon leader. Hawker knows that Rodgers isn't good and tells Bill that he wishes Bill could lead, but he can't because he's not an officer.

In battle something happens that Bill doesn't think Hawker is going to make it out of. Hawker surprises him by landing back at Pleiku. Hawker orders Bill to take an R&R in Hawaii and then to apply for commission so that he can command the platoon when he returns.

Bill arrives at his mother's house in Hawaii, and she tells him that she had hoped his father would come home at the same time. In Hawaii Bill has a little trouble readjusting. He goes to the officer's club and can't get a beer and becomes really furious.

When Bill gets home his father is there. They call a truce and his father says how much Bill has matured. That night at the club, Bill's father tells another general how well Bill is doing. The book ends with Bill dancing with the general's daughter.

Elliott, Ellen. (1968). *Vietnam Nurse*. USA: Arcadia House.

Joanna Shelton, an Australian nurse, is summoned to the American embassy in Saigon, where she is told that her missionary/physician father is missing. Dr. Shelton had been trying to arrange unofficial talks between Washington and Hanoi. The American ambassador asks Joanna to help find her father and take up his work.

Dr. Steve Donovan, a friend of Joanna's from Sydney, offers to accompany Joanna on her mission to find her father and set up negotiations. Joanna meets Captain Wayne Moore, the Green Beret who will lead the unit. Seven people will go in all, each of the soldiers being veterans of the Korean War. They talk about the small likelihood that Dr. Shelton will still be alive.

Joanna and the unit are dropped in the plateau country near Djiring. She is struck by the toughness of the Green Berets. Steve shows his ignorance of the jungle by making noise and attracting attention. As they stop for the night, Moore assures Joanna that she'll be protected. As she and Steve talk, she speculates on whether or not he still loves her and whether or not she could love him. While they're talking and cuddling, Steve again asks her to marry him.

Private Koerner spots a battalion (of NVA? VC?) moving close by. The unit stays put and Koerner tries to lead the VC, who have spotted him, away from the others. Joanna is concerned that Koerner is sacrificing his life, but everyone assures her that he is quite capable.

Koerner joins them later that morning, saying that he killed a few VC. The unit makes its way through the rain, with Joanna hating every second. They come across a village and the soldiers come at it from all angles while Steve and Joanna wait in the bush. Moore finds a boy, Dai Thu, who speaks some English. Dai Thu takes Steve and Joanna to his mother who is very sick and in need of treatment. They treat half of the village. Joanna suspects that Dai Thu is VC because of his strong reaction to her comments about the evils of communism. Wayne is skeptical. She is convinced that the VC might strike at any moment.

At 4 a.m. the entire group is captured. Joanna is awakened by being kicked. Dai Thu indeed has brought the VC to the village. The head VC, Commissar Phat, claims to have seen Dr. Shelton close to Dalat, several days prior. While Phat and Joanna talk alone, she tells him of her father's mission. Phat says that it would be quite impossible for the North to agree to negotiation. Joanna faints.

Joanna wakes up and is being carried by Wayne and Roswell. Wayne ignores the VC and calls Steve back to look at her. Wayne tells her that they're going to Dalat because someone there wants to talk to her, but they won't say if it's her father. While they're trekking through the jungle, Steve tells her that this might be their last time together and again asks her to marry him. She feels indebted to him, but she continues to ask herself if she's in love. She says yes just to stall him, thinking that they'll never get away from the VC. They continue to slog through the monsoon. When they stop for a rest, Phat politely checks on Joanna. Steve acts macho and ridiculous. Phat punches him. Steve returns the punch and knocks Phat out. The other VC kill Steve on the spot.

They bury Steve while the VC eat dinner. The men fuss over Joanna and Wayne wants her to take a sedative, saying that they can carry her the next day if necessary. The men compliment her on being tough. When they stop for the night, they talk about their probable future. Wayne tells Joanna about the rough treatment prisoners often get. The food that the VCs give them is inedible. In the morning they resume their forced march. Caught out in the open moving up a hill, the VC and their prisoners are the target of an American air strike. Even though the Americans are in the middle of the VC, no Americans are hurt. Napalm is dropped but there are no fires. Phat demands that Joanna nurse all of the wounded VC.

Joanna begins treatment and convinces Phat to let the Green Berets help. Phat comes to get Joanna for her to treat Dai Thu, who has been crushed by a falling tree. Phat tells her that Dai Thu is the illegitimate son of Huynh Tan Suu, a high-ranking member of the National Liberation Front. Phat demands that she operate, even though Dai Thu is so injured that he will likely die. Phat tells her to do a good job because the VC have her father.

Joanna and Wayne prepare for the surgery. Phat tells Joanna that her father is indeed in Dalat and that he is well. When Phat leaves, Wayne confesses his love for her and she returns his feelings. They complete the surgery. Joanna gives instructions about how to care for Dai Thu until a doctor can come. Phat tells Joanna that Huynh Tan Suu is waiting in Dalat to thank her.

When they arrive at the VC compound outside of Dalat, Suu comes out. He is old-world charming and asks Joanna to eat with him. Joanna meets her father at the table. He and Suu are old friends. After discussing the war, Suu agrees to release the Sheltons and the Americans. Wayne tells Dr. Shelton that he and Joanna want to be married.

Butterworth, William E. (1969). *Stop & Search: A Novel of Small Boat Warfare Off Vietnam.* Boston: Little, Brown.

Eddie Czernik is a third-generation Bohemian who plans to be a game warden like his father and grandfather. As he learns to pilot small boats for his father, he eventually gets a license to be a charter boat skipper. At college he majors in marine biology and is on a Navy ROTC scholarship. He is supposed to go to Bethesda for his commission when he graduates.

Not surprisingly, Eddie graduates early and can't be commissioned. He goes into the navy as a seaman apprentice and after basic goes straight to Vietnam to a small boat (river patrol) program, skipping any sort of advanced training. There is no mention of any preparation for Vietnam. Up to this part of the story, there has been no mention of the war or the antiwar movement.

Aboard the PCF-16, the crew's job is to stop and search any Vietnamese craft in the Mekong Delta and the surrounding ocean. Occasionally, they find someone carrying supplies for the VC. There is little spit and polish on board, as the skipper (Lieutenant Russell) is very laid-back. The crew functions well together. Everyone gets along and pulls together. After an ambush in which the Russian gunner's mate is killed, Eddie begins to lose his innocence about the war, although no real information is given about what Eddie thinks. Chernoff's replacement, Emmons, is a by-the-book jerk. In another ambush, Chief Asher is killed and Russell is seriously hurt. Emmons and Lieutenant Potter take over. Eddie borders on disrespect thinking that people should be leaders because of ability, not length of service or rank.

He is eventually commissioned as an officer and is sent back to skipper the boat. Emmons becomes his chief.

Dean, Nell M. (1969). *Nurse in Vietnam*. New York: Julian Messner.

Lisa Blake is a young air force nurse who volunteers to come to Clark Air Force Base in the Philippines because her boyfriend was killed in Vietnam. While meeting her roommate Nancy, Lisa makes many racist remarks about Asians in general. Colonel Phelps gives Lisa a long and detailed tour of the hospital.

Mace Thomas, a wounded Green Beret, steals Lisa's compact so that she will have to visit him in the hospital to get it back. She's not interested in Mace because of Clint, but he seems persistent. Lisa falls into the routine of the hospital. Somewhat forced situations occur so that some character can explain some hospital or military information to us. Mace is eventually transferred to Okinawa to recuperate.

Lisa is pulled from her regular duties to go as a replacement to pick up a planeload of casualties in Saigon. With a five-hour layover, she goes into town to see the Servicemen's Recreational Center, where Clint had written many of his letters. She manages to waste enough time that she can't get back to the airport before the flight, which then must be delayed. Lisa is reprimanded upon her return to Clark.

Lisa visits a Filipino nurse, Erlinda, who has quit her job and gone home to take care of her mother, who has cholera. While in Lemery, a volcano erupts and Lisa and Erlinda have to pitch in to help the refugees. After she returns to Clark, Mace notifies her that he is coming for ten days before he returns to Vietnam. They spend those days dining and dancing and going on romantic excursions—all properly chaperoned. While viewing the rice paddies, he kisses her and asks her to marry him. She accidentally says "Clint" and Mace quickly turns peevish.

Trying to forget Mace, Lisa and Nancy throw a going away party for a nurse who has been transferred. Party conversation revolves around work and different medical procedures. Finally, Lisa gets another chance to go on an air evac flight to Biên Hoa. When they arrive, the plane is grounded because a bird has gotten in the jet engine, which allows Lisa to spend some time in a "field" hospital.

Lisa bums around with nothing to do for several days. She gives shampoos and sets to the other "girls," and they talk about movie stars and fashions. Finally she gets so bored that she volunteers to help at the hospital. The second she volunteers, the doctor in charge asks her to accompany a surgeon to a remote village on the Cambodian border to "patch up" and transport by helicopter a severely wounded soldier (could it be Mace?). The helicopter is shot down in "enemy territory," but no one is hurt in the crash.

Several of the crew are wounded as they try to kill the five or six Vietnamese who shot down the chopper. Eventually the five Americans walk ten hours without incident into the village that they were going to. When they arrive they find three Americans waiting for them. The doctor goes to look after them and Lisa sets about to make an adequate operating room. Of course, Mace turns out to be one of the Americans—but not the one who's hurt. He tells her that they've been there for some time and that there isn't a radio and that no planes ever come. He also suggests that a search party would see the burned wreckage of the helicopter and assume that everyone aboard was dead.

Lisa and Dr. Gregory work tirelessly through the day treating the wounded Americans and the lepers. After days go by and no one comes, Mace decides to go alone back to the helicopter to see if he can fix the radio. Dr. Gregory gives an amputee, Lieutenant Colt, a transfusion of his own blood and later passes out. Mace returns three days later than he had promised. The radio is built MacGyver-like out of wood and wire. Immediately a chopper is sent. Everyone returns to Biên Hoa safely. The last line: "Their hands clasped tighter. Somehow she knew Mace was right. Someday, someday, they would be together forever" (p. 192).

Combat Novels—Vietnamese Perspective Subcategory

Dunn, Mary Lois. (1968). *The Man in the Box.* New York: McGraw-Hill.

Chau Li is an adolescent Montagnard boy whose father has been tortured and killed years before by the VC. One morning the VC soldiers appear in his village with a beaten American prisoner in a small bamboo cage. Chau Li wants to rescue the prisoner—not because he is an American, but only because he couldn't help his own father when he was in the same box. He knows that he is risking his life, but he cannot let the man in the box die without trying to help.

He has something of a plan to take the man to a cave his father had shown him. At the last minute, Chau Li's friend Ky comes back and helps him get the man out of the village. Amazingly, Chau Li gets David to the cave. Chau Li is a whiz in the jungle. He kills a monkey and gathers many edible plants and herbs for medicine. He also completely covers his tracks, knowing that the VC will be looking for him.

When they run out of food, Chau Li ventures into a village some miles away to try to get some. An old woman, rumored to be crazy, feeds him. It turns out that her son is a sergeant in the VC "army." She helps Chau Li by lying to people in her village about him already leaving. She gives him many supplies.

Chau Li returns safely to the cave and David. He tells David that he has overheard some VC soldiers discussing the fact that American Green Berets and the ARVN will soon be at the village where Chau Li has been. While Chau Li is out trying to find wood to make David crutches so that he can go back to the village (the VC have broken all the bones in his feet), he is grabbed by ARVN and American soldiers. The ARVN think he is VC and want to kill him. A black Green Beret scares Chau Li, but won't let the Vietnamese hurt him. Chau Li tells David of the incident and David assures Chau Li that they were actually friendly Americans. David asks Chau Li to go back to America with him to be his first son.

Chau Li and David start down the mountain to the village where they hope the Green Berets will be. David's crutches are too short and he is far too weak to travel. They eventually make it into the village. David tells Chau Li to stick close, because he doesn't want them to get separated.

The medics take care of David and call for a helicopter to take him to Da Nang. Chau Li is to go with David. At the last minute, an ARVN chopper shows up. As David is being loaded on board, there is a VC mortar attack. Just as Chau Li attempts to get on with David, who is drugged, the Vietnamese crew shoves him out saying No *Mois*. John Louis takes over guardianship of Chau Li until they can get him to Da Nang to meet up with David.

Chau Li goes back to the house of the woman who helped him in order to urge her to come inside the compound for the night. They are sure there will be a VC attack, and he wants her to be safe. She thinks the VC won't hurt her because of her VC son. What she really wants is to be left alone.

In the night the VC attack. The Americans and villagers are brave and steadfast in their defense of the village. Just when it seems that all is lost, there is an American air strike. Some soldiers and villagers are killed by accident. Riley, John Louis, Doc, everyone Chau Li knows among the Americans is killed—some by the air strike. The entire village and much of the surrounding jungle is destroyed—to a great extent by the American napalm and bombs.

Chau Li is hysterical. Someone tries to lead him to safety in the jungle, and he throws a grenade at him, realizing that the person is VC. Too late he realizes that it was Ky. Chau Li finds a sampan on the river and dazedly gets in it. He floats all night and awakens the next afternoon. When he realizes that Da Nang is at the end of the river, he heartens.

Graham, Gail. (1972). *Cross-fire*. New York: Pantheon.

Harry wakes up alone in the jungle. He recounts what he remembers of his patrol and then nothing. Harry is convinced that the woods are filled with VC and that perhaps he is in a trap. He hears someone and is attacked by a young girl. He talks to her, but he is surprised and irritated that she doesn't speak English. She has a baby, but he doesn't know if she is the mother.

As they are "talking," Harry hears a sound and whirls around firing wildly into the bushes. The girl, Mi, screams and he immediately assumes that she is VC as is whoever is in the bush. When the person in the bush doesn't come out, Harry holds his M-16 to the baby's head ordering her to tell the person to come out. Several other children join Mi.

The next chapter is Mi's account of the bombing of her village, as the narration shifts to her viewpoint. Each chapter alternates between Harry's and Mi's third person limited narration. Mi recounts the story of how the unnamed village is bombed while she and her siblings are out in the rice paddies. They are the only survivors of the bombing.

Harry wonders what to do with the kids. He continues to be irritated that they're afraid of him and that they don't speak English. He vows not to fall asleep so that he can watch them all night.

Mi and younger brother Ton sneak away in the night. Ton wants to kill Harry, but Mi won't allow it. They take Harry's gun and most of his supplies. Ton reveals to Mi that Hung Ba, an old man in the village, is VC and is training many of the children so that they would be ready to fight the Americans. Ton gets all of the children out of the shelter and they start across the swollen river to get away from Harry.

Harry awakens and finds that the kids have taken his things. He immediately thinks of them as "stupid, thieving gooks." He can't fathom why or even that they would dislike or distrust him. He wishes that he had killed the kids and contemplates doing just that. When he finds them trapped in the river, he is furious that Mi doesn't immediately trust him. He also punches Ton in the face while the kid is in the river, making him nearly lose consciousness, in order to "teach him some manners." Bong falls in the river and nearly drowns. Harry saves her with mouth-to-mouth. Her leg is broken. Ton tries to kill Harry with a rock. Harry deflects, but tells Mi that he will kill Ton if he tries anything else. Mi supposedly understands. He ends every sentence with "Do you understand?," knowing full well that she speaks no English. Harry sets Bong's leg. Mi takes him to the remains of her village and he understands what has happened. He is horrified.

Ton is angry that Mi has taken Harry to the village. She thinks her relationship with Harry has changed, and Ton accuses her of wanting to marry him for his money. After a fight, Ton sulks in the jungle. The baby has a fever and begins to have seizures. Mi is upset and Harry holds her hand. They supposedly communicate through this touch, but what he doesn't know is that touching is culturally insulting. Mi lets it slide. The baby eventually dies.

Ton digs a grave for the baby. Harry continues to be furious with Ton, thinking about beating him for having an inappropriate attitude. Harry doesn't know how to react to the baby's death and burial. He wants Mi to know that he cares, that he is sorry, but he doesn't know how to show it.

Harry gets really mad at Ton for not behaving the way he wants and picks Ton up and shakes him and basically humiliates him. Ton leaves after a big fight with Mi. Harry builds a stretcher for Bong and they decide to cross the river in order to get to Cai Nuoc, where Harry believes they'll find help. While crossing the river, B-52s spot Harry and Mi. Ton stands out in the open shaking his fist at the planes. When Harry tries to get him to cover, the B-52s return and hit Harry with strafing fire (which is not something B-52s would have been capable of doing).

Mi is furious with Ton and blames him entirely for Harry's being wounded. She tries to make Ton see that Harry was trying to save his life when he rushed out. They don't know what to do with Harry, and he dies during the night without having regained consciousness. American paratroopers drop into the area and start shooting at anything that moves. Mi, Ton, and Bong are all killed.

Terry, Karl. (1974). *Children of the Dragon*. San Francisco: People's Press.

Much information about the war and Vietnamese culture is conveniently worked into this story. North Vietnamese children are sent into the countryside to avoid American bombings of Hanoi (much like the English children during World War II). Tri comes from Hanoi to Dai Lai to stay with Hoa and her grandmother, Te.

Te tells the kids a bedtime story about the legend of the giant yellow turtle who gave Le Loi (farmer in 1407) a golden sword to drive out the Chinese invaders. She remembers her mother telling her stories about the Chinese, Mongol, and French invaders.

The next morning, Hoa and Tri do chores around the house and take care of the animals. Hoa explains about the loose pants and straw hats that are worn in the country. On the way to the rice fields, Hoa and Tri talk about how much they love Ho Chi Minh (Uncle Ho—a term of respect) and how he protects Viet Nam. At the rice fields, Hoa and Tri work with other villagers to maintain the paddy dike system. She explains how the people have used this irrigation system for thousands of years. She also tells Tri about filling the bomb craters with lotus and making them fishponds. While they're enjoying their idyllic pastoral scene, American bombers fly over. Everyone runs in terror to the nearest cover. Hoa runs out to herd the water buffalo to cover as well. The planes fly on.

That night, Mother Huong's sister Ly comes for dinner and brings fish. They talk about their villages being cooperatives and how that works so much better now that the resources are pooled. The next day Hoa and Tri go to school. They wear branches to camouflage themselves. Hoa explains about the foxholes under the school desks. The school grows its own lunch food. Hoa tells about how everyone can go to school now because it's free.

During a geography lesson, Tri talks about Hanoi and what a beautiful city it is. The children discuss how the factories were moved from Haiphong to the country and how they're better now that everyone owns them. After school, Hoa and Tri go to visit Hoa's brother Kim who is in the hospital after being badly burned in a bombing raid. That night, Tri and Hoa work on math homework and remind their mother that Ho Chi Minh's Study Rules say they can stay up as long as they want if they're studying.

Months later, Tet (the Vietnamese New Year) is celebrated. During the Tet theater, Grandfather Ahn gets a copy of the newspaper. The play stops as he reads that North Vietnam and the United States have signed an "agreement to end the war and restore peace in Viet Nam." Tri heads for home the next day. Te reminds him that although the bombing has stopped, the war is still going.

Clark, Ann Nolan. (1978). *To Stand against the Wind.* New York: Viking.
This is a framed story told in one long flashback. The novel opens very confusingly with Em and his family in an ugly room in America preparing to observe a ceremony that honors ancestors. It is Em's responsibility to write his memories as part of the ceremony.

Flashback—We are taken back to Em's house in his unnamed village. He thinks of how similar all Vietnamese houses are. He remembers how his rice farmer father occasionally went into Saigon to work as a mechanic and how his father insisted that Em's older siblings attend school there. Em's mother is required to accompany them although she does not approve. No one cares what she thinks. Em is left in the hamlet with his grandparents. He is given the responsibility for the water buffalo that is used in farm work and comes to think of it as a pet.

Em manages to avoid school in Saigon because his uncle is a scholar and can teach him in the village. Eventually, Americans come to Vietnam to "help run the government" and to train Vietnamese soldiers. When they come to the hamlet, people are afraid of them, but gradually everyone gets along. Sam, a reporter, is a particular friend of Em's. Sam begins to work in the rice paddies with Em and his grandfather. Sam tells them that he wants to know about Vietnamese people so that he can write a story for his magazine. Sam convinces Old Uncle to teach him Vietnamese.

Although no specific date is given, Em describes the war as worsening. Em perceives the VC to be everywhere—even in his own hamlet. Mother writes home and says that American money is ruining Vietnam and Saigon and that she doesn't want to stay there. Father is upset because she doesn't want to do what he says is right. Sam volunteers to get an army jeep and drive Em, Father, Grandfather, and Old Uncle into Saigon to see how things are—knowing that Mother is correct.

When they arrive in Saigon, the place is full of dangerous street kids and beggars. Americans are everywhere and they aren't as friendly as they had been earlier. Grandfather decides that Mother and the children must come home. Sam takes them to an orphanage and a hospital before leaving Saigon. Everyone but Sam is surprised about the changes in Saigon. They retrieve Mother and the older kids and go back to the hamlet. Chi-Bah is finished learning how to be a secretary and wants to work for the Americans. Elder Brother and Father both want to join the ARVN.

Sam visits the hamlet as often as possible and stays two or three days at a time. Everyone is sad and nervous about the war. Mother and Grandmother dread when Elder Brother will leave for the army. They both speculate about the possibility of a Matchmaker coming to arrange a marriage for Chi-Bah, who is fifteen.

Chi-Bah accepts a marriage proposal through the complex Vietnamese customs of betrothal. There are many visits, etc. Anh-Hai suggests that perhaps he and Sinh should go into Saigon and find out how long it will be before they are to be called to be in the ARVN—just in case it is less than two months—the normal period of Vietnamese engagements. Sam arrives and brings wedding presents, saying that he might not be able to come back for the wedding. He gives Chi-Bah and Sinh letters to send to Sam's parents asking them to welcome Chi-Bah and Sinh if they should ever need to come to America. They thank him for the gift, and Sinh says that they won't ever leave Vietnam.

Sam is worried about Anh-Hai and Sinh—thinking that they will probably have to leave to join the army within the next weeks. Old Uncle is worried about the war that Sam says is getting worse by the hour. He sees strange things in the stars. The family horoscope just stops and his suddenly veers in a different direction.

Anh-Hai and Sinh find out that they will be called to the army in two weeks, so the wedding must be hurried. The older people are scandalized, but Grandfather thinks that the stars agree with the idea of going ahead. The wedding and wedding preparations are described in minute and ponderous detail. Father has a plan to go to Saigon to be the major's chauffeur, Sinh and Anh-Hai will be in the army, and Chi-Bah will be the major's secretary. That way they can stay together. They return to Saigon after the wedding.

After all the activity, the house seems quiet. Life settles into a routine of making repairs after the nightly bombings. There is much concern about the rice farming and *many* pages are devoted to explaining every detail.

Sam comes back after a long absence. He volunteers to stay at the hamlet as long as the family needs him. He will work in the fields with the men. Sam stays and works in the fields planting rice. The narration says that the war really has had little effect on the day-to-day lives of those living in the delta. Sam brings Father and Chi-Bah home to help with the rice harvest. They can stay for three days. Anh-Hai and Sinh are off fighting. More laborious description of rice harvesting. After the harvest, there isn't time for the usual celebrating. In three or four weeks it will be Tet, the Vietnamese New Year. Long descriptions of Tet preparations are included. The family is briefly reunited for Tet.

Life returns to as normal as possible. One evening, Sam races to the hamlet on a motorcycle. He is visibly upset, but manages to tell the family what he knows. He says that Chi-Bah heard a rumor that Saigon was going to fall. When she went to find Sinh, she was told that neither he nor Anh-Hai were there and, no one knew where any of the soldiers were. Also that Father was killed when the palace where he worked was bombed. Everyone in the family is crushed. Chi-Bah is in a Saigon hospital. No one knows exactly what to do.

Shortly, Em returns from the rice fields. As he approaches, he smells a strange burning smell that he doesn't recognize. The entire hamlet is gone. Everything has been burnt and bulldozed. The place is filled with ARVN and American soldiers. Sam is there screaming. The family has been killed in the bombing. The American captain tells Sam and Em that the village was full of VC. The captain tells Em that he must leave his buffalo and go to a refugee camp. The buffalo is to be shot since it could be food for the VC. Sam reaches out to grab Em and is shot at the same time that the buffalo is killed. Only Grandmother and Old Uncle are left alive. The few people from the hamlet are herded into a refugee camp.

The refugee camp is only about twenty miles away. The refugees aren't ill-treated, although they are crammed together in an ugly and barren place. They are given seeds, but no land or water. They are given enough food to keep from starving. A month or so later, Chi-Bah appears with "John," the American captain who killed Sam and Em's buffalo. Chi-Bah resents the family's reaction to him as someone evil. She also reports that Anh-Hai is dead. Nothing is said about Sinh. Em is now the head of the household.

Chi-Bah sends the letters to Sam's parents that he gave her as a wedding present. There are plenty of refugees and plenty of American relief workers trying to get things straightened out. Finally they come to America.

Pevsner, Stella, and Tang, Fay. (1997). *Sing for Your Father, Su Phan*. New York: Clarion Books.

The story begins as Su Phan waits for her father's ship to return from Haiphong in North Vietnam. His trip has taken longer than usual and she is worried, but he returns safely. Later Chung Bo tells the family that he was detained in Haiphong by communist officials who threatened to seize the ships and goods. They were only allowed to leave when they paid a huge bribe.

The family is somewhat apprehensive about future trips, but Chung Bo assures them that since he's a man, he knows what he's doing. He takes extra supplies for extra bribes. Local boys tell Su Phan that the war is getting closer and closer and that soon they'll all be involved. Mama and Grandma reassure her. Chung Bo's ships are late and everyone is tense.

The family finally receives word that Chung Bo's ships have been seized by communist officials. No one knows exactly what's happened to him. He finally appears to tell that he and his crew were taken captive, but that the Americans bombed the place where they were being held and they managed to escape. Chung Bo tells the family that the communists will no longer tolerate free ship trade, so he decides to open a store. Americans bomb the village and scare the family to death. Even though everyone is wary about the war, the children begin school again.

There is increasing fear and gossip about the war approaching. One night the state police burst in and seize Chung Bo because he hasn't joined the communist party. The soldiers ransack the store and home—destroying much and stealing the rest.

The family is devastated and terrified. The children return to school only to be taunted by their former friends about their father's arrest. The whole family is so weighted down with grief that they become listless and uninterested in anything.

One day at school, the sirens go off, warning of approaching bombers. The students and teachers walk into the jungle to hide. The planes pass overhead on their way elsewhere. This continues daily until finally the bombers do drop some bombs that land beyond the village. Everyone is terrified.

Grandmother decides to leave to live with friends where it's safe. She argues with the whole family, but leaves anyway. They are all surprised that she has actually gone. Su Phan is especially disgusted that they've let her leave. The children begin to pressure their mother to move away into the jungle. The school has been moved and many of their neighbors have also gone. Voong is afraid that if they move, then Chung Bo won't be able to find them. The village itself is bombed and shrapnel comes into the house, but no one is hurt. The family moves to the settlement where the grandmother is already living. The other villagers help them to build a small shelter. No one is happy, but they try to settle in anyway.

Three years pass since Chung Bo's arrest with no word of him. The family tries to make do with Voong Nhi Mui selling dim sum at a nearby village. Mother announces that she has found out which prison Chung Bo is in and that she intends to visit him. She leaves in the morning and the children stay home to work.

Soon after Voong Nhi Mui leaves, Su Lenh becomes ill, which makes the making and selling of dim sum quite difficult. In the boat returning from an island where the girls have been picking wild onions, bombers are seen overhead. They lie down in the boat, in order to avoid attention. When the planes are gone and they sit up, they cannot see land and are terrified. They row, but they still can't see land. They finally make their way home.

After six weeks, Voong still hasn't returned. Grandmother visits, hoping to see Chung Bo. She is full of dooming assumptions. Mother returns and is completely exhausted. She reports that the police have no intention of releasing Chung Bo because he hasn't learned his lesson.

The children return to school and life goes on. In 1969 everyone learns of Ho Chi Minh's death. The children are afraid that they are leaderless. Each year Mother goes to visit Father in prison and comes back looking more broken. The children want to come. Voong is afraid that Senh Hau will be taken for the army. He is convinced that the recruiters frequently come to the school and take boys younger than him (he is 15). He stops going to school. They decide that he will go out with the fishermen each day to avoid the army.

One day, Mother just collapses. Chung Bo has been imprisoned for seven years. Su Phan and her sister fantasize about their lives after the war—children, marriage, travel, peace. On the way home from doing the village laundry, the sisters see an old man coming up the street. They assume that it's someone's grandfather coming to visit. They chat briefly with the old man before they realize that he is Chung Bo, their father. The family is thrilled to have him home. The rest of the village doesn't react as warmly. They appear to be afraid of Chung Bo.

Since there is fear and suspicion in the old village, the family moves to the village where Grandmother lives. Things are more hopeful there.

Combat Novels—Platoon Subcategory

Haldeman, Joe. (1972). *War Year*. New York: Winston.
Haldeman, Joe. (1978). *War Year*. (2nd ed.) New York: Pocket Books.

Draftee John Farmer arrives at Cam Ranh Bay and is quickly sent to the Central Highlands, to Camp Enari near Pleiku. After a week of intensive training, John and Willy Horowitz are assigned as combat engineers to B Company and sent to Ban Me Thuot. The commander at Ban Me Thuot complains that his replacement soldiers are being kept at Enari as clerks. Later that same day, John and Willy are sent on to a firebase—2124—or the Alamo. The Alamo is occupied by A Company and B Company.

As soon as they arrive, John and Willy are put to work constructing a bunker with the other engineers, Pop, Fats, Prof, Doc. The atmosphere is casual. Everyone is drinking beer and talking as they work. The lieutenant seems as laid-back as everyone else. Suddenly word comes in that A Company has run into a platoon-sized ambush. Willy, John, Prof, and Doc prepare to go out and blow an LZ (a landing zone for helicopters).

When they get out into the bush, the chopper drops them off, then speeds away. The engineers are supposed to cut down trees to make cover. There are many wounded men gathered near the LZ, including one who has had both of his legs blown off. Eventually, a dustoff comes to take them away. What's left of A Company sets up a "patrol base" in the bush and stays for three days while awaiting supplies and replacements from Alamo. Since many of the engineers from A Company were wounded or killed in the ambush, Willy, John, and Prof are temporarily assigned to stay.

Several days are spent wandering around the jungle, rather routinely. Then suddenly as the Company is digging in for the night, they are attacked by faceless Vietnamese whom we never even see. After a large firefight, in which several Americans are killed, John and Willy go back to B Company. The firebase has moved from Alamo to Plei Djaran—a pleasant place with good food and nice scenery. After a month, John and Willy are sent again to join A Company.

After a couple of weeks of boredom, Prof steps on a mine while walking point. He is killed horribly and John is seriously wounded by little frags from his chin to his feet on one side. We follow John on his trip on a medevac to a field hospital and then to a larger stationary hospital. At the hospital John sees an NVA prisoner waiting to be operated on for a shoulder wound. John gets through his two surgeries and begins to heal enough so that he can use crutches to go to the PX (post exchange) or the Club. After a week or so, John is sent to the convalescent center in Cam Ranh Bay because the hospital space is needed for Vietnamese civilians who have been attacked by the VC.

John enjoys being at Cam Ranh. Chow is good, there is hot water in the showers, and there is an air-conditioned library. After several weeks of physical therapy, the doctors take away his crutches. The first day he is expected to do PT (physical training—standard military exercise), go on a mile run, and participate in sandbag detail. On that same first day, John goes to his physical therapy appointment at 1300 and misses the 1330 formation. If you miss formation, you're automatically put on the roster to be shipped out the next day. When John realizes he's to be shipped out, he tries to explain the situation to the sergeant in charge and asks to see a doctor. No one will listen and bureaucracy wins out. John is sent back to Pleiku in the morning even though he can barely walk.

After a short while in (Camp Enari) Pleiku, John accidentally fails to salute a general's jeep and as punishment is sent back out to the firebase—although he is assured that they have seen little action in his absence. The next morning, Willy wakes John up at the firebase. Willy tells John that John will probably have to take over his position as "field squad leader" because Willy is eight days short and will be on the next helicopter out. John and Willy stand on the pad together and Willy takes off.

The (1972) Ending:

Seconds later there is an explosion and John realizes that the helicopter has been shot down. Everyone runs out of the firebase to the burning wreckage. John is hit in the leg again and finds out from the medic that everyone on the slick (helicopter) burned to death.

After getting home, John tries to readjust and refuses to answer a letter from Willy's parents.

The (1978) Ending:

The chopper takes off safely and John is indeed made squad leader. The company leaves a few hours later to set up a company-sized ambush about two klicks away. Nothing happens that night, so the exhausted company starts to come back to the firebase. They are ambushed on the way because they are tired and careless. Most of the company is killed. The captain calls for artillery on their own position. He orders John, the only surviving engineer, and some others to break through the line to blow an LZ. The sergeant wants the others to come back and help with the fighting, so John stays out alone trying to set the charges to blow an LZ. An NVA officer and four men come up. John kills the officer and the men throw a grenade toward John. The explosion sets off all of the explosives. John is killed, and since he's the narrator, the story essentially stops here.

Myers, Walter Dean. (1988). *Fallen Angels*. New York: Scholastic.

Perry ends up in Vietnam through a paperwork screwup. He has a bad knee and isn't supposed to ever see combat. But after a couple of weeks in Saigon, Perry and Peewee are transferred to Chu Lai, where they are sent out by truck to Alpha Company, which is in the "deep boonies." They finally arrive in their squad and meet the black sergeant (squad) and white lieutenant (platoon) in charge. On their first day in the boonies, they are airlifted out on patrol. The first patrol is uneventful, but after being dropped off by the chopper, walking the one hundred yards back to camp, a man is killed by a mine. The squad goes on several hearts and minds missions (an attempt to win the affection and trust of the Vietnamese peasantry) into local villages.

After several weeks of not leaving the camp, there is an engagement close by and the entire company is sent out. A few tense hours pass and the company is brought back in. Sergeant Simpson hears that lurp (long range reconnaissance patrol) teams are being brought in, which he takes as a very bad sign. Several weeks pass again at the camp. Captain Stewart brings in a TV crew to interview everyone and then makes the squad go out on patrol so that the crew can go. After that patrol, Perry realizes that the captain has sent in an inflated body count.

The company stays in camp a lot. There is a fight between Walowick and Johnson over a racial slur. The platoon commanders talk among themselves about Captain Stewart getting them all killed. Perry has to go out on ambush with Charlie Company since he missed a patrol with his own squad. On ambush with Charlie Company, Perry meets Lieutenant Doyle, who isn't interested in the war and is only interested in getting home in one piece. He calls in artillery or Willy Peter (white phosphorous, an incendiary artillery round that is extremely destructive) if there is any kind of skirmish. When a firefight erupts, Charlie Company lets go with everything including Willy Peter only to find out that they've just killed most of the first platoon. Everyone takes it hard.

The squad goes on a pacification mission and gets along fine. They are set to go on another, but Captain Stewart gets them out of it. They assume it's because you can't get a body count on a pacification. A few days later, Echo Company visits the same hamlet and several men are hit. Alpha Company is ordered back into the hamlet to set up an ambush to wait for the VC. They go and the VC surprise them by appearing from a tunnel. Then the platoon opens up but most get away. As the squad edges away from the village to the LZ, Lieutenant Carroll is hit. They back into the village destroying it. When the choppers come moments later, the door gunners kill everyone and level everything—in a village that the troops were supposed to be protecting. The chopper takes the entire squad straight to Chu Lai, where Lieutenant Carroll dies.

Several NVA regulars are captured and the companies expect large movement soon. Lieutenant Carroll's replacement, Lieutenant Gearhart, arrives. The squad doesn't know what to think of him at first. Captain Stewart gets more and more gung ho and the squad worries that in his zeal to be promoted, they will be put in unnecessarily dangerous positions.

Rumors that the war will soon be over abound shortly before Christmas 1967. The South Vietnamese officers are all going home for Tet. Lots of VC activity in Cambodia is spotted. Marines in Khe Sahn are trapped. People don't know if it's the NVA trying to get into a good position before the Tet truce. The squad begins to hear about truce violations and are sent out to stop traffic between two hamlets. They are separated from the rest of the platoon. Gearhart is trained in reconnaissance, so the squad is to be sent out as a lurp team to replace one that had been completely wiped out. They find that Captain Stewart volunteered them.

When they reach their place of ambush, they realize that it is to be a joint venture with a group of ARVNs. Simpson and the other men don't like the plan that Gearhart has laid out. They don't trust him. As they lie in ambush, a VC company comes through. The squad is exposed when a flare lights up the area. Through the ensuing firefight, the squad realizes that they're significantly outnumbered. They fall back and try to get to a pickup zone and call for a chopper. Gearhart does a few brave things, but the men aren't sure about him—especially when they realize that he accidentally set off the flare. Even though they have no idea how many may have been killed, Captain Stewart files a body count of twenty-eight.

There has been much movement, and one of the hamlets where the platoon has worked is being harassed by the VC. The Airborne are supposed to go in and secure the hamlet, and then Alpha Company is supposed to protect it until the VC are no longer a threat. But on the way to the hamlet, word comes over the radio that Alpha Company is to secure the hamlet instead of the Airborne. When they arrive, the VC have already killed most of the people in the hamlet. The men check all of the huts, and there is generally great anguish over the destruction and the senselessness of it. Perry kills his first man up close. Finally, the wounded are taken out and the hamlet is set on fire. The Vietnamese are evacuated. The company is really shaken up.

The whole "outfit" was being sent to Tam Ky to act as ARVN advisors, with Alpha Company going first. Feelings run badly against Captain Stewart. When they arrive at Tam Ky, they realize that it's very far out. The hooches don't seem like they'll stand much in the way of fire. The squad goes out to lay an ambush, and thankfully, when the VC come, Gearhart knows not to open up. It turns out that it is nearly a battalion that and the squad would certainly have been wiped out. There is resentment in the company that the ARVN aren't doing their share and that in general they are cowardly and inept. The men find out that Stewart is volunteering them everywhere so that he can be promoted. The entire company goes out on a sweep, but after they are on the ground, they run into a huge force of VC. Men from other squads are killed. Johnson, Brew, and Perry are all hit. Brew dies in the medevac on the way to the hospital. Perry is hit in the leg and wrist. In a hypocritical and disgraceful ceremony, Perry and some other men are given their Purple Hearts.

After a few weeks, Perry is returned to the company, which is significantly reduced in size. The men tell Perry that Sergeant Simpson has gone home and that his replacement, Sergeant Dongan, has put black soldiers in all the dangerous positions. No one likes him and there are several near confrontations between Dongan and Johnson. The black guys all pledge their loyalty to Johnson. On guard duty, Dongan at least proves that he knows what he's doing when he kills a VC sapper. A Vietnamese woman and two children come to the camp. She is interrogated and released. As she leaves camp, she hands a guy from Charlie Company one of the children whom she has mined. Many men are killed as are finally the woman and the other child. Everyone is deeply demoralized.

Captain Stewart and an ARVN colonel fight over who will lead an assault up a hill. The Vietnamese colonel gives Stewart a direct order. They plan to use artillery to soften the area, then go in and draw fire. They are finally sent in by chopper. Gearhart moves the men around, trying to draw fire. When basically nothing happens, the squad moves back to the command post. The ARVN colonel then wants his men to take the hill for credit. As the ARVN start out, they are ambushed and almost all are killed. Alpha Company must take a VC-controlled village in order to secure an LZ. They eventually do and there are many wounded. Dongan is killed.

Word comes that an NVA battalion is on the way and everyone has to leave quickly. The GIs gather and burn their dead; the ARVN leave theirs. On the way to another pickup zone, the ARVN who are in front come under small-arms fire. Everyone dives for cover. Johnson tells them to get up and keep moving. Stewart tells them to stay down and look for the sniper. The squad keeps moving. The squad comes upon an NVA platoon in a clearing and pins them down, killing many. A jet drops napalm on the rest of the NVA. When they finally reach the pickup zone, the ARVN are already there. An ARVN commander has his men encircle the GIs so that the ARVN can get out first. When the choppers come, Gearhart has his men put their hands up so that the chopper crew can see what's going on. The door gunners fire on the ARVNs as do the GIs. They fight any ARVN who tries to get on the chopper.

When they return to the base, Monaco starts having flashbacks—not dreams. He starts firing inside the hooch, thinking he sees VC. Walowick says that he's had them too. The squad finds out that once again there has been a hugely exaggerated body count.

Squads are low on men and on the next patrol, Lieutenant Gearhart has to go out with another squad because they only have five men. Brunner is then squad leader. When they get to the river that they're supposed to check out, there is a ridge that flanks it. Everyone is nervous because there is no cover and plenty of places for VC to hide. They run into a small force and kill them all, losing no men. On the way back to the LZ, Peewee and Perry are sent to check out a low spot in the ridge. As they near the top, they hear a firefight, but all around the river—not up to the ridge.

It's dark and silent and Peewee and Perry are separated up on the ridge. They don't know if the squad is even still alive or where they might be, or if the VC know that they're on the ridge. When they hear Vietnamese voices, they open up. A flare goes up and they can see that there are many VC. Peewee and Perry move away from the ridge and find a spider hole; but they assume that the VC will know about it too. They make it through the night. Peewee is stabbed seriously in the stomach by a VC checking out the hole. When Peewee and Perry finally get back to the LZ, they see Monaco sitting alone by a tree and realize that the VC are holding him as a trap. When a chopper comes down, the VC will kill him and the crew. Perry and Peewee manage to open up just as the chopper comes, and Monaco is barely saved. Perry is hit again as he gets on the chopper.

Perry and Peewee go to the hospital at Chu Lai. Peewee is set to go home. They find out that Captain Stewart has been promoted. After a month in the hospital, Peewee and Perry are sent home together.

Emerson, Zack. (1991). *Echo Company #1—Welcome to Vietnam.* New York: Scholastic.

The story begins as Michael gets off the plane at Tan Son Nhut in Saigon. He quickly displays his petulant attitude toward the army. The internal narration from Michael's point of view shows him to be basically a cynical smart-ass. On the truck trip, he expresses his very derogatory views of the Vietnamese. After a few days with a replacement battalion, he joins *Echo Company* based in Chu Lai in I Corps, close to the demilitarized zone.

At Chu Lai, Michael goes through some orientation/training before joining the rest of Echo Company out in the field. This includes first aid, LZ info, patrol stuff, packing, booby traps, Vietnamese culture and history, etc. Then he and Bear are sent out to the field. They meet the lieutenant and are assigned to their respective squads. They are told that they are doing some regular search and destroys, and will be back to the firebase in five or ten days.

Sergeant Hanson tells Michael that they're staying in that night, because they have to hump a long way the next morning. Michael shares a hole with Snoopy and is absolutely paranoid and terrified. He hears things and when he doesn't hear things, he wonders if everyone else is dead. Emerson does a good job of conveying the absolute terror. The next morning, everyone is up and ready to hump. Michael learns about taping things down, how not to drink, where to walk in the patrol, etc. The patrol is presented as terrifying, with Michael not knowing what to do or how to do it. Everyone is as helpful as possible. After lunch, the heat and the weight of the pack finally get to Michael, who faints. He is embarrassed, but no one gives him a hard time.

Days later after humping since morning, the squad comes upon a village. Second and 3rd squads are waiting on the other side and 1st platoon is supposed to sweep through it pushing anything dangerous into 2nd and 3rd. In the village, nothing momentous happens. The huts are searched, but the people seem to have no reaction. Eventually a tunnel is found and it is blown up. J.D. and Finnegan clown around with the kids in the village. While everyone seems to be relaxed, a guy from 2nd squad is searching a rice container that is booby-trapped. Most of his arm is blown off. The people in the village nervously claim not to be VC. Some men in the squad want to destroy the village, but Hanson won't let them. Finally after the dustoff, the order comes from the commanding officer to torch the village, and then the VC sympathizing villagers can be relocated. Michael is really upset at the notion of being ordered to set fire to people's houses and refuses to take part.

That night, the whole platoon sets up camp together. Michael is still mad and doesn't want to be with any of the men. First squad is going out on a night patrol—Michael's first. Lieutenant Brady tries to reassure

Michael that the "zippo raid" was just SOP (standard operating procedure). Michael isn't convinced.

After Michael goes out on his first nighttime patrol without incident, the squad gets word that the whole platoon will be spending the day and night at the NDP (night defensive position). This is a mixed blessing—more restful, but sitting ducks. Command wants them to stay until someone can figure out where the VC mortars are. They expect resupply that day and use up their few remaining supplies and blow an LZ. They all try to get as much sleep as possible, knowing that they'll most likely be hit again that night. They go out to blow some timber for cover and almost have a race riot when a redneck makes a racial comment. Resupply comes and everyone gets mail, food, water, and beer. Three new guys come in with the chopper and Michael marvels at how much a veteran he feels. The new guys think he's old.

That night, Michael and Snoopy are on guard watching the perimeter when the mortars start. No small-arms fire. The overwhelming air power knocks out the guns and the choppers strafe the woods. Hanson tells them that they'll move out at 0600. First and 2nd platoons are supposed to chase a large group of VC through a valley, while 3rd platoon polices the NDP and catches up later.

After a few hours of humping, with 1st squad (really J.D.) on point, J.D. motions that he sees three VC. The other squads try to flank them. In the ensuing firefight, there are two confirmed VC kills. No one in 1st platoon is wounded other than a few scratches. They wait for about twenty minutes for 2nd platoon to meet up with them to pursue the VC.

While waiting, J.D. heads for a shade tree and steps on a mine. He is completely liquefied and splatters over most of the group, completely covering Finnegan, who was standing quite close to him. Viper helps Michael to clean up what's left of J.D. and put it in a body bag. Viper tells Michael not to make friends in Vietnam. Then Viper goes on to tell Michael that Snoopy is often really careless and that he and Hanson watch him all the time. This really creeps out Michael. Lieutenant Brady asks Viper and Michael to act as if the body bag is heavier than it really is as they walk it over to the medevac. Finnegan is freaked out, but everyone tries to get it back together and they go off to meet 2nd platoon.

Emerson, Zack. (1991). *Echo Company #2—Hill 568*. New York: Scholastic.

Hill 568 begins about an hour after the end of *Welcome to Vietnam*. Finnegan is still completely freaked out after J.D.'s death. A new lieutenant from 3rd platoon, Kendrick, is hateful to Finnegan. Michael jumps up, getting in Kendrick's face. Sergeant Hanson intervenes just in time. Hanson pulls Michael out in the jungle and tells him to cool it.

The next morning, Hanson asks Michael to start being permanent point for the squad. (J.D. was the last point.) Michael refuses, saying that he doesn't have enough experience, but acquiesces when Hanson agrees to teach him. The next chapters detail the misery of humping in the rain with leeches, bad food, and no sleep. Michael is still sick after J.D.'s death. He can't eat, there's not enough time to sleep, etc. The weapons platoon catches up with the rest of the guys, so now the whole company is together. After they dig in, resupply and mail come. Michael and Kendrick have another confrontation. First squad is going out on ambush that night. On the ambush, 1st squad is joined by Bear and Thumper. Hanson is point; Michael is slack. They get dug in by a creek and wait. While Michael is on guard he hears a noise. He doesn't know whether to wait; if he shoots too soon, he'll give away their position. Finally a trip flare goes off and everyone starts shooting. No one is injured. Michael is terrified.

When they return to the NDP in the morning, they are told that 1st squad will go out on patrol again that night and that the whole company will be lifted out the next day to go to Que Son (not Khe Sahn), where they will have a new area of operation. The entire battalion will eventually meet up there. Upon arrival in Que Son the squad finds the construction of a large firebase.

Life at the firebase quickly settles into a boring routine—but still better than humping. Delta Company comes in and everyone waits for Bravo and Charlie. No one knows why the whole battalion is being assembled. Two days before Thanksgiving, Michael walks point for the first time, with he and Hanson switching off each hour. After a few pointers from Hanson, they leave. When they get back to the firebase without incident, the platoon sees that there is a field kitchen and that steaks are being served. The old guys know that it means that the battalion is going to be sent to do something really bad. Michael is unable to relax after walking point.

The battalion's mission is to secure some hill in the Que Son mountains. Intelligence reports that a fortified NVA company is using the hill as a base for operations. The mission is to clear and secure Hill 568. As they prepare to go, everyone really loads up on ammunition, carrying far more than usual. Many are also carrying small weapons—pistols, knives, things for close-in fighting. The plan is that bombers, heavy artillery, and gunships will soften the area first, then the troops will be lifted in, clearing and driving any remaining NVA into the A and B companies waiting for them down the road. It rains heavily the morning of the assault and no one knows whether or not it will be canceled. It's not.

The slicks drop them in a really hot LZ. They are mortared immediately and Hanson tries to move them away from the area, assuming that the mortars are zeroed in. Michael is separated from his squad, and even from the platoon. People are dying all around him. Delta starts up the hill for the initial assault. Echo stays back, but is ready to act as reinforcement. Almost immediately word comes back that Delta is completely pinned down, with heavy casualties. Echo takes only weapons and heads out from another direction to help them get out. They come under sniper fire trying to get to Delta because they've run into a bunker complex. As they're pulling back, Michael realizes that they've left some people. In the heat of the moment Hanson volunteers the squad to get them. No one is injured and Bear and Moretti from 2nd squad are rescued. There is a massive bomb/napalm strike.

Michael is surprised to see that the air strike doesn't seem to have made any difference to the NVA. They pop up and begin firing immediately upon the return of the soldiers. Everyone pulls back for the night. Echo is down to about seventy men (should be ninety to a hundred); Delta is even lower. They dig in to spend the night before trying to take the hill in the morning. Shortly after midnight, sappers try to break through the perimeter. When the battalion starts up the hill in the morning, they are hit really hard as they come upon an unassailable bunker complex. It seems that the men just snap—having had enough. They start doing things like charging the bunkers and throwing in grenades, standing in front of bunker openings and spraying in with M-60s from the hip. In the middle of it all, Michael's M-16 jams. There are continual assaults. A large group of NVA almost flank the platoon. Everyone is terrified and people are dropping all around. Wounded and dead are everywhere. Even after all of this, they start up the hill again.

Everyone gets separated again. Michael finally has had enough and when he doesn't recognize anyone around him, he charges up the hill, hoping to find the squad or at least the platoon. He gets a radio and has a confrontation with an officer in a chopper. While there, Kendrick tries to make the guys charge. Michael is on the verge of mutiny, completely refuses to obey and get killed. He comes up with a plan instead for the lieutenant to call in an air strike, but for the planes just to pass and not drop anything. When the NVA are ducking, the Americans will attack. It works. They make it to the top of the hill. It seems to be over. Michael finds the squad. Everyone is alive. Finnegan took some shrapnel in the shoulder. Hanson has broken ribs.

Emerson, Zack. (1991). *Echo Company #3— 'Tis the Season.* New York: Scholastic.

The story opens at Christmas in the base hospital at Pleiku. Lieutenant Rebecca Phillips spends many of her off-hours in the hospital trying to cheer up the wounded men. After a trying morning shift, she gets something to eat and goes back to her hootch. She, like the men, is perpetually exhausted. We find out that the battle from *Echo #2—Hill 568* was at Dak To and that many American men were wounded by friendly fire from a gunship. We are also told that Rebecca had a boyfriend who was killed at Phu Bai in 1966 and that her brother, Doug, draft-evaded into Canada.

Rebecca spends a lot of time talking about triage decisions—about how head wounds aren't generally treated, about how soldiers are left to die, about how anyone who would take a long time to work on is left so that people with a better chance can go first—all of which really bothers Rebecca. That night on her shift in the ER, some field casualties are brought in. One is expectant (mortally wounded and therefore not treated) and she must wait with him until he dies. Unfortunately, he was still partially conscious. She thinks about Bobby, her dead boyfriend, and wonders since he was a head trauma case if he died like this.

When Rebecca's shift is over, she goes to check on the men in the wards instead of going to bed. The major sees that she's still at the hospital and Rebecca is *ordered* to leave. She doesn't seem to be able to be realistic in her work habits.

On her day off, Rebecca goes to the officer's club and gets good and drunk, fending off lecherous doctors. The twenty-four hour Christmas truce goes into effect, but Rebecca has to work. Most people are gone: patients sent home, staff on R&R, or at the Bob Hope show. Rebecca gets pretty homesick thinking about her last Christmas with Doug and her parents. She tries to stop feeling sorry for herself, thinking about the men out in the field and how much worse it must be for them.

In the morning, Rebecca stays around to hear the Christmas Eve party gossip—new couples, etc. A chopper pilot friend rushes in looking for a corpsman, saying that he has been called out to get a soldier who stepped on a mine. He can't find a corpsman and Rebecca offers to go with him since there is a cease-fire. It's against regulations, but she assumes that she'll be back before anyone notices that she's gone. It is strictly forbidden for nurses to go on medevac runs.

During what seems like a routine flight, the chopper is hit. The co-pilot is killed instantly and Wolf crash-lands, but not before he can radio their position. Wolf has two compound femur fractures, a serious chest wound, and dies almost immediately. Moments later, Rebecca hears Vietnamese voices outside. She grabs the medical bag and Spike's gun and gets out of the chopper before they can get to her.

The VC blow up the chopper and don't see Rebecca in the bush. She is smart and gets away. Her nose and her ankle are broken, but she walks anyway. She knows to stay off the trails as she goes deeper into the jungle, deciding which supplies to keep and to leave. After several hours of moving through the jungle, she has to stop. While she's sitting, a teenage Vietnamese soldier comes upon her. They both appear frightened and hesitant. They both point their pistols at each other. Rebecca tries to get him to leave, but he doesn't speak English. They stand there for hours. Rebecca keeps talking, trying to figure out what to do. They finally sit. They're about five feet apart. Rebecca knows that this has to be over before dark. This confrontation with them sitting and staring at each other lasts for more than forty pages. She finally gets sick of the whole thing and starts to put her gun down and get up. Her leg is asleep and she lunges. The boy is startled and shoots her in the arm. She shoots and hits him three or four times. He takes quite a while to die.

Rebecca spends the night there and treats her own wounds as best she can. In the morning, she takes the dead kid's gun and sets off again (with a bullet wound to the arm, broken nose, eyes nearly swollen shut, broken ankle). She gives some serious thought to killing herself but doesn't and keeps moving. Finally, she crawls into the muzzle of an M-16. An American soldier.

Echo Company. First squad. They're all really taken aback. After the squad has found Rebecca in the bush, Hanson immediately wants her to give him the gun. They're not ready to lift her out and she doesn't want to be defenseless and refuses. He insists. She pulls rank. She refuses again and keeps the gun. Viper tells them to grow up. She doesn't want Hanson to report that he's found a woman because of all the attention it would stir up. Michael is very nice and respectful. Hanson settles down and agrees to tell Lieutenant Brady that they have wounded—but not her specifically. She doesn't want anyone to know exactly what happened, so she tries to get the medic to give her some forceps so that she can pull the bullet out of her arm herself. She only agrees to let them make her a litter when Viper tells her that her slowing them down might get them all killed.

When the medic on the dustoff realizes that she's a woman, she manages to get him not to say anything. When they land at her hospital, they wheel her in as just another soldier. Major Doyle and Captain Stockman agree that her bullet wound will be listed as a frag wound. Captain Stockman takes the gun that Rebecca still has and hides it.

Emerson, Zack. (1992). *Echo Company #4—Stand Down*. New York: Scholastic.

The story starts right after the squad has found and medevaced Rebecca in *Echo #3*. Michael thinks about Hill 568 and how they gave it up shortly after all of the bloodshed in *Echo #2*. Rebecca is the only topic of conversation for the squad, and it is established that Michael developed an immediate crush on her. Finnegan and Michael talk about the fact that Rebecca had a gun—and *not* an American one. They also mention that her wound was gunshot—not frag.

When the New Year's truce (January 1, 1968) starts, the squad spends the day playing cards and drinking beer. The next couple of days are spent around the firebase listening to rumors about who was going to do what and when. One afternoon, an older, bristly, lifer-looking type comes into the 1st squad's bunker and announces that he is the new platoon sergeant, which had previously been Hanson's job. He makes several racist comments.

The next morning after Quigley's arrival, the platoon goes out on patrol with 1st squad in the lead, which meant Michael on point. Michael interestingly describes what he does on point—trying to become part of the rhythm of a place in order to see what doesn't belong there. On the patrol, Michael sees a very small footpath. Lieutenant Brady wants them to follow it. Michael nearly steps in, but figures out that there's a punji pit (a disguised pit lined with poisoned spikes) in the trail. He's a little freaked out, but he is good enough to catch it. HQ wants them to stay on the trail. Michael continues on point, knowing that where there's one booby trap, there's another. He assumes that they might be approaching a bunker complex. Michael finds unnatural twigs. Hanson finds one trap and Michael finds another. Although he hates point, Michael is really good at it.

Michael gets two letters—one from his old girlfriend Elizabeth and one from Rebecca. He keeps thinking that he's over Elizabeth since she really hurt him. She seems *completely* over him. In fact her letter just asks him to talk about his feelings about the war for her sociology project. She says that she has joined the antiwar movement and is very judgmental about his involvement. Then he opens Rebecca's letter and is disappointed to find that it's just a short, impersonal note. He doesn't know that in *Echo #3* she vowed not to get close to anyone else while she was there. Michael is really devastated by both of these letters.

On patrol another squad finds a big and recently used bunker complex. They gather up documents to send to intelligence and destroy everything else. Someone finds a tunnel and a little guy goes in it and finds some rooms. Michael writes one sentence to Elizabeth blowing her off and sends an extremely polite note to Rebecca letting her know how much he appreciated her note.

There's a rumor that the company is going to stand down in Chu Lai, which would be pretty amazing. Because of the Tet truce, they think they won't be needed for a while. It's nearly Michael's nineteenth birthday, and his mother sends him a package that he refuses to open until his actual birthday (because of bad luck). He gets a letter from Rebecca on the night before his birthday that consists solely of "!." On the night of his birthday, everyone cuts Michael some slack and gives him little things—pen, pound cake, book. Michael opens his box and is pleased with all the little things. And for the best news, Quigley tells them that they're to stand down in Chu Lai in two days.

They are transported to Tam Ky and are trucked fifty miles to Chu Lai. Michael thinks this may be good, since he's not sure people can behave coming straight out of the bush. As they get closer to "civilization," Michael starts getting nervous. He hasn't been around people for a really long time.

On arriving at the barracks in Chu Lai, everyone is made to turn in his grenades and guns, so that no one would get drunk and stupid. Michael keeps an NVA pistol, refusing to be unarmed in Vietnam. After a shower and new uniforms, Brady tells them that there won't be any work, but that they're not allowed to leave the base. Before they're allowed to play, there's a formation. Michael wants to get over to the hospital to see Rebecca, but he has to go to the formation. Most of the squad is given the Combat Infantry Badge, and then Michael and Hanson are given the Bronze Star for the hill battle. Despite his indifference to the army, Michael is impressed—especially when he finds out that Kendrick is the one who put him in for the medal and that Kendrick had actually asked for a Silver Star.

Michael finds the hospital and looks for Rebecca. Captain Stockard and Major Doyle won't let him see her. Only after he tells them that he was the one who found her, do they give him any information. Michael and Rebecca's meeting is awkward and they only exchange "How are you's?" and then he leaves. Michael is too tired, sad, and disappointed to even get out of the hospital. He sits down on the floor of the hallway, and Major Doyle comes out to try to comfort him. They have a strange conversation where several times she pulls rank in order for Michael to remember where and who he is. After Major Doyle leaves, Michael goes back into Rebecca's ward. They have a terse confrontation. It seems that neither knows what the other wants. She finally agrees to meet him later for a sandwich in the medical officers' mess. They sit trying to have a conversation, but it doesn't really seem to be working. When Michael hears gunshots (they turn out to be from a Western movie), he shoves Rebecca off her chair, covering her with his body, and pulls his own pistol. He is completely humiliated and begins to wonder if he's going crazy.

They finish their strained dinner. Michael wants to go out with her and she wants to go home—alone. She finally tells him that many guys, each day, try to get her to spend time with them and that she just can't do it. She finally agrees to allow him to come back to the nurses quarters with her. It gets too late for him to get back by curfew and she asks him to spend the night. Finally, she tells him that he can sleep in her bed. While they're lying there, she tells Michael that Major Doyle completely covered for her being in the bush. She stayed in the OR and insisted that they took shrapnel out of Rebecca's arm. The next morning, he passionately kisses her good-bye. He feels better than he has since coming to Vietnam. Michael runs into Major Doyle leaving the nurses quarters. She's not happy, but she doesn't report him.

When Michael makes his way back to the other guys, he finds that they spent the night drinking heavily and fighting. He tells Snoopy that he spent the night with Rebecca, but that nothing happened. Snoopy asks if he'll see her again and he says yes.

White, Ellen Emerson. (1995). *The Road Home.* New York: Scholastic.

Part One: The War

Part One starts shortly after the Christmas where Rebecca had been shot down and injured (basically *Echo #3*). Tet had turned into a major offensive and the hospital was swamped. Rebecca continues to receive many letters from family and Michael because of her injuries. People work in the hospital for twenty hours a day in miserable conditions. Rebecca takes Darvon for her badly healing ankle and drinks regularly.

Finnegan comes in wounded and tells Rebecca that Michael shot him to get him out of the field. Everyone at the hospital gets more and more ragged and tense. MLK is killed and racial tensions get worse.

Michael is brought in with an AK (above the knee) amputation. He doesn't want to see Rebecca and she is very upset. Hanson is also brought in with extensive abdominal wounds and missing an eye. They were both hurt when Michael missed a booby trap on patrol.

Michael is bitter and doesn't want anything to do with Rebecca. He is getting ready to be airlifted out the next afternoon. Their relationship is very strained. Michael sees Hanson before he leaves, and Hanson assures him that he doesn't blame him for the mine.

Rebecca settles into a mind-numbing routine. Snoopy shows up on his way back to the World. He asks about Michael, not knowing that he hasn't contacted Rebecca either. They're both horrified that Michael has left the others hanging. Rebecca finally gets her orders to go home.

Part Two: The World

Rebecca arrives in California and is told not to respond to antiwar hippies who surround the airport. She makes her way through airports and tries to readjust thinking paranoically about everyone she sees. Her parents pick her up at the airport. She assumes that a preppie guy is about to spit on her suitcase.

Arriving at the house, Rebecca doesn't know how to act. Her mother is a little smothering and her father is tense—their relationship has long been strained. Rebecca and her mother establish a truce as they get used to each other again. Rebecca tries not to drink as much as she wants to. Rebecca refuses to leave the house and sometimes doesn't even leave her room. She doesn't call friends to let them know she's back.

Rebecca visits her KIA boyfriend's mother and some of her friends. She is extremely uncomfortable and hypersensitive about any comment that anyone makes. Doug, Rebecca's draft-evading brother, calls from Canada to check on Rebecca—to make sure she has made it home from Vietnam all right. The family assumes that the FBI will show up to question the family again. The whole family is tense and snappish.

Rebecca occasionally talks about the medical side of Vietnam. Her doctor father continues to disapprove of Doug and of Rebecca's over-stepping medical activities. Rebecca receives a letter from Maggie Doyle mentioning how difficult it is to fit back into American life.

Mom plans a huge family get-together as a good-bye to Rebecca as she leaves for her last seven months of army life at Fort Dix. Doug calls again and gets to speak to Rebecca. Mom and Dad agree to arrange a lawyer to negotiate on Doug's behalf, if necessary.

After finishing her tour at Dix, Rebecca returns home to near-constant drunkenness. Her father begins to question her about her plans for life, but Rebecca refuses to plan anything. She mentions that she's vaguely thinking about returning to Vietnam because she feels too hopeless and adrift. Her parents react violently. Her father confronts her about the constant drinking. Her parents suggest that she consider medical school and offer their emotional and financial support. Instead, Rebecca tells them that she must leave. She doesn't know where she's going or when she'll be back, but she leaves, nonetheless.

Rebecca drives to Colorado in search of Michael. Even though she doesn't have an address, she manages to find Michael's house. Mrs. Jennings immediately recognizes Rebecca and is thrilled to see her. Michael is very hostile and asks her to leave. They go for a drive and he is relentlessly obnoxious. Finally, he softens and lets her see his stump. They acknowledge how the war has damaged them and vow to get to know one another again. Michael's parents are astonished at the change in him. He becomes more outgoing and cooperative after Rebecca arrives. They begin to talk tentatively about their war experiences and eventually decide to move back to New England for Rebecca to attend medical school.

Response to the War Novels

Crosby, Alexander. (1971). *One Day for Peace*. Boston: Little, Brown.

The story opens as Jane's mother tells her that Jeff, Jane's friend and milkman, has been killed in Vietnam. Both Jane's mother and father express anger over the war and the U.S. involvement. Jane's father suggests that she write a letter to the president, their representatives, and the newspaper. He also suggests that she and her friends think up some way to protest the war. She finally gets an "answer," from the president, which she realizes is not an answer at all. The letter thanks her for her input, when actually all she had done was ask a question. The government also included some bulletins and pamphlets. Jane is completely disgusted by the idea that not only are there typos in the form letter, but that no one really addresses her question. Jane asks her schoolmates about doing something to stop the war. Some support it, but even those that don't doubt that they could possibly do anything to make a difference. Jane responds that *maybe* nothing would be accomplished, but *surely* nothing would be accomplished if no one tried. Jane is discouraged, but on her way home from school she runs into Donald Lehman. She asks him about helping her, and to her surprise, he agrees. He also suggests that they include kids from the black junior high.

Jane goes to see Fred, Jeff's nephew, in her first trip to the black neighborhood, the Hollow. Jane notices as she bikes to Fred's that everyone she sees is black and that they all sort of stop to look at her. She's starting to feel uncomfortable and unwelcome, but she finds the house and Fred. He is interested but brings up the notion that things aren't so great for blacks here in the United States, but he agrees to join and to bring some Hispanic friends with him.

The group decides on a parade with a band and signs. Donald knows all about getting permits. Roberto knows a band. The group, now called the Winchester Peace Committee, is very enthusiastic. Donald, Fred, and Jane go to the police department to get a permit for their parade. Police make Jane nervous, so Donald does the talking. The police sergeant assumes that someone has put the kids up to this. He takes their fathers' names and asks them to wait. They talk to the police chief, and when he realizes that Donald's and Jane's fathers are lawyers, he asks if this is a "test case." The kids say that they just want a permit. Chief Christman sends them to the mayor's office to talk to Jess Epstein, an administrative assistant.

At the mayor's office, the secretary tells them to go away and only come back when they have an appointment, because Jess Epstein is far too busy to see them. The mayor comes in the waiting room and Jane recognizes him. They tell him that they need a parade permit and they all go to the mayor's office. The mayor and Mr. Epstein listen patiently to the kids and ask how the committee got started. Jane tells about Jeff. The mayor tells the kids to call him "Alger" since he thinks of them as friends. He says that they can have the permit and that he will also issue a proclamation at the parade. Epstein warns him about the upcoming election and that people might be put off by his involvement. He says that he is going to do what he believes. Jane's father is impressed and both parents join the committee.

When Jane gets home from school the next afternoon, a reporter and a photographer are waiting for her. They have the mayor's proclamation and want to know about the parade and the committee. The next day the headline reads: MAYOR PROCLAIMS PEACE DAY, SIX CHILDREN PLAN PARADE.

The next day, after the article was printed, kids have mixed reactions at school. Mr. Hudgins, the principal, calls Jane in and tells her that she is out of line and threatens her that if she comes to be known as a troublemaker, she could be ruining her whole life. Mrs. Wertheim, the German teacher, however, tells Jane that she is proud and will join the parade. The local minister encourages Jane's mother to make her stop.

When Mr. Simon comes home, he is *really* furious about the principal. He calls Mr. Hudgins and confronts him about threatening Jane. When Hudgins denies the charge, Mr. Simon asks that he call Jane back to his office to tell her that the peace committee is just fine. Mr. Simon threatens him with the school board and a restraining order. Mr. Hudgins apologizes and tells Jane to forget the whole conversation.

The committee grows by leaps and bounds, adult and child. Letters to the editor of the *Gazette* pour in—some good, some bad. The American Legion calls for the district attorney to investigate the "juvenile radicals." Things begin to get a little tense. As more and more negative letters are published, people rally around the kids, calling to ask how they can get involved. They are told to make a sign and join the parade.

The day before the parade, Donald is attacked on the way to Jane's and is rescued by Fred and Roberto. Jane is nervous about the parade and possible resistance. Mr. Simon tells Jane that he called around getting doctors and lawyers, etc. to agree to march. He even got the local congressman to join. At the staging area, everything goes well. Many kids from the black junior high come. Jane meets Grimes, the trumpet player, and agrees that he is far-out. Jim Eady, the reporter, tells Jane that there are seven hundred people there including some people from the Washington news, CBS, and Associated Press and suggests that there is probably also the FBI. Mr. Tarantino brings the tree on his grandfather's pushcart.

The march begins. Erickson's factory is the first building they come to. Roberto tells everyone to keep an eye on the building. As they pass, a huge, white peace sign is unfurled from the roof. Roberto says that his priest had arranged it with some of his parishioners. When they pass some construction workers, Grimes plays "America the Beautiful" and calms everything by being funny. The workers laugh and encourage the march. Jane blows them a kiss. Someone throws a few bottles and cherry bombs, but is arrested. It seems that nearly everyone joins in the end of the parade as it passes. Thousands of people end up in the park.

Mr. Tarantino brings the tree and starts his speech about coming to the country as an immigrant. He goes on to say that the war is wrong. Then he says that Jane should speak before they plant the tree. She thanks everyone and then gets the rest of the committee starters and Theresa up on the platform. Grimes gets everyone to sing "Where Have All the Flowers Gone?" while he plays. Everything is just beautiful. Some people hang around after the march and watch the tree being planted.

Wolitzer, Meg. (1984). *Caribou.* New York: Greenwillow.

This story set in 1970 opens with the Silverman family watching son Stevie's birth date chosen first in the draft lottery. In one second, the entire world has changed for Stevie, and really for the whole family. Stevie is terrified and nearly hysterical. When all of the relatives begin to call, Stevie takes off on his bicycle.

No one talks about Vietnam until months later when Stevie has to go for his physical. Dad tries to make the best of the situation, saying that being in the army and going to war is not the end of the world. Stevie refuses to go to the physical and decides to go to Canada. He admits that he isn't interested in the antiwar movement, but he is afraid of being killed. Dad is furious and Mom is spineless.

At school, Becca decides that she is angry with the country and on the spur of the moment won't stand for the Pledge of Allegiance. She gets in some minor trouble, having to stay after school to write an explanation. She tells the teacher that she is angry because Stevie is nice and now he will have to leave. The teacher is sympathetic and Becca decides that she'll stand the next day because once was enough.

In February, Stevie decides that it's time to go to Canada. There is no talk about how he's arranged things or where he's going to stay. So we have a long-haired man of draft age with steamer trunks buying a one-way ticket to Montreal, and nothing is said about it. During their last dinner together, Stevie and Dad get into a minor confrontation. The next morning, Mom drives Stevie to the bus station. Dad comes out and wishes Stevie luck before they leave.

Becca finally gets a letter from Stevie—addressed just to her. He tells her that he's fine. Becca replies that she's still mad at Dad for not being more supportive of Stevie and decides to start saving her money so that she can go visit Stevie in Montreal.

There is an annual art contest at Becca's school. The winner paints a mural in the cafeteria and wins $100. This year's theme is "My Country, 'Tis of Thee." Even though Becca doesn't feel patriotic, she decides that this would be a good way to earn the money to go see Stevie. Becca is a finalist in the art contest and has to come up with some idea for the mural. She recalls a Memorial Day parade that the whole family attended several years back and decides that a patriotic parade with bands and flags, etc. will be her entry. Becca wins the contest and will paint her mural. Becca writes to Stevie asking if it would be okay for her to visit. She asks Mom to talk it over with Dad.

Becca begins the actual painting of the mural. She decides that it's time to ask Dad about Canada. She asks Mom to help her convince him that night at dinner. Mom seems reluctant and almost scared. Dad says no without giving any reason. Mom is absolutely no help.

Becca is a wreck at school. She is finished with the mural except for the flags. She isn't sure that she even wants to finish it because she feels so unpatriotic. That night she has an idea. At school, Becca goes to finish the mural. She is scared and a little excited. Stevie's letter told her to find her own way to make a statement and this may be it. Becca paints peace symbols on all the flags at the parade in the mural. The drama teacher sees her and wishes her luck at the unveiling the next morning.

When the mural is unveiled, the principal is horrified and angry. The parade is still a marching band and clean-cut families, but they are holding flags with peace symbols on them. No one claps. Becca is called to the principal's office. The kids seem to approve. Becca's teacher defends her. She suggests that the flags be painted over, but that Becca not be punished. The principal calls Becca's parents. At dinner that night, Becca can't tell what her parents think. Dad says that she's becoming very independent. After dinner, Mom is really upset, and she convinces Dad to let Becca go to Canada because she wants peace in the house.

Stevie picks Becca up at the bus station in Montreal. His hair is long, and he is driving a van covered with peace signs borrowed from his French-Canadian roommate Michel. They tour the city and Stevie plays Becca the new songs that he has written. Becca has a wonderful time in Canada. When it's time for Becca to go back home, Stevie takes her to the bus station. Right before she gets on the bus, he hands her a small statue of a man carved out of caribou bone—an old artifact that isn't supposed to leave the country.

Nelson, Theresa. (1989). *And One for All.* New York: Orchard Books.

Every night Mr. Brennan watches the news to keep current about the war. Mrs. Brennan and Mrs. Daily are both worried about their nearly draft-age sons. On a report about an antiwar demonstration, Mr. Brennan gets really upset and blames the protestors for prolonging the war.

Wing Brennan and Sam Daily, despite being best friends, often argue. It is established that Wing is very much behind the war effort and that Sam is very against it—claiming the war is actually a civil war in which we shouldn't be involved.

Wing's younger sister Geraldine finds out that Wing has been kicked off the basketball team until his grades come up. He hasn't told anyone and has stayed after school every day in order not to. The Brennans are angry about Wing's deception. Mama is particularly worried about his grades because of graduation and college. Wing insists that he isn't going to college, but they all know that if he doesn't go he'll be drafted for sure. Wing, however, doesn't seem to care.

On the first snow day, everyone stays home from school, and things seem back to normal. Sam tries to convince Wing to let him act as tutor. Wing doesn't want to, saying that the nun who won't let him play really just has it in for him and won't change her mind, but Wing finally agrees.

Sam and Wing study together. Dad makes the whole family sit together to listen to LBJ's State of the Union Address. He tells Wing and Sam that he knows that they'd come to the defense of their country if called. Later in January, Wing gets suspended for fighting with another boy, for making a snide remark about LBJ. Dad is just as mad as Wing about the remark. Sam convinces him to go back to school and take his exams.

Mama plans a surprise eighteenth birthday party for Wing. As Wing arrives home that evening, he really is surprised. Geraldine notices that he looks a little funny. Wing and Sam disappear from the party. Wing tells him that he's joined the marines because he flunked his English exam and won't be let back on the basketball team. Sam and Wing have a vicious verbal fight, and Sam tells Wing that he has stupidly thrown his life away. Wing is viciously defiant to Geraldine, who hopes his joining up was some sort of misunderstanding. Parents are somewhat upset: Mom is crushed; Dad seems more upset that Wing didn't ask permission first. Wing later finds out that he has passed all his subjects with Cs and even a D in English, so he could have stayed on the team.

Wing sends a letter from basic training at Parris Island. Dad tries to put on a happy face, but is obviously worried about Vietnam. The Brennans come across Sam at a shopping center handing out flyers, which they assume are raffle tickets or something. When they realize that they're antiwar flyers, Dad is furious and makes the whole family leave. Geraldine wonders if Sam is a traitor. Dad is completely disgusted.

Wing comes home for a visit before shipping out to Vietnam. None have mentioned Sam in their letters. Mr. Zatarian, whose son is in Vietnam, tries to have Sam arrested for getting people to sign a petition outside a grocery store. The Brennans refuse to go to Sam's graduation. Sam is awarded a scholarship to Georgetown. When Wing gets home, everyone is thrilled. He wants to see Sam and everyone is worried about the boys' reactions to each other—especially since Wing doesn't know of Sam's antiwar activity. They all express their horrible disappointment in Sam. Wing goes to Vietnam.

Geraldine is worried about Wing. He writes that his best friend is killed and he begins to question the sensibility of the war. She goes to church to light candles for Wing. She is disgusted that Wing might be ready to forgive Sam and agree with him. On the day before Easter the news comes that Wing has been killed. That night Geraldine decides that she's mad at Wing for going to Vietnam and getting himself killed. Then she decides that it's all Sam's fault that Wing is dead. She gets on her bicycle at midnight and rides to the Daily's and demands to see Sam. She tells Mrs. Daily that Wing is dead, and Mrs. Daily tells her that Sam is back in Washington for a march.

Geraldine goes to Washington on a bus. She gets a map to the White House, where she assumes the march will be. Geraldine sees a "hippie" girl and assumes she must be a friend of Sam's. The girl tells her to look for a march over at the Washington Monument. She finally finds Sam and in the middle of the candlelight march, she realizes that the protestors are okay. Sam guesses that Wing is dead.

Sam borrows a friend's car and drives through the night to get Geraldine back home. He reminisces about his father's death in Korea. He died accidentally when coming back from a weekend pass; his jeep driver turned onto a bridge that was about to be blown up. Mrs. Daily wants Sam to call him a hero, but Sam doesn't think he is.

Geraldine begins to see that Sam was in the antiwar movement not to overthrow the government, but instead to protect the soldiers, to make sure that they all came home safe. At Wing's funeral Sam speaks about Wing as a friend. He and the Brennan family reconcile.

Rostkowski, Margaret. (1989). *The Best of Friends*. New York: Harper.

This is the story of Sarah and Dan Ulvang and their friend Will Spencer. Dan and Will are seniors and Sarah is a junior. Dan is as competitive and controlling as Sarah and Will are easygoing. Mr. Ulvang is a controlling bully who has pushed Dan into skydiving as a hobby. Dan is terrified, but won't refuse his father.

Sarah helps Kris pass out antiwar literature at a local college where Mr. Ulvang works. Dan spends much of his time studying to maintain his 4.0 average for his father. When Dan gets his AP scores, Dad forces him to open them in front of people. Dan scores 5 of 5 in English and history and 4 of 5 in calculus. Dad says that he's disappointed in Dan and tells Dan that he should be disappointed as well. Not only does Dan not stand up to his father, it doesn't even seem to occur to him to do so.

During her antiwar afternoon with Kris, Sarah expects to be either encouraged or yelled at, but doesn't count on being ignored, which is generally what happens. Will and Dan eventually stop by and as soon as they arrive and begin to talk to Sarah and Kris, Mr. Ulvang sees them. He is insulting and dismissive, but doesn't throw a temper tantrum. She urges Dan and Will to read some of the literature. She insists that "we" are killing many Vietnamese civilians.

Will is not a strong student and is taking many junior-level classes including a history class with Sarah where Dan is a student assistant (and martinet). Will refuses to let Dan help with a term paper for the class and wants to do it himself. Dan thinks that Will just doesn't bother to try and is unconcerned about his grades.

Dan meets Will and Sarah at the Peach Palace, where Will works, that evening. One of the guys talks about joining the army when he graduates instead of waiting to be drafted, which Dan thinks is stupid. Dan is concerned that if Will doesn't make good grades, then he won't get into college and will be drafted. Will appears unconcerned.

Mr. Ulvang bullies Dan into taking a math class over the summer after high school because of Dan's disgraceful AP performance. Dan refuses to stand up to his father, and when he reads an antiwar pamphlet he realizes how his father completely dominates his life.

Sarah sees Dan reading the *Life* issue that shows all the dead for a week. Dad comes in. When Sarah says that it's sad, he replies that the soldiers are getting some recognition. Sarah asks about recognition for soldiers who died in other weeks and for the Vietnamese dead. He says that he's proud of the dead. He tells about how the draft board (of which he is head) is inundated by people trying to get out of the draft. Then he tells about someone who returned his draft card, refusing induction and goes on to say that this person will be prosecuted. Sarah questions her father about his role in the draft board—asking if he feels guilty. He assures her that he does not and tells Dan and Sarah that they shouldn't question the government and that we must fight for democracy. Dan says that there is no democracy in Vietnam and that it's partly because of us. He also questions the domino theory and communist containment.

Will talks to Joe who has just joined up and who is excited about going to Vietnam. Dan asks Joe about the war and Joe defends it as us defending our way of life. Dan tells Will everything will be better next year when they're at the university, but Will tells Dan that he won't be going because he's not college material. Dan is really angry with Will for being impressed with Joe's idiotic macho posturings.

Dan vows to learn as much about the war as possible. He refuses to talk to his father about it. Sarah continues to confront Dad briefly about her antiwar stand. Dan wonders about what Will really thinks about the war and if he's saying that he won't go to college just to stick it to Dan.

Will takes Sarah to the prom. Dan interrupts them dancing a slow dance, insisting that he give Will his eighteenth birthday present. Will is reluctant to quit dancing, but Dan insists. Dan gives Will a parachute jump even though he knows that Will is not only not interested, but has flatly stated many times that he would never do it. Will angrily allows Dan to bully him into it. Sarah tries to apologize for Dan, but Will says he doesn't want to talk about it.

Will goes ahead with the jump, which terrifies him. He gets more and more furious with Dan and after they land, they have a fistfight. Will tells Dan that they are no longer friends. Will goes straight to an army recruiter's office. He doesn't seem to know why he's joining—only that he wants to do something himself without anyone telling him to do it.

Will tells Sarah about enlisting and she is furious with him for having done it with no real reason. She also assumes that he's really joined to get back at Dan for the jump. Sarah tells Dan about Will's enlistment and they are both distraught. Dad says that we need more men like Will and is very proud of him. After the three of them have a terrible fight, Sarah tells Dan that it's easy for him to be judgmental since he has a college deferment. She also chides him for not acting on his antiwar beliefs.

Dan turns in his draft card to his father and says that he refuses to carry it any longer. Dad won't take it so Dan tears it in two. Will thinks about his impending enlistment. He can still change his mind, although no one knows that. Sarah tells Dan that she's proud of him and will help in any way she can. Will leaves for basic.

Jones, Adrienne. (1990). *Long Time Passing.* New York: Harper.
    The story is told in one long flashback and begins with Jonas receiving a letter from Gideon Brophy summoning him back to Passot, California, for the settling of his aunt Hester's estate. Jonas returns to Passot hoping to see Auleen. The earlier part of the novel begins with seventeen-year-old Jonas arriving at Hester's house in Passot. She is to be his guardian because Jonas's mother is dead and his marine father, Hugh,

has taken an assignment in Vietnam. Hugh expects him to enlist on his birthday, but Jonas isn't interested. He becomes friends with Gideon, a one-armed man who lives on the beach, of whom Hester doesn't approve. Through Gideon, Jonas meets Auleen, a high school senior who is involved in the antiwar movement and who intends to attend Berkeley in the fall.

Auleen introduces Jonas to people in what she calls a "commune." He has mixed feelings about the antiwar activities, having always lived on military bases and been surrounded by military people. Jonas is introduced to Davey, an antiwar leader. Auleen impresses upon him the sacrifices and risks that are involved in antiwar activity—mentioning specifically People's Park and other instances of police brutality.

Hester forbids Jonas to see Auleen or Gideon, claiming that they're not socially acceptable. When Jonas refuses, Hester writes to Hugh, who insists that Jonas cooperate. Jonas decides that he is in love with Auleen and intends to accompany her to Berkeley, where they can live together. Jonas has mixed feelings about the antiwar activity, but takes part in his first peace march in Berkeley. He thinks his mother would have been proud and his father horrified.

After several weeks in Berkeley, Jonas gets a call from Hester telling him that his father is missing in action in Vietnam. Auleen goes on, as planned, to a Ban the Draft rally in Oakland where some "commune" members intend to burn their draft cards, and Jonas goes back to Passot to try to get more information about his father.

Jonas is worried sick about his father and doesn't know what to do. He eventually decides that instead of going into the marines through OCS (officer candidate school), he will just enlist because he wants to join quickly in order to get to Vietnam fast so that he can look for Hugh. Hester tells Jonas that Hugh would be proud that he's enlisting. Jonas becomes convinced that his father's survival depends on him and that when he can finally "measure up," everything will be fine and he and Auleen can be together.

Jonas is unable to contact Auleen. He remembers his halfhearted participation in the peace rally as if it had been a major commitment, when in fact he was there to be with and impress a girl. He wonders if he has betrayed anyone with his marginal participation. He speculates about the true nature of heroism. After not being able to contact Auleen in

Berkeley, he leaves for San Francisco to enlist. He gets his head shaved and a uniform. He wanders around San Francisco and then takes a bus to Berkeley. He finds Auleen and they plan to meet at a cafe. Jonas sits nervously awaiting Auleen. She is very surprised and politely tells him that it's a ridiculous notion that he'll be able to wander around Vietnam searching for his father and probably a fruitless one even if he were allowed. He remains firmly convinced that it will be possible. They have harsh words, but Auleen tries to stop them so that their last hours won't be spent fighting.

He asks her to wait for him. She tells him that they're awfully different and that she's going to Canada with Davey and had hoped that he'd come too. She says that she won't promise to wait, that things will change, and that she may never come back to the States. Then she leaves him there. Jonas reports to his personnel carrier and they ride through a demonstration on the way to Pendleton. He imagines that he sees Auleen.

The story then flashes to the present as Jonas arrives in Passot. He is recently divorced again and unable to stop his restlessness after the war. Jonas finds Gideon, who is happily surprised to see him. Auleen arrives unexpectedly but doesn't seem to have any real reaction to seeing Jonas. Jonas tells that Hugh's body was found shortly after his arrival in Vietnam. Auleen and Davey had been married and living in Canada, but had finally divorced. Auleen and Jonas leave Passot together.

Qualey, Marsha. (1994). *Come in from the Cold.* Boston: Houghton Mifflin.

Part I: American Casualties

Maud's sister Lucy, an antiwar activist, goes underground when she is implicated in the death of secret service officers. But then Lucy is killed while setting a bomb in a physics lab at the University of Minnesota. Maud and her college professor father are crushed by Lucy's death and both fall into depression.

Part II: Body Count
Shifted point of view to first person, Jeff

Jeff gets the kids in his high school to pass a resolution condemning the war in Vietnam. We meet Jeff's older brother, Tom, and his divorced mother. Tom is a marine who hasn't yet gone to Vietnam. He resents Jeff's antiwar sentiments, as do most of the people in his northern Minnesota town, Red Cedar.

Tom is killed in Vietnam. People gather at the Ramsey house and Mom tells that she and Paul had just gotten engaged earlier that afternoon. Tom's body was sent back from Vietnam accompanied by several soldiers.

Because of his depression from the war and Tom's death, Jeff stops going to high school. His mother and stepfather are on their honeymoon, so they aren't there to supervise. Jeff's friend Gumbo is really worried about Jeff's mental state. Reverend Roger comes to the house to check on him. They have a tense talk and Roger tells Jeff that his family won't even speak to him because of his antiwar attitudes. Roger persuades Jeff to go to the University of Minnesota for the moratorium for which Maud had been given the flier at the beginning of the book.

Roger picks up Jeff to go to UM. Roger points out the physics building. Jeff remembers that one of the bombers was killed during the bombing, about the same time as Tom's death. After some speeches, they begin to march through town and are confronted by anti-antiwar people.

Part III: Peace Comes Dropping Slow

Maud and Jeff meet when Maud drives up to Red Cedar with Natalie. Maud seems to have the same trouble seeing the relevance of school after the death of a sibling that Jeff did. They meet at a local bar. She doesn't know how much to reveal about Lucy. He talks about Tom and about how protest is patriotic.

Maud helps Jeff work on posters for the protest and the VFW Loyalty Days and stays for the protest. She and Jeff hand out black armbands. Only about thirty protestors show up, but many VFW come. The parade is comprised of units of veterans and local school bands. The protestors have a flag too. After the parade, some of the flag wavers attack Jeff and try to take his flag away. He's hurt bad enough to be hospitalized.

Maud is working at the community center when word of the Kent State murders comes over the radio. Everyone is floored. She and Jeff agree to go to a demonstration in Minneapolis together. There is a general outrage about Kent State.

Jeff speculates that the real antiwar action isn't marches but the things you do every day. They hitchhike back to the car and get picked up by some hippies in a van. They've started a commune, but have taken the day off to come down for the march.

Jeff visits the commune and really likes it. Maud and Jeff fight because she's committed to a play at the senior center and won't blow it off to go with him. Maud gets a call from Jeff's mother, who is wondering where he is. Jeff has quit school and left campus. Maud doesn't know anything about it and is quite worried. They both assume that he's gone to the commune—The Woodlands. Jeff's mother also tells Maud that Gumbo has taken off for Canada because of his low draft number.

Jeff and Maud eventually live happily ever after at the commune.

Wolkoff, Judie. (1980). *Where the Elf King Sings.* New York: Bradbury Press.

Marcie knows that her father is getting ready to have another bout of depression. The family car has been repossessed and he has been ranting, raving, and pacing at night. He was fired from his job at Willowmart a month ago and seems to think there's some sort of conspiracy preventing him from getting another job. At Vanessa's recent slumber party, Dominique told Marcie that her father was nothing but a drunk. When Marcie gets home, Mama is getting ready to leave for her waitressing job. Daddy has been gone since early in the morning. No one knows where he is, nor is he expected back. Younger brother David tells Marcie that he overheard Mama telling Grandma (Daddy's mother) that if Daddy started drinking again she was leaving.

At 3:00 a.m., Marcie is awakened by shouting and screeching tires. Daddy is obviously drunk and out on the street yelling at a cabbie. Marcie both pities and hates her father. She remembers her grandma talking about flashbacks and always making excuses for her father. She also remembers some of the flashbacks that Daddy has had.

After an afternoon out, Marcie and David dread going home, not knowing what condition they might find their father in. They know that Mama will have gone to work and that they will have to fend for themselves for dinner. When they approach the house, the door is wide open and hanging on one hinge. The house has been ransacked, and they both immediately assume Daddy is responsible when they see empty liquor bottles in the sink.

When they can't get Mama on the phone, Marcie calls Grandma, who comes to get them. Grandma refuses to think that Daddy might have had anything to do with the house and blames Mama for not being at home. Both kids resent Grandma for refusing to see the truth about Daddy.

When Mama calls early the next morning, Grandma doesn't even answer the phone, but Marcie gets it. Mama says that Daddy still hasn't come home. Marcie assumes that when and if he does, Mama will make him move out. When Marcie comes back into the bedroom, Daddy is sitting there watching David sleep. She expects him to act as if nothing has happened, which is what he normally does in this situation. After an ugly confrontation, Mama tells Daddy that she's brought his stuff over and that she'll get a court order to keep him away from the kids. Daddy pleads with her to let him explain. She ignores both him and Grandma. Grandma tells Mama that she is cold and cruel and isn't being fair to Daddy.

After several weeks, Daddy stops writing to them. He wrote daily at first, telling them that he's at the VA hospital and that he's been to several vet "rap sessions." Mama refuses to answer Daddy's letters and doesn't know if she'll stay with him even if he does get better.

Marcie gets a letter from Daddy. He apologizes for not having written more often. He does some explaining and tells her about the flashback that caused the incident at the house. He promises to try to stay sober and get his life together—not the same huge promises he normally makes. Marcie thinks he sounds more real than he has in a long time.

Grandma calls and says that Daddy borrowed her car and took off. He was depressed about the date and she doesn't know where he went. When she speaks to the minister from the rap session, he tells her that Daddy was really upset about some anniversary. Grandma is afraid that since Daddy was so depressed, he'll try to hurt himself. Marcie tells her that she thinks Daddy has gone to his friend Eggie's grave. Grandma comes to get them and they eventually find the cemetery. Grandma finds Daddy's friend John Eggleston's grave. They see footprints but no Daddy. Grandma finds an unopened whisky bottle. They find another set of footprints coming to Eggie's grave from the other side. The two people left together.

When Grandma brings them home, Mama comes in with a man she introduces as Kurt Scoffield, a friend of Daddy's. She tells everyone that she and Kurt had driven Daddy up to a VA hospital that afternoon. She says that he'll be in a special Vietnam ward getting psychological help for his PTSD and medical help for his alcoholism. Mama says that Daddy will be in a psychiatric ward for up to a year.

The family finds out that it was Kurt who found Daddy in the cemetery and got him home safely. Kurt says that last night at the rap session, Daddy broke down talking about Eggie's death (he has never told any of the family). Kurt says that Daddy was reliving the experience. Kurt explains Daddy's story. He says that Eggie's unit was choppered in to help. During a firefight, Daddy fell into a "pangee trap." Eggie stepped on a mine as he ran to help Daddy. Eggie's body was completely destroyed.

Marcie is really upset by the scene that Kurt has described. Mama says that she didn't know what the scar on Daddy's leg was until Kurt told her the story. Eventually the family visits Daddy at the VA hospital and the story ends on a positive note.

Bograd, Larry. (1986). *Travelers.* New York: Lippincott.

Jack Karlstad, a second-generation vet, is a high school senior in a run-down mining town in Colorado. His fighter-pilot father was killed in Vietnam when Jack was only four (in 1972). A.J. Karlstad was well liked in his home town and people compliment him to Jack often, even though it confuses him—making him both sad and resentful. Jack's best friend is Wendell Nast, a jerky, raunchy, sexist son of the local mine boss.

When Wendell comes up with a plan to have his parents pay him to drive to his grandparents' in San Francisco, he invites Jack along. Jack decides to go so that he might look up some of the men that A.J. mentioned in letters to Jack's mother. Jack doesn't know what to expect from these men, but he wants some information about the father he doesn't remember.

Jack sets out to learn about his father. He talks to several people who knew his father and comes to learn that A.J. started the war with blind patriotism, but reconsidered his position. Upon returning home Jack decides not to register for selective service, instead writing a letter identifying himself as a conscientious objector. Jack also decides to take over his grandfather's farm.

Dawson, Candy Boyd. (1987). *Charlie Pippin*. New York: Macmillan.

Charlie Pippin chooses to join the war and peace group for her sixth-grade current events/social studies project. Charlie is interested in learning about the Vietnam War because her father, Oscar, is a vet and he generally refuses to talk about his experiences there. Other group members are dismissive of Charlie's ideas, saying that the war happened a long time ago and that no one is interested, but Charlie is determined.

Although Charlie is close to her mother and grandparents, she has a very strained relationship with her father. He appears to be hypercritical of her behavior and accomplishments at school. When he discovers that she has chosen the Vietnam War as a project topic, he is very angry and tells her that he will not help or participate in any way.

Mom's sister Jessie calls to say that Uncle Ben (also a Vietnam vet) is coming to visit. Oscar doesn't like Ben, claiming that he is irresponsible and flaky. Mama Bliss (Oscar's mother) tells Charlie that she may learn about Vietnam, but in order to understand, she will have to talk to real people. Mama Bliss asks why Charlie is determined to do a report about the war, since it will obviously upset her father. Charlie merely says that she feels that it's important for her to learn about Vietnam.

Uncle Ben finally arrives. Charlie tenses, but Dad is friendly to him. Charlie's sister Sienna tells everyone that Charlie is doing a report on Vietnam—Ben is approving and Dad is furious. Dad thinks that no one needs to think about Vietnam, but Ben thinks that everyone should be educated. They fight about Vietnam. Dad says that we must help people resisting communism. Ben says that there was no support for the war and that we needed to focus our attention at home. Ben argues that a disproportionate number of black soldiers were killed, also that the country/government betrayed the soldiers by sending them to die and then not supporting them properly.

Charlie wants to interview Uncle Ben about his experiences, and even though he is agreeable he continues to cancel every meeting that they arrange. Charlie researches the war and she wonders about the materials' neglect of black Vietnam vets. She realizes that she needs to learn more about communism for much of this to make any sense.

Charlie finds, in Mama Bliss's dining room, an old newspaper article with a picture of a black soldier holding another black soldier, comforting a wounded white soldier, and sobbing. Charlie realizes that it is her father. The article tells how Daddy was a hero rescuing these men and others. Daddy's leg is wounded and Charlie decides that that must be how he got his limp. She also reads that both of the other men in the picture eventually died. Charlie wonders why no one ever told her about her father being a hero.

Charlie interviews Granddad, asking what he knows about Daddy in Vietnam. Granddad talks resentfully about the treatment of black soldiers and about the treatment of Vietnam vets. Charlie realizes that there's a lot she doesn't know about her father and begins to understand why he might not want to think about her project.

Uncle Ben calls and invites Charlie to go to Washington for the weekend with him to see Aunt Jessie. He says that her project inspired him to go to "the Wall" for the first time and he wants her to go. Charlie is convinced that her father won't let her. He is ugly about the whole decision and indeed won't let her go, even though Mom thinks it would be a good idea.

Charlie desperately wants to go. She tells her parents that she'll be spending the weekend with a friend and tells Uncle Ben that she can go. Only after they arrive in Washington do Ben and Jessie realize what Charlie has done. Her parents are furious.

Uncle Ben approaches the directory of names and takes a piece of old paper out of his pocket. Jessie shows him how to use the directory. They find the names and their locations on the Wall. Charlie looks up the names of the two men who had appeared in the newspaper picture with Daddy. Charlie is in awe of the Memorial, reflecting on its vastness. She overhears the conversations of other people looking up names. Ben finds the names he is looking for. He stands crying as Charlie hugs him. She leaves him in his space and goes off to look for her father's friends' names. She gets a park ranger to make rubbings of the two names on the Wall. She leaves an origami flower in the crack of the Wall and takes some pictures. She takes Ben an origami crane, a symbol of peace, to tape to the Wall. He does and thanks her. Charlie remembers having read that some people didn't like the design of the Memorial. But she thinks it is not only appropriate, but beautiful and touching.

When they get back to the house, Mama Bliss and Granddad are waiting. They seem quite angry too—especially Mama Bliss. Daddy tries to get Charlie to explain why she did it. She apologizes for lying, but says that no other trip would have been like this one, and Ben agrees. She says that she needed to see the Memorial because of her project. Charlie is sent to her room and Ben leaves. Shortly, Granddad comes in. He asks Charlie why she didn't tell Daddy about looking for his friends, which is what he guesses she did. She shows him the rubbings and he says they are powerful.

Days later Charlie gives the rubbings to her father. They talk about the article. Daddy says that the three of them had been like brothers and that they had vowed to come home together. She tells him about leaving the flower. Daddy cries and is visibly moved.

Jensen, Kathryn. (1989). *Pocket Change*. New York: Macmillan.

The story begins when we meet high school senior Josie Monroe. Josie is close to her vet father and her young stepmother, Marsha. Dad begins to act strangely—taking days off, even though he's a real workaholic. Marsha refuses to acknowledge that anything is going on. Each day Josie thinks that Dad acts a little less rational. He eventually accuses Josie's quiet, shy boyfriend, Brian, of being dangerous and orders Josie never to see him again. Dad becomes secretive and distant and has flashes of real rage toward Josie. Dad and Marsha fight.

Josie stops to pick up milk and bread on the way home from school. A car backfires and she sees her father in a ball on the street rocking back and forth. People surround him, thinking that he must be on drugs. He doesn't appear to recognize Josie. Josie wonders if perhaps her father is taking drugs or is drinking heavily. She thinks that Marsha is being secretive and wonders how much to trust her. Marsha still acts as if nothing unusual is happening. Josie is really distraught over the fact that she feels as if no one is being honest with her. Dad becomes violent and nearly punches Josie, but punches a wall instead. Josie is afraid to be home with Dad.

Josie avoids Marsha and Dad. She is afraid of her father and doesn't really trust Marsha anymore. Josie rummages through Dad's things and finds an article about Vietnam vets going back to Vietnam. Downstairs, she and Korean friend Mary read the well-worn article, which has several parts underlined. It mentions vets suffering from Agent Orange exposure and PTSD.

Josie is somewhat relieved that her father's erratic behavior might have some sort of Vietnam-related cause. When Dad returns home Josie opens the door for him, thinking now that she understands, maybe things will be OK. Dad mumbles something in Vietnamese and reaches out to touch Josie. He doesn't really even seem to see Josie and Mary. As soon as he focuses on Mary he bolts upstairs. Mary suggests that Josie call the police or something, because he is obviously crazy. Josie thinks he just needs some help. Mary tells Josie that she won't come back to the house.

Josie tells Marsha about the incident and becomes really frustrated when Marsha won't acknowledge that there's even a problem. Mary tells Josie that Josie's father has been prowling around the neighborhood at night looking in windows. They are quite afraid of him and think he is unbalanced. Brian urges Josie to call the police or someone. Josie finally gets through to a vet counseling center. They talk about PTSD and flashbacks. Dr. Whitehead tells her that her dad must come in and want to be helped. He also tells her that she should call the police if she feels threatened.

That afternoon, Dad comes home and acts normally. He says nothing about where he has been, but appears to be in a good mood. After hearing some combat footage on TV, Dad grabs Chrissy and swears that he won't ever let anyone hurt his son. Marsha finally says that Dad has had nightmares for years, that he doesn't always recognize her, and that he has started keeping a knife under his pillow. She thinks he is afraid of the VC coming back to kill him and maybe thinks of himself as going out to hunt them.

When Dad flees the house, Josie goes after him. She finds him close to the beach, having an extended flashback. She manages to convince him to come home. Josie calls Dr. Whitehead and he tells her that things are *very* serious and that Dad really needs to come in for help.

The next day, all seems normal. Marsha wants Josie to take Chrissy to a neighbor's and not to leave him alone with Dad. Josie asks Dad if he remembers the flashback and he does. She asks him what happened. He says that she would hate him if she knew some of the things that happened in Vietnam. He tells her about a young girl that he killed and finally admits that he doesn't understand what's happening to him. She suggests that he get some help, but he flatly refuses.

When Josie returns home one night, she sees that the police have her street blocked off from either side. Dad breaks out a window and shoots a few rounds. The cops start to bring in sharpshooters. The officer in charge unsympathetically tells Josie that they really just want to get Dad to a hospital and that no one will hurt him if he throws out his gun. Josie doesn't for a minute believe that the police have any experience disarming Vietnam vets or any stake in getting Dad out unhurt. When Josie realizes that Chrissy is in the house with Dad, she manages to break away from the police and get to the house.

The police are staying back, but Josie doesn't trust them at all. Josie gets into the basement and then comes up into the living room. It's all dark. She finds Dad. He recognizes her. She goes upstairs to check on Chrissy, who is asleep in his bed. Josie goes back down and tries to tell Dad that there are police outside, not VC. He seems to waver between flashback and reality.

Suddenly, Dad realizes all of what has happened. He throws out the gun and prepares to go out. He tells Josie that she must hate him. Dad goes out and the police slap handcuffs on him and take him away. Josie assures him that she still loves him.

Five or six months later Dad is in a nearby veteran's hospital. The VA sends Marsha a monthly check. Dad might come home later in the summer or early in the fall. Marsha is in therapy; Josie refuses to go.

Antle, Nancy. (1993). *Tough Choices: A Story of the Vietnam War.* New York: Viking.

The story starts as the family is at the airport to meet Mitchell, who is returning from Vietnam. Emmett (brother) refers to Mitchell as "G.I. Joe" and both Lee Ann (Mitch's girlfriend) and Mom get very angry. Samantha (sister) thinks that she will never forgive Emmett if he ruins Mitchell's homecoming. There are protestors at the airport, and Samantha angrily states her defense of the soldiers and the war. Samantha moves her mother aside, assuming that she will get into an argument with the protestors too. Samantha drags Emmett ahead and they meet Mitch first. They're all happy to see each other. Samantha vows never to think about Vietnam again.

On the way to the car, the family is accosted by protestors who single out Mitch to call a baby-killer. Everyone, especially Mitch, is really shaken. The protestors are presented as hysterically vicious. Emmett and Mitch nearly have a scene at the car when Emmett calls Mitch "G.I. Joe" and tells him that he doesn't believe in war. Mitch, the peacemaker, manages to smooth things over.

Mom tries to get Samantha to persuade Mitch to tell her all about Vietnam. Mom is surprised and a little offended that Mitch thinks she won't understand. Emmett makes signs for a die-in. He and Mitch have a confrontation about the causes of the war and whether or not the American soldiers kill civilians, just as the VC do. Emmett tells Sam that he is afraid to be drafted. Sam goes to check on Mitch while he is sleeping and comes across pictures of Jim Smith, Mitch's best friend in Vietnam. Mitch is worried about him, since he's still there. Mitch hears a car backfire while sleeping and immediately jumps up to find his gun. He knocks Sam down and scares her, although he seems quite good-natured about it.

Emmett tries to get Sam to come to the die-in, but even though she is curious, she is afraid that Mitch will be angry. Mitch tells her that she will have to decide for herself what to do. She finally decides to go, although she is really skeptical. Emmett asks Sam to squirt fake blood on him. She does, is somewhat upset, and moves to the edge of the crowd, where she meets a man in a wheelchair who lost both legs in Vietnam. He tells her that Mitch probably misses Vietnam and that he will take a long time to adjust. He tells her to be patient with both of her brothers.

The man hears sirens and assumes that the police will come and arrest the protestors if they don't leave. Mitch, Lee Ann, and Sam try to find Emmett to get him away before the police come. People do start to leave and Emmett reluctantly agrees to go. They have a minor reconciliation.

Lee Ann asks Sam privately about whether Mitch talks to her about the war and tells Sam that he doesn't tell her anything. They both wonder if he'll ever be the same as he was before. Lee Ann finds a letter from Linda Smith and is furious. She is ready to make a scene in front of the entire family. Mitch assumes that she is writing to tell about the trip that they're planning to visit Mitch, but of course, it's actually that Jim was killed in Vietnam the day after Mitch left. Mitch takes the news badly.

Mitch is quiet for a few days, then he seems to have a change of heart. Sam comes home from the store and finds the house in an uproar. Emmett is screaming at Mitch that he's an idiot. Mom says that Mitch has decided to leave early and asks Sam to try to talk him out of it. She goes up to his room and finds him in his uniform and packing. He has, of course, decided to go back to Vietnam—because he claims that the war brought out the best in him. Sam thinks he's doing it to spite the protestors, but he tells her it's because he enjoyed having friends.

Index

Air America, 90
alcohol. (*See* drugs)
American cultural myth, 18-21, 217-18
And One for All, 67, 107-8, 127, 151, 171-72, 198, 204, 283-85
Appy, Christian, 155, 159, 161, 221

baby-killer, 176, 179, 180-81, 205, 299
Baritz, Loren, 7, 19-20, 158
Benjamin, Walter, 20
Best of Friends, 67-69, 74, 77, 105-6, 151, 170-71, 198, 204, 216, 285-87
body counts, 143, 204, 266

Cambodia, 58-59, 70, 84-85, 90
career military, 119-20, 129, 149
Caribou, 70-71, 105, 112, 170, 197, 281-83
Carr, Edward, 41-43, 223
Charlie Pippin, 71-72, 74, 155-56, 178-79, 203, 294-96
Children of the Dragon, 58-60, 70, 73, 76, 93, 166, 190-91, 203, 253-54
Come in from the Cold, 69-70, 174-75, 180, 205, 289-91

Cross-fire, 56-57, 92, 118-19, 130, 140-41, 158, 188-89, 202, 251-53
cultural continuity, 21
culture war, 4-7, 9, 209-10

Dittmar, L., 211
Divine, R. A., 43-44, 46
Downey, Sharon, 113-14, 117, 119, 124, 127, 219
draft, 158-59
draft evasion, 170, 196, 203
drugs, 70, 104, 109, 137, 142, 149, 152, 157, 173, 202-4, 220, 260, 268, 272, 277-78, 291, 293

Eagleton, Terry, 16-17, 222
Echo Company, 63-65, 73, 99-103, 112, 122-26, 129, 146-49, 166-67, 195-97, 203-4, 266-76

Fallen Angels, 61-63, 95-99, 112, 120-22, 142-45, 155, 166-67, 193-95, 201, 203-4, 262-66
FitzGerald, Frances, 23-24, 44, 213
flashbacks, 152-24, 203
fragging, 98-99, 144-45, 160, 204
French colonialism, 58-59, 67
friendly fire, 97-98, 102

About the Author

Deborah Wilson Overstreet is an assistant professor of English education in the Department of Curriculum and Instruction at the University of Southwestern Louisiana where she teaches undergraduate and graduate courses in English and reading methods and adolescent literature. She received her Ed.D. from The University of Georgia in English education in 1994. Her research on Vietnam literature and other subjects has been published in *The ALAN Review, SIGNAL*, and *Statement.*